Creating Your Family Heritage Scrapbook

From Ancestors to Grandchildren, Your Complete Resource & Idea Book for Creating a Treasured Heirloom

MARIA GIVEN NERIUS
BILL GARDNER

PRIMA PUBLISHING
3000 Lava Ridge Court ❧ Roseville, CA 95661
(800) 632-8676 ❧ www.primalifestyles.com

Library of Congress Cataloging-in-Publication Data

Nerius, Maria.
   Creating your family heritage scrapbook : from ancestors to grandchildren,
   your complete resource & idea book for creating a treasured heirloom /
   Maria Given Nerius
      p.   cm.
   Includes index.
   ISBN 0-7615-3014-2
   1. Genealogy. 2. Scrapbooks. I. Gardner, Bill. II. Title.
   CS14.N47.   2000
   929'1—dc21   00-061143

01 02 03 04 ii 10 9 8 7 6 5 4 3 2 1
Printed in the United States of America

How to Order
Single copies may be ordered from Prima Publishing, 3000 Lava Ridge Court, Roseville, CA 95661; telephone (800) 632-8676. Quantity discounts are also available. On your letterhead, include information concerning the intended use of the books and the number of books you wish to purchase.

Visit us online at www.primalifestyles.com

Dedication

If happy memories could magically become a road, and if tears of missing you became a bridge to heaven, I would dance my way through the stars and bring you back home with me. Until then, to my parents, family, and rather eclectic gathering of friends, words fail me in expressing just how much you mean to me—other than simply I love you. I dedicate this book to you.

—MARIA GIVEN NERIUS

If it weren't for families, we wouldn't be here. If it weren't for the memories they've given us, we wouldn't have written this book. And if it weren't for an extended family of dear friends, I wouldn't have near as many memories to cherish. To all of them, and especially to Maria for involving me in this project and for extending her very dear friendship, I dedicate this, my first coauthored book.

—BILL GARDNER

Contents

Foreword vi
Preface xi
Acknowledgments xvi
Introduction xvii

1 Genealogy and Heritage Albums Combined:
   Bringing Family History to Life, by Maria Nerius 1

2 Grassroots Research, by Maria Nerius 31

3 Internet Genealogy and Other Shortcuts, by Maria Nerius 73

4 The Art of Preserving Our Memories, by Maria Nerius 91

5 Photos: Picturing Your Family Through the Years,
   by Maria Nerius 125

6 Journaling: Words from the Heart, by Maria Nerius 155

7 Tools of the Trade, by Maria Nerius 175

8 Designing Your Heritage Scrapbook:
   Themes and Techniques, by Maria Nerius 207

9 Creating Your Heritage Scrapbook:
   Composing the Pages, by Maria Nerius 237

10 Memory Quilts and Memory Crafts, by Bill Gardner 261

11 Family Reunions: Staying Connected All Year Long,
    by Bill Gardner 275

Appendix A: Online Information 301
Appendix B: Glossaries 306
Appendix C: Organizations and Societies 319
Appendix D: Supplies and Resources 333
Appendix E: Helpful Documents and Forms 347
Index 359

Foreword

by Judy Svoboda

From very early times, people have been interested in tracing their ancestors. After all, if a person was of the right line, he or she could be king or queen, or at least a member of an illustrious family. These early genealogies were simple recitations of names, part of the oral tradition, which documented the lines of the privileged. They contained few references to specific dates and places. These stand in contrast to the genealogies being written today. Today's family histories cover all segments of society from rogue to the honored. The emphasis is no longer only a search for "connections." Today, by and large, genealogists are more attracted to the personalities on their pedigree, the everyday person.

My interest in genealogy or, perhaps more correctly, family history, started some forty years ago while in undergraduate school. Research for a paper I was writing on the Old Northwest Territory led me to the map room on the third floor of the University of Illinois Library. There, on an 1870s plat map of DeWitt County, Illinois, I saw the name of Fredrick Trummel, a man I had never heard of before but one that carried *my* rather unusual last name. Curious, I contacted my father, who identified this Fredrick Trummel as my great-great-grandfather. I was hooked. I wanted to know more about this man. Though responsibilities of school and family kept me from research for several years, I remained curious to know who this man was and why he left Europe to settle on the prairies of Illinois in the 1860s.

If you have picked up this book, you probably have some of the same curiosity. Who were the people who preceded you? You may already consider genealogy your hobby. If you do, you can count yourself among millions. Depending on who you believe, genealogy is the second or third most popular hobby in the country. Part of this popularity can be credited to Alex Haley's book *Roots* and to the TV miniseries based on it. That series made people aware of the fact that all families, regardless of social position, have interesting stories to tell. Another part has to do with the availability of records and the ability to access these records.

Genealogy's popularity as a hobby certainly has been bolstered by the advent of the personal computer and the Internet. Genealogical software can be used to manage the data and to organize that data into charts and graphs, all of which was once done with pencil and paper. Several programs will produce indexed genealogical reports based on the family data entered. The Internet makes it easier to network with family members and other researchers, professional and hobbyist, allowing the researcher to compare notes. Also on the Internet the researcher will find land records, out-of-print family histories, online classes, information on migration trails, historical maps, professional standards, and U.S. Census records, all available in minutes. Huge databases, including the Social Security Death Index and the LDS (Latter-Day Saints) Ancestral File, are now available online. The way one does genealogy has been changed by such technology and will continue to be. On the horizon, for example, is the use of DNA to document familial relationships. The recent Thomas Jefferson family studies is a case in point.

A question often asked of a genealogist is: What do you get out of all this research? Besides always having a project on the table to keep the mind alive and well, genealogy will expand your knowledge. As you do research, you cannot avoid picking up a bit of history, psychology, sociology, law, accounting, diplomacy, geography, library science, religion, and language.

Genealogy also offers an opportunity to understand the past. One of the first things discovered after undertaking a genealogical project is that genealogy goes beyond a documented pedigree chart. The chart will show the names of the direct ancestors and some vital information about them: birth date and place, marriage date and place, and death date and place as well as the name of their spouse. Once you have filled in those blanks, you have a basic outline of these people, but they are just stick figures. By expanding your search to include the whole family and its personality, you put flesh on these figures. You discover that a stick figure had a life. It was a farmer, a carpenter, a lawyer, or a housekeeper. It had some siblings, one was a preacher, another died in infancy, and a third "went west." It attended the Quaker Monthly Meeting and was admonished for wearing a red hat. It bore nine children, including a set of twins. One of those twins came in the cornfield. That baby was wrapped in the apron and taken to the cabin where the other twin was born some thirty minutes later. It woke up one morning in a sod hut in Nebraska only to discover its hair was caked with the mud that had dripped from the ceiling during the rainy night before. It lost a leg at Antietam or Gettysburg or Vicksburg. These are no longer stick figures; these are real people. They are "whos," not "its."

When we take this broader approach to research, we do more than increase our knowledge base. First, we learn a little bit more about ourselves, why we are the way we are. For example, I have been accused, by some (actually, my husband), of being just a bit stubborn. Did this tendency come from my father's very German grandfather who stood on his German homestead and declared that he would depart this land if Bismarck took one more pig? Well, Bismarck did, and so did my ancestor, ending up in central Illinois in 1861.

There is more to discover about yourself than a few personality traits. Health issues can be more effectively dealt with if one has knowledge of a family's health history. Is the family prone to heart disease, certain cancers, or depression? Does a certain condition run in the family? Who are possible donors of bone marrow or a kidney? Knowledge of a family's health history improves the care.

Self-knowledge, then, is one of the major attractions of genealogical research. And we get a bonus. Genealogical study also makes the researchers more understanding of those they live with. You can better relate to others if you understand a bit more clearly their roots. In one family there was animosity between the children and the father, a quiet man given to spurts of temper not against the family but against things. The children nonetheless were alienated. As an adult, one of the children became interested in the family history and conducted interviews with family members. When interviewed, her mother commented that the high school sweetheart that she fell in love with was not the man she married. What happened between her high-school days and her marriage was the war in the South Pacific. Her eighteen-year-old sweetheart was part of the first wave of marines on the Sullivan Islands. How much easier it was for the children to forgive their father's isolation when they realized that his anger was not directed at them but at the images he could not erase from his mind.

People are drawn to this hobby for rewards other than discovering themselves and understanding others. Some feel that in this age of family instability people wish to rediscover the joys of family. Reunions and family newsletters are more and more common. Each offers us an opportunity to expand our families, to meet new people with a common experience. I have never understood why, but there is truth in the old adage that blood is thicker than water. Maybe it is some personality link or just a knowledge that we share the same genes. Whatever the attraction, it is there. Several years ago I made a tour of the Midwest just to meet some distant cousins with whom I had corresponded over the years. I was amazed by the fact that none seemed a stranger in spite of the fact that this was our first meeting.

I also think that genealogy is appealing because it puts each of us into history, albeit vicariously, through our ancestor. It makes us part of the human race, part of something that is larger than our own lives. We become connected to history. The Salem witch trials are much more astonishing when your eighth great-grandmother was labeled a witch herself. How real the trek across the Great Plains becomes when you read your great grandmother's account of dances along the Little Blue River in Kansas and of stacks of bones of fallen cattle along the Humbolt in Nevada. I felt the impact of World War II as I read my grandmother's description of the day she put her last born on a train to boot camp in 1944. He was but seventeen. If you read cemetery records, you can feel the pain of a father who buries his infant son and wife on the same day. We learn that the people in the past were much like ourselves and they dealt with life as best they could.

One of my favorite records that illustrates how names on paper can become human is an 1880 census return for Cox's Bar Precinct, Trinity County, California. There we find one Robert Martin, forty-four, with his wife, "Walty," thirty-six; daughters Carrie, Minnie, and Annie; and sons Lorenzo, Robert, and William. Also in the household is a grandson Oscar, age six months. For each entry, the census taker has dutifully entered the place of birth, plus the birthplaces of each individual's father and mother. The elder Robert was born in Pennsylvania, and the rest were born in California. Each child's father is correctly recorded as being born in Pennsylvania. When census taker recorded the birthplace of grandson Oscar's father, there is this rotation, probably given by the elder Robert: "Never had a father. Came by chance."

Whatever draws you to genealogy, the search becomes addictive and never ending. Each time one question is answered, two more are posed. For each grandparent who comes out of the woodwork, two more are waiting to be found. It only takes ten generations assuming you don't have cousins marrying cousins, before you have more than a thousand ancestors on your pedigree chart.

And it is yourself that is often overlooked in your research. I have a golden rule for genealogists: "Do for your descendants what you wish your ancestors had done for you." Leave behind stories and photos, records and memorabilia so that you emerge as a personality, not a few vital statistics. That is the purpose of this book. Get out the shoe boxes, the old pictures, the letters, the old silver, whatever you have that might offer clues to events and dates and to personalities of your life. A membership pin in the VFW suggests military service. A Rose Bowl program might suggest a university affiliation. A dish with a foreign trademark might suggest a country of origin. Treasure these objects. These are the connections to the past and the ties to the future.

Preface

by Bill Gardner

For more years than I can remember, more than my own forty-five years, my paternal grandfather's family has held a family reunion in June. My grandfather and his seven siblings took turns hosting, so every eight years, it was right in my own backyard. (We lived one block from my grandparents but could cut through the neighbors' backyards to get to their house.) There under the huge oak tree we would all take turns cranking the ice cream maker. We had no use for those electric machines. Our ice cream was truly made by hand! It tastes better that way.

As my great aunts and uncles grew older and eventually died, one of their offspring stepped in to host the reunion when it would have been their parents' turn. Since I now live in another state, I haven't attended one of the reunions in years. I believe there are five generations represented each year at the gathering. Between reunions the family always kept in touch with the "round robin," a letter that began with one of the siblings and passed onto the others. (You'll hear more about round robin letters in chapter 6 as you learn how to journal family heritage.)

PHOTOGRAPHS AND MEMORIES UNITE FAMILY

I believe it was having such a tight-knit family that may have prompted my aunt to want to learn more about her ancestors.

When my dad's mother died in 1988, I remember going through her things and looking at dozens of black-and-white photos of people I didn't know. Fortunately, my dad knew most of them. Unfortunately, we didn't know about acid-free inks and the like back then. The photos were identified using regular ballpoint pens. Still, the photos will survive for many more years, though not as long as we might like them to.

Even though I don't know much about my dad's family, I had the joy of knowing his mother and learning from her my appreciation for all things handmade—those things created with love and compassion and someone's own two hands. Something like a scrapbook or family heritage journal.

I was fortunate to live in the same town with all my grandparents. My dad has lived in the same town all his life. My mother and her family arrived in town when she was fourteen. For several years we lived one block from my dad's mother and grandmother, who lived together in a house my dad's grandfather built. Then we moved across town to a new house one block from my mom's parents. It was a small town, so when I say across town, it was all of about eight blocks.

I remember Great-Grandma Merkel sitting in her rocker in front of the window in their house at the top of the hill on the corner. Every time we drove by or rode our bicycles by, we made sure to look and wave. I remember spending countless hours mowing her lawn, trimming the hedge, picking grapes, or just sitting and talking.

What I truly regret is never having quizzed my great-grandmother about her family. She lived to be ninety-five and died when I was in college. She spoke fluent German, and I never took the opportunity to have her teach me.

FAMILY HISTORY COMES HOME

While it's fun to remember and preserve memories from last year's birthday or family Christmas celebration, it's also fun, as well as important, to explore your family's roots and record its history. Just who is that in that black-and-white photo and how are they related? Or are they related? Sometimes it's just as important to remember family friends and record their relationships to members of the family.

Do your kids know their grandparents? Did you know your grandparents? My paternal grandfather died when I was two years old; I know little about him, and there are few photos of him. That's why when Maria and I began writing this book I decided to interview my father and ask him about his family. About all I know about my grandfather is that he was from Chicago and worked in the printing industry.

On the other hand, one of my mother's sisters, Judith Svoboda, who wrote the foreword to this book, is a genealogist and has traced my mother's family back to the 1700s. She traveled the country researching our ancestors, discovering that they once owned thousands of acres of land in Virginia. I've often wondered if that land had remained in the family over the generations and those hundreds of years, how much of it would actually be mine now!

While dear Aunt Judith traced our family's roots, no one has ever compiled the family tree in photos. I knew my mother's maternal grandfather, but I never knew her paternal grandparents. I don't even recall seeing photos of them. I do know that they were farmers in central Illinois and that much of the family never strayed far from there. There's something about a photo that seems to make one feel closer to the people in the photo. Had I had photos of those family members, I would have at least known what they looked like, and I could ask my mother what they were like.

 ## THE HOTTEST INTERNATIONAL TREND

I enjoy my work in the creative industries for many reasons. Spotting creative trends is one of the best moments. Being on the cutting edge of what the public wants is incredibly satisfying. As editor of *Craftrends*, the leading craft industry trade magazine, I've witnessed the evolution of scrapbooking. It's a phenomenon like none other I've seen in the craft industry in the past twenty years, and it's an activity the whole family can enjoy. I've seen popular crafting activities like macramé and fabric painting reach their pinnacles, though they continue to be an activity many crafters enjoy. Needlework activities like cross stitch and knitting are also enjoyed by countless creative people, but scrapbooking appeals to the masses, and I truly believe it has the potential to last forever.

Scrapbooking tugs at the heartstrings. A scrapbook truly affects everyone who sees it. Creative people embraced this activity as a way to not only display their creativity, but as a way to explore their feelings and build long-lasting keepsakes. The heritage scrapbook is not only a cherished collection of memories, but a book filled with family history.

In the past, genealogy has been an activity left to the professionals or to those who can dedicate massive amounts of time to tracing personal family roots, but modern technology has made this search less intimidating and documentation more accessible. It occurred to me that scrapbookers would want to combine the two personal adventures.

THE EVOLUTION BEGINS

Scrapbooks and their pages can be simple or complex. They can be colorful or monotone. Some are funny; some are sad. All bring back and preserve memories that will live for generations.

The evolution started simply and with some anxiety. Taking scissors to photos was intimidating to most when they first began scrapbooking. But the more they learned, the more they realized there was only so much sky or grass one really needed in a photo! Many people began scrapbooking by preserving memories of classic celebrations like birthday parties, vacations, and good friends getting together.

As those shoeboxes and drawers full of photos slowly began emptying and scrapbooks were created, scrapbookers became more confident in their abilities to produce fun, creative, and beautiful keepsakes. To build confidence, most scrapbookers work backward in time, starting with recent photos first. The evolution continued with the introduction of new tools such as punches and oval and circle cutters, new papers, and new confidence. That's when scrapbookers finally turned to old black-and-white photos of their ancestors—parents, grandparents, great-grandparents, aunts, uncles, and cousins. Scrapbooking became a history project. Heritage scrapbooking was born.

THE YEARBOOK OF YOUR LIFE

Remember your high school yearbooks? Well, that's what a scrapbook is only it can contain a lifetime of memories rather than just one year's worth. And it's all about your family and close friends, not a bunch of strangers. Chances are, the sentiments you record in your family heritage scrapbook are more heartfelt than those words scribbled in your yearbook by people you may not even remember!

It's amazing the memories just writing this preface conjures up for me! Some are simple and some are complex. Some are funny; some are sad—just like the family heritage scrapbook pages I plan to create. I hope reading this book will give you many reasons to pause and recall similar recollections of your own family.

This book gives you all the information you need to research your own family and gives you the know-how with suggestions and ideas for creating your family heritage scrapbook—for creating your family's own historical document.

Dig out those photos and start recording your family's heritage for future generations, as well as for you.

Acknowledgments

We would like to acknowledge the following people and companies who helped us with important information, generous materials, quality supplies, needed photographs, personal stories, amusing insights, and unselfish considerations—or who just lent an ear when we needed a friend to listen: Ken Nerius; Tenon Thompson; Mom and Dad (Mary Jo and Lawrence Gardner); Claude and Helen Given; Bill, Tollee, Stephanie, and Kelly Given; Ron, Mary Jo, Tess, and Andrew Given; Brenda Given; Elizabeth and Clem Conklin; Sandy Cashman; Andrew Williamson; Kelly's Crafts; Barb Lashua; Fiskars; Hot off the Press; un-du; Archival Mist; Miriam Olson; Cousin Jeff Given; Uncle Ron Given; Aunt Wanda Cusack; PlaqueMaker.com and Kyle Sherman; OTT-Lite; Wayne Schwartzman; McGill Inc.; Craf-t Products; Petersen-Arne; Clearsnap; All Night Media; Paper Adventures; Ranger Ink; Dorothy and Pud Williams; Wayne Given; Carmen Carr Walker; Dr. Barry Cole; Dr. Thomas Priest; Marynell Christenson; Mike Irish; Dave O'Neil; Russel and Marilyn Russell; Steve and Vivian Summers; Jeff Nerius; 3-L; The Family Tree Maker; The Huffmans; Jamie Hart; Bo; Moe; Sam; Max; The McAteers; Ingrid Ginther; Steadtler; Ami Simms; Vivian Ritter; Mary Leman Austin; Aunt Judith Svoboda; Aunt Sharon Harker; Cousin Deborah Svoboda; Uncle John Trummel; Dennis DeYoung; Craftrends Magazine; Primedia Consumer Magazine and Internet Group; The NAMES Project; Arnold Grummer and family; the Snyders; Ben Walker; the Kastlers; the Imros; Aunt Barbara; and all those friends and family who have provided many, many wonderful memories over the years.

And a very special thank you to James Thomas Given. Without his compassion for the author's voice and legal acumen, this book would never have been written or published.

Introduction

What exactly is family heritage? Often out of the mouth of babes do we adults hear the real definitions of words. Several years ago, a friend's son stood before me proudly proclaiming, "I am Mathew James McAteer, and I live at 1234 Penguin Drive in Palm Bay." He continued without taking a breath, "If I'm good, you can call my mom at 725-8444, but if I'm being bad, you are suppose to call my favorite Aunt Maria at 725-0792. She'll know what to do." His cocky smile and sure stance told me that all was just right in his six-year-old world. He had a name. He had a home. And he had family who loved him very much—even a favorite aunt who would bail him out of any boyish mischief that might come his way (and she wasn't even blood kin). It was as if all those he loved and loved him back tenfold were right there beside him to protect and celebrate his very being. Such pride. Such confidence. Such pure joy. That's what family heritage means to me. A sense of being. A sense of who I am and all I might yet become and accomplish. A strong foundation beneath my feet and a sturdy roof over my head with lots of interesting closets, windows, and doors. I feel at home no matter where I am because a part of my family and my heritage is deep inside of me making even the strangest of destinations more welcoming.

Many might find my thinking interesting for a person who lost her father before she reached her fifth birthday and who grew up with a mother who struggled constantly to keep a stable home. Even though I have three older brothers, they were gone and off to college before I turned thirteen. It was just Mom and me against the world. Not your traditional image of the classic American family, but still a very valid one.

✿ SUCH A MIXTURE IS A THING CALLED FAMILY

My mother became a naturalized U.S. citizen after coming to the United States from Germany after World War II. My father's family was a rather quiet group whom I didn't even really get to know until I was well into my twenties because of assorted real and imagined family differences and too many miles that separated us. Yet, my childhood did instill in me a great sense of family heritage. I knew my father's family came from Ireland and there was a bit of the blarney in my DNA. I was born with that stoic determination that so many German genes know well. I had wonderful friends, whose parents took seriously the fact that if I didn't have a "complete" family, they would make sure I had a loving adopted one surrounding me at all times.

As I grew older, however, I began to feel a strong need to preserve and capture some of the moments and memories of the heritage that surrounded me. Of course, I'm an American, but my family roots stretch wide, with my great-great-grandfather's Ireland and my mother's beloved Germany. I found I had an interest in these countries and what it might have been like to live there as my ancestors did. I had a gift for the written word but was often terribly shy in a group of people, too tongue-tied to speak up without blushing. Did anyone else in my family have such traits? When I looked into the mirror, I most definitely saw my mother's freckles, but did my eyes look like my father's? Did my hands resemble the small delicate hands of my grandmother? I didn't really know. Each of us has some questions and curiosities about our family and family history. It's human nature!

✿ AGE-OLD NOSTALGIA IN A NEW CENTURY

As we enter a new millennium, each of us should make the time to find out as much as we can from family and close friends about all the milestones and world events that took place in the century we have left behind. We must also understand that just as family members are born, other family members will die. It's so important that we not let our ancestors' memories, recollections, and precious moments be lost to future generations. Many of you will discover that your ancestors crossed mountains, rivers, and even oceans to make a home for future generations. And don't forget, too, that you and your life should be lovingly recorded for your children and their children.

Countless books have been written about historical events. Countless movies have been made to retell the stories of the pioneers and newsmakers of their day. The future will be full of articles and notations of world happenings. But as good as these resources and fountains of information may be, nothing can compare to hearing history and family moments from the voice of a loved one. Nothing can compare to reading in your grandmother's or great-grandfather's own handwriting his or her viewpoint or opinion on his or her life and how it was a part of the whole of our world.

You'll discover a very special inner satisfaction when you come to understand that you set a goal to create a family tree with a heritage album and succeeded. Please understand that this is not meant to be a project completed in a day or even a week. In some cases, it may take a time to track down a document or tidbit of family information. There may even come a time when you must acknowledge that you've hit a wall while trying to locate a family fact or figure. Tuck this unfinished task away for a while and come back to it at a later date.

Hopefully, genealogy and family heritage scrapbooking craft will be something you can return to time after time and make a part of your leisure activities. Each bit of information will open new insights. Each photo and the journaling that will accompany it will be unique and different. It's a hobby that keeps changing and improving as you add new tools and supplies.

❧ A Brief Background

Bill Gardner and I took a certain approach to presenting the information in this book.

Include Special Friends

First, we consider close friends as extended family and assume that you will, too. So many of us have dear childhood friends who are still a part of our everyday lives—the friend who was there in first grade when you desperately needed a lunch buddy to trade sandwiches and laughs with, or the chum who survived junior high with you and never once pointed out a pimple outbreak in mixed company, or a college pal who pulled all-nighters with you as you studied for an advanced economics course you both were convinced you would never need in this lifetime.

Don't forget to include friends of your parents and grandparents who may have been part of a baby-sitting circle or weekly game of bridge. Neighbors, too, often become good family friends who can give new insight and information about your family. Many of our fathers have old military buddies who were there for each other. In small towns or the big cities, people find each other and develop close friendships. In short, I hope you will agree that often our family members are our best friends and sometimes best friends become our families; therefore, this book will often include ways to bring friends into your family history. At other times Bill and I will just assume you understand that if you prefer to list your friend Jamie in your family tree rather than Uncle Wizen, you are quite free to do so. This is not rocket science. You aren't presenting your heritage album to the National Association of Perfect and Proper Genealogists' annual "Let's Find Out What's Wrong with This Person's Family Tree" award ceremony. This is *your* personal quest. It should make you happy.

Beware of Selective Memory

A phrase has become common (at least in my family) to describe what others might view as an inaccurate presentation of fact: *selective memory*. Selective memory explains why, when you get three or four relatives in a room and ask them to tell exactly what happened at the last family reunion, you'd swear each one attended a different event! With a little comparison, the truth usually lies between the extremes.

Pets Are Family, Too

Some family members have four legs and know more family secrets than Great-grandma Anna! A family's dog, cat, bird, bunny, or turtle often do play a very significant role in the family unit, and these special adopted members of the family will not be overlooked in this book. Bill and I will never claim that family pets are human, but we'll never deny it in this book, either.

1

Genealogy and Heritage Albums Combined

Bringing Family History to Life

What makes this book so special is that for the first time, family genealogy research and family heritage scrapbooking have been combined to give you the best resource for documenting your family history. Every bit of information Bill and I could gather from reading genealogy articles, conducting personal interviews with experts and family historians, asking in-depth questions of manufacturers and experts in archival products, and conducting time-consuming searches on software and the Internet have been put into this book. It's easy to read, easy to follow, and easy to apply, so you can spend your time creating your family heritage scrapbook.

Although I can't promise swift results in your tracing family roots, I can and do promise many little victories and successes. With care and determination you may discover old family photos, diaries, love letters, postcards, family vacation slides, or 5mm movies. I, for example, was nearly twenty-three years old before I had my own copy of a photograph of my father. My dad was the photographer of the family. Since he died quite young there were few photos of him. But when I told one of my aunts I didn't have a picture of my dad, she sent me a wonderful photograph of my father with his dad and all of his brothers and sisters. The copy was not all that clear and just a little out of focus, but I felt like I'd been given the crown jewels. For the first time, I knew without a doubt I had my father's compassionate deep brown eyes. Sure, I knew things about my father—I listened to my brothers tell tales of camping and fishing adventures. I had also read a WWII POW's diary in which my father had written words of encouragement. I even had vague memories of walks and talks with my dad. Yet, the photo brought all of these pieces together for me. That's the power of a photograph. That's the power of seeing proof as well as hearing it and reading it. That's the power of combining genealogy with a heritage memory album.

The search into family history can be a very emotional process. Be prepared to experience surprise, frustration, anger, joy, and amazement.

The search into family history can be a very emotional process. Be prepared to experience surprise, frustration, anger, joy, and amazement—one at a time and sometimes all at once. No person is perfect, nor is any family without some secrets that might be best left to lie.

Your approach, attitude, and tone will set the mood for this family exploration. Be respectful of the fact that in your search you may innocently and unknowingly touch upon sensitive issues or bring back an unhappy memory for a loved one.

Be patient and take time to truly listen to everyone you approach for help and information.

Years ago, my brothers and I gathered for a very sad occasion: our mother's funeral. After the services, we all met at an uncle's home. My brothers knew most of the relatives who had come together, but because I was so much younger than my brothers, most of these relatives were strangers to me. Appropriate for the baby and only girl in the family, I felt very sorry for myself and frankly, I was feeling quite lonely in this crowd.

I offhandedly mentioned to my brothers my feeling of being the obvious black sheep of the family. I expected the appropriate sympathy from my older male siblings and, as usual, wasn't treated with kid gloves or treated to any cotton candy. My oldest brother laughed and said I was nuts—that *he* was the black sheep of the family. My middle brother rolled his eyes and said that if anyone was the black sheep of the family it was him. My youngest older brother crossed his arms over his chest and said he was the black sheep.

Interesting, don't you think? We were four grown children arguing over the rather unappealing title of black sheep of the family. We ended up agreeing that the title was obviously rotated between all my mother's beloved children. It made me look around the room of strangers and suddenly feel a kindred spirit. How many of them felt they were the black sheep of the family? How many of them were thinking, *Who is that stranger?* as they looked at me? Family will gather

(continues on page 6)

WHY DO A FAMILY HERITAGE SEARCH?

To help you focus on the research and exploration ahead of you, it's important to be honest with yourself and consider all the reasons you have for wanting to trace your family tree. It's important that you also have some idea of what you want to place in your heritage memory album. How many of the following statements will you check off as reasons for your interest in family genealogy and memory albums?

1. I want to find out more about my family history—where we came from and what we've done in our lives.

   Yes ___   No___

2. I'm hoping to find some long-lost relative who is going to be so charmed with me that I'll be left a million dollars in his or her will.

   Yes ___   No___

3. I'd like to create a special gift to give my children, my parents, or another family member.

   Yes ___   No___

4. I'm curious whether my family has any famous or infamous members. I'm almost positive I'm related to the queen of England, but I need more proof.

   Yes ___   No___

5. Knowing who my ancestors are will help me know myself better.

   Yes ___   No___

6. I just love history.

Yes ___   No___

7. I'm an organized person who enjoys solving puzzles and mysteries.

Yes ___   No___

8. I'd like to find a few photos and mementos of my ancestors.

Yes ___   No___

9. I can't afford to hire a private investigator, so I'm going to have to do all the research myself.

Yes ___   No___

10. I'm creative and love trying new things. I can't wait to put together my first heritage memory pages.

Yes ___   No___

11. My mother bought me this book for my birthday, and it would be a never-forgiven insult to her if I didn't at least attempt a family tree.

Yes ___   No___

If you checked yes for statements 1, 3, 5, 6, 7, 8, and 10, this book will help you meet your expectations. The others just show that you have a great sense of humor—a valuable asset if the going gets tough during your research.

❧

(continued from page 3)

in the good times and the bad times. Don't ever miss an opportunity to make a few statements, ask a few questions, and listen to each other.

Keep in mind, too, that you may also help heal some old wounds, shed some comforting light on unnecessary family mysteries, and help turn a negative memory into a positive one.

It's human nature to want to share information, insight, and a bit of gossip with the ones we love about those we love. Be patient and take time to truly listen to everyone you approach for help and information.

 ## SORTING OUT WHAT YOU SEEK

Each of us at some time in our lives has wondered, *Who am I?* Undeniably, a part of who we are is linked to our family. Several reasons account for wanting to research and discover more about our family histories. Family genealogy and the creation of a family heritage scrapbook will sharpen your wits, strengthen your research skills, and let you get creative with color and balance as you put those memories and photographs together in an album.

Appreciating Our Past and Future

Many people feel that by charting the past they have a better understanding of the future by being able to see just how far the family line has come. America is such a melting pot of cultures, traditions, and people that few of us can claim pure Native American roots. More than likely your family tree may contain ancestors from various nations, including a few countries that may no longer even exist or might have undergone a name change or two. There is no negating that a very personal pride results from seeing a family tree with a solid rooted foundation and limbs and branches jetting up and out, from being able to say, "This is me. This is my family!"

Bridging Distances and Generations

Families today can end up all over the globe due to career or military obligations. It's more common than ever to pack up your life and possessions and move across the state, across the country, or across the ocean. Besides being so mobile, we are also a high-tech society that has forgotten for the most part the pleasure of writing a long letter and, in turn, reading a gossipy letter of happenings in the family and neighborhood from home.

Gathering and preserving your family's precious memories may bring you closer to your relatives, including distant or fragmented ones, in both spirit and community. Many doors of communication can be opened, and bridges can be built to narrow generation gaps. Tracking family genealogy and recounting stories along the way brings the past to life for young and old alike.

Each of us at some time in our lives
has wondered, Who am I?
Undeniably, a part of who we are
is linked to our family.

If you are lucky enough to have other family members who are also interested in family heritage, don't hesitate to lighten your research load by sharing responsibilities and including everyone who wants to help. A young child may love coloring a few family trees for the heritage album. A teenager might enjoy spending a few hours on the Internet finding a lost relative or locating important information. Dad might enjoy a few hours on the computer finding great clip art or fonts that will be included in the album. This should be a family event. Including the family makes each member feel like they contributed to creating the family heritage scrapbook.

Enjoying New History Lessons

We can glean unique insight into the past with information not just about family members but about the world as a whole. There is a good chance one of your relatives fought in World War I or II. It's possible one of your family members can be traced back to the Civil War, the Revolutionary War, or, for some, wars of other countries on what at the time was your relatives' native soil. Some of your relatives may have waltzed at grand balls or jitterbugged at a USO dance, or maybe they did the Monkey in their socks. Do your children remember a dance called the Bump?

> ### *It's not the quantity of family history but the quality of your research that will make a mark for you and your family.*

It's not the quantity of family history but the quality of your research that will make a mark for you and your family. Each of us comes from unique situations and family member combinations. None of us will have the same look or feel or feelings in our heritage scrapbook, just like not one of us will have an identical family tree. As my mom used to say, "It is the differences that make life interesting."

LEAVE YOUR DOUBTS AT THE DOOR

If you are beginning to think this is too big a task or that you aren't creative or artistic enough to create a heritage album, stop those negative thoughts right now. I have never met anyone who couldn't do this, didn't enjoy doing it, or wasn't thrilled with the results! The goal of writing this book is to let you know that no matter what the size or what the personal circumstances of your family are, there are ways to explore your roots and preserve precious memories for yourself, your family, and future generations. That goal seems quite grand, but I have personal and occupational experience in genealogy and the glorious world of scrapbooks. It's a love that has grown stronger over the years, and it's very easy to share this joy with you. You'll find the more you give in your family research, the more you will receive back from your family members.

CRITICAL FIRST STEPS

To start your family history research, it is important that you have a focus, or you will soon be overwhelmed with information. Literally thousands of books, magazine articles, Web sites, historical societies, and libraries are filled with information on genealogy and preserving family memories. This book will give you focused information concentrating on the beginner's level of genealogy, with resources to expand your search as you wish, as well as information about how to preserve the artifacts you uncover.

Here is an overview of the important beginnings of your family heritage research into six steps:

1. Learn a few pertinent terms.

2. Create your family heritage file.

3. Understand genealogy's basic coding system.

4. Determine what you know right now.

5. Narrow your search.

6. Evaluate the information gathered.

Step 1: Learn a Few Pertinent Terms

You should become familiar with a few key words right off the bat before you even start worrying about family genealogy and heritage. This is a brief list of commonly used terms; a more comprehensive glossary is in the back of the book.

Acid-free: A term describing materials with a pH value of 7.0 or higher. Materials with a pH level of 7.0 are neutral, and those with a pH level greater than 7.0 are alkaline.

Archival: Originally a term meaning that a material or product is permanent, durable, or chemically stable and that it can therefore be used safely for preservation purposes. No standards exist that describe how long an "archival" product will last.

Archives: A repository containing primarily the retired official records of public or private agencies.

Compiled service record: Military records that have been abstracted from various original documents into one record and filed alphabetically by the soldier's name.

Compiled source: Information abstracted from various original documents into one record; secondary source.

Conservation: Care and treatment that attempts to stabilize items such as paper documents, photographs, textiles, or memorabilia through chemical means or by strengthening items physically, which results in sustaining their survival for as long as possible in their original form.

Family group sheet: A page (often a preprinted form) listing a family unit: father, mother, and children of that union, with the dates and places of birth, death, and burial given for each individual, in addition to other information and source documentation.

Family history: The study of the genealogy of one's family with emphasis on accumulating information on the events and circumstances of their lives, rather than mere dates, places, and lineage.

Family History Center: A genealogy library operated by the Church of Jesus Christ of Latter-Day Saints (LDS; also known as Mormons), where any visitor can access the extensive records amassed by the LDS Family History Library in Salt Lake City, Utah.

Family History Library: The repository of the largest collection of genealogical materials in the world; operated by the Church of Jesus Christ of Latter-Day Saints, located in Salt Lake City, Utah; open to the public; distributes copies of microfilmed records to Family History Centers.

Lignin: A substance that gives plants and trees their strength and rigidity, and also binds wood fibers together. When wood is broken down to make paper, the lignin becomes unstable. Paper that contains large amounts of lignin, such as newsprint, is very acidic and will turn yellow when exposed to light and humidity.

Lignin-free: Paper containing a maximum of 1 percent lignin.

National Archives: The repository for documents relating to the history and people of the United States.

Neutral pH: The center reading of 7.0 on the pH scale of 0 to 14. It is neither acidic nor alkaline. For manufacturers, the acceptable pH neutral range is from 6.5 to 7.5.

Personal Ancestral File (PAF): A widely used genealogy computer program; available from the Church of Jesus Christ of Latter-Day Saints.

pH: Measurement of the degree of acidity and alkalinity. On a scale ranging from 0 to 14, pH 7.0 is neutral, above 7.0 is alkaline (or acid free), and below 7.0 is acidic. Paper with a pH below 5 is considered highly acidic and should not be used in scrapbooks.

(continues on page 14)

TRACING THE LIFE OF A NAME

As you read through older records, you'll often find words and names spelled in a variety of ways, even in the same document. Even in more recent records, you may come across typos and other inadvertent spelling errors. While misspellings of words may only be slightly bothersome, spelling problems related to names can make deciphering records and tracing families difficult.

In 1997 I needed a passport to travel to Europe for vacation. I called my brother Ron, the lawyer, to ask for help locating a copy of my birth certificate (the original had been destroyed). My brother said he'd file the request with the appropriate county in Indiana.

The copy of my birth certificate arrived several weeks later. I excitedly ripped open the envelope with delightful visions of my European vacation in my head only to look down and see my name listed as Marie Isabelle instead of my real name, Maria Isabella. I was devastated! All through my childhood my older brothers would tease me by calling me Marie rather than my real name. Those memories only added to my disappointment. All my life I was Maria Isabella—I positively was not a Marie. This felt like some kind of horrible cosmic joke. I felt as if my identity had vanished. I couldn't possibly be a Marie!

Ron reassured me that indeed I had always been called Maria and that all I needed to do was take some other form of documentation with me to the county clerk's office. He was confident that my passport would read Maria Isabella . . . not Marie Isabelle. My big brother was right. The clerk's office staff was very understanding and I had no problems proving indeed I was Maria when I showed them a baptismal certificate, voter's registration, social security card, and driver's license. I came a little over-prepared, but I wasn't going to take any chances!

Whether it is your surname, given name, or middle name, our names make us individuals and give us identity. The point I'm trying to make is that errors do happen. More than likely the nurse who took down my name couldn't understand my mom with her thick German accent. Mistakes happen. Just be prepared.

Name spellings weren't standardized until more recent generations, so many people spelled even their own names in a variety of ways. In addition, many people couldn't write, and those who wrote for them when the need arose sometimes had minimal spelling skills and just spelled phonetically, writing down what they heard. More drastic name changes often took place when a family immigrated to the United States. The family may have Americanized its name by dropping syllables or difficult letter combinations, translating their names to English, or changing them completely. In addition, immigration officers often made mistakes or had to guess at more difficult name spellings, doing their best to spell out what they heard. Finally, spelling mistakes exist simply due to human error. Record keepers and transcribers aren't any more perfect than the rest of us! Keep this in mind as you research your surname.

All kinds of records were prone to spelling mishaps, including vital records, church records, and the immigration and census records mentioned already. Throughout all of these documents, the following pairs of letters were often confused due to verbal miscommunication, depending on the accent of the person who was saying the name and the person who was writing it: *b* and *p, d* and *t, f* and *p, f* and *v, g* and *k, j* and *y, s* and *z, v* and *b, v* and *w,* and *w* and *r*. In addition, the *c* and *s* combination could become *ch* or *sh*. Also, double letters could turn into a single letter, and vice versa.

Vowels were prone to change as well. *I, ie, ey,* and *y* were often interchanged, as were *o* and *oe, a* and *ay,* and other similar vowel combinations. *E* could be added to or dropped off of the end at will (and the same goes for *s*). Vowels could also be dropped out of the middle of a name, leaving several consonants in a row. These are all letter changes to keep in mind when you are looking for a family name in a record set.

Let's take a look at an example. My father's family originally had the surname O'Givens. For whatever reasons, my branch of the O'Givens dropped the *O* at the beginning of the surname and the *s* at the end. In many of the search engines and indexes, many alternate spellings have developed:

Original: O'Givens (or in other explanations to the roots of the name it was MacGiven)

Current spelling: Given

Alternate spellings: Giveen, Givan, Givens, Gibbon, Green, Gwen

(continued from page 11)

Photo-safe: Any material that is chemically stable.

Preservation: The act of stabilizing an item from deterioration by using the correct methods.

Surname: Last name; in the United States, usually the same as the father's surname.

Step 2: Create Your Family Research File

Your next step is to keep a notebook or get file folders, which I will dub your family research files, that will hold all the information you discover through the process of collecting your family history. Designate a safe place to keep these family research files—a drawer, a shelf, or your nightstand. You can use your computer as your family research files, but keep in mind it's not easy to get your computer to open up and store precious, original copies of your family documents. You'll want to find a safe place near your computer, such as a filing cabinet, to keep the original copies you gather.

You'll save time, effort, and frustration by completing this step before continuing. Otherwise, it's too easy to misplace important research or get distracted by other activities going on in your household. Give yourself a break, and make it as easy as possible to keep track of the information you will gather by creating a family research file.

Step 3: Understand Genealogy's Basic Coding System

Genealogy is a very well-organized science. It has to be—with so much information, it would be impossible to locate any fact without a universal coding or indexing of family histories. In general, almost every index will use the three following ways to organize information: surnames, dates, and places. Most indexes that vary will explain in detail how to request information if it is formatted differently.

KEY INGREDIENTS FOR YOUR FAMILY HERITAGE SCRAPBOOK

Chapter 6 will cover in detail all the supplies you will need to create your family heritage scrapbook, but here's a list to get you familiar with what you'll need:

✳ Copies of family documents and important papers

✳ Photographs organized and identified

✳ Memorabilia collected through the ages included kid's artwork, postcards, or movie tickets

✳ Album in which to store your scrapbook pages

✳ Acid-free, lignin-free, and photo-safe papers on which to create your pages

✳ Page protectors to prevent damage by handling or accidents

✳ Acid-free and photo-safe pens, markers, and inks

✳ Sharp scissors or other cutting tools for cropping and cutting photos and papers

Surnames

Write the surname (last name) in all capital letters; this makes it easier to scan genealogical records. The family name or surname is key to locating records and documents. Next write the first name, and if the person had a middle name, include it also. In cases of common surnames, it is often the middle name that will help correctly identify whether you are related to someone. It's important to note a maiden name for married females in the family.

Example 1: NERIUS, Maria Isabella Given

Example 2: GARDNER, Bill

(continues on page 21)

CHECKLIST FOR YOUR FAMILY HERITAGE HUNT

Important information, including that in this listing, may already be tucked safely away in your own or a relative's home. Keep this list in your family research files to help remind you of information you should be looking for to complete your family tree, pedigree charts, and family group records.

Birth, Childhood, and School

- ✿ Baby books
- ✿ Birth announcements
- ✿ Adoption records
- ✿ Guardian papers
- ✿ Report cards
- ✿ Honor roll certificates
- ✿ Awards and honors
- ✿ Programs
- ✿ Publications
- ✿ Handouts
- ✿ Alumni lists

- ✿ Fraternity or sorority brochures
- ✿ Diplomas
- ✿ Yearbooks
- ✿ Test books
- ✿ Newsletters or bulletins
- ✿ Graduation announcements
- ✿ Trade or vocational school pamphlets
- ✿ Diaries
- ✿ Dance cards
- ✿ Transcripts
- ✿ Ribbons or trophies

Church, Religious, or Spiritual Activity

- ✿ Family Bible
- ✿ Baptismal record
- ✿ Christening announcement

- ✿ Confirmation record
- ✿ Ward and branch records
- ✿ Written history of church

✤ Parish records

✤ Bishops transcripts

✤ Parish vestry books

✤ Marriage bans

✤ Quorum records and biographies

✤ Church census records

✤ Ordination record

✤ Church bulletins

✤ Prayer or mass cards

✤ Funeral announcements

✤ Programs

✤ Church newsletters

✤ Tithing records

✤ Ordination certificate

✤ Ministerial papers

✤ Mission release

Employment or Career

✤ Social Security card or number

✤ Citations

✤ Honors

✤ Achievement awards

✤ Retirement announcement

✤ Retirement records

✤ Union papers

✤ Trade announcements

✤ Pension records

✤ Severance notices

✤ Apprenticeship forms

✤ Severance papers

✤ Income tax forms

✤ Résumés

✤ Company newsletters

✤ Agreements

✤ Training documents

Military

✤ Selective Service records

✤ National Guard service documents

✤ Citations

✤ Service medals

(continues)

(continued from page 17)

- ❀ Disability records
- ❀ Uniforms
- ❀ Ribbons
- ❀ Insignias

- ❀ POW diaries/journals
- ❀ Pension papers
- ❀ War rosters or memorials
- ❀ Firearms/swords

Other Official Documents and Records

- ❀ Wedding announcements
- ❀ Wedding guest books
- ❀ Anniversary announcements
- ❀ Divorce papers
- ❀ Obituaries
- ❀ Funeral service guest book
- ❀ Memorial cards
- ❀ Wills
- ❀ Bookplates
- ❀ Naturalization papers

- ❀ Passports
- ❀ Visas
- ❀ Alien registrations
- ❀ Vaccination or immunization records
- ❀ Receipts
- ❀ Club membership cards
- ❀ Denizen papers
- ❀ Marriage certificates
- ❀ Birth certificates

Land, Property, and Assets

- ❀ Deeds
- ❀ Land grants
- ❀ Water rights
- ❀ Mortgages
- ❀ Town histories

- ❀ Cemetery records
- ❀ County histories
- ❀ Orphan court records
- ❀ Census records
- ❀ Passenger lists

- ✻ Leases
- ✻ Tax documents
- ✻ Titles
- ✻ Estate records
- ✻ Check registers
- ✻ Canceled checks
- ✻ Bank books
- ✻ Driver's licenses
- ✻ Motor vehicle registrations
- ✻ Stock certificates
- ✻ Savings bonds
- ✻ Safety deposit box receipt or key

- ✻ Insurance records
- ✻ Contracts
- ✻ Summons
- ✻ Subpoenas
- ✻ Ledgers
- ✻ Business licenses
- ✻ Occupational licenses
- ✻ Trade certifications
- ✻ Hunting and fishing licenses
- ✻ Tax notices
- ✻ Loans
- ✻ Abstracts of title

Health

- ✻ Medical records
- ✻ Hospital records
- ✻ Insurance documents

- ✻ Immunization papers
- ✻ X-rays
- ✻ Vaccination records

Other Great Resources

- ✻ Greeting cards
- ✻ Journals
- ✻ Diaries
- ✻ Letters

- ✻ Postcards
- ✻ Photographs
- ✻ Autograph albums

(continues)

(continued from page 19)

- ✿ Calendars
- ✿ Schedule organizers
- ✿ Newspaper clippings
- ✿ Scrapbooks
- ✿ Engraved items
- ✿ China and serving pieces
- ✿ Quilts
- ✿ Needlework samplers
- ✿ Pressed flowers
- ✿ Ticket stubs

- ✿ Family bulletins
- ✿ Family histories
- ✿ Local area histories
- ✿ Family traditions
- ✿ Travel logs
- ✿ Family coat of arms
- ✿ Insignias
- ✿ Souvenirs
- ✿ Plaques

(continued from page 15)

Dates

Specific dates are important because this information can help you form a time line. Narrowing down the year, month, and even the day can help you focus in on the time period and help you disregard information that took place before or after the event you are looking for. You may only know the month or the year. Don't disregard this information; place it into your family research files. You can always remove it or delete it later.

Dates are listed by day (number), month (abbreviation), and year (number). Note that this is the reverse of the order civilians usually use in the United States:

Example: 02 Nov 1959 rather than 11/2/59

Places

Places are recorded by city/township, county, state, and country. This information can help you track official records often kept at the town or county level of government. It can also help you track a family's movement during a lifetime.

Example: Palm Bay, Brevard, Florida, USA or Palm Bay, Brevard, Florida, by way of Warsaw, Indiana

Step 4: Determine What You Know Right Now

Before you gather information from relatives, historical societies, or computer programs, organize the information you already know about your family. You may be pleasantly surprised that you have a substantial head start with the amount of information at hand. See the sidebar "Checklist for Your Family Heritage Hunt" for some ideas, but don't let its length intimidate you: Remember to keep only those items that you deem personally important for your family heritage scrapbook.

There are two universal methods of documenting family genealogy information: the pedigree chart and the family group record.

Before you gather information from relatives, historical societies, or computer programs, organize the information you already know about your family.

Pedigree Chart

The first tool used to organize this family information is called a *pedigree chart.* The information included on this chart includes the following:

Full name

Born

Place

Married

Place

Died

Place

Most of the genealogy indexes and search engines are organized in the same fashion as this chart. You'll quickly adapt to the indexing and organization of genealogy if you use the Pedigree Chart and Letter to Request Information for Pedigree Chart provided at the back of this book. Start small, and your search skills will develop and become second nature.

Family Group Record

The second paperwork tool is a chart called *family group record* that will prove vital in your family heritage search. Basically the same information is recorded onto this form as was listed in the pedigree chart; however, the family group record organizes the information by

immediate family unit. The information included on this form includes the following:

Husband (or wife, plus any children)

Born

Place

Married

Place

Died

Place

Father's full name

Mother's full name

You will want to fill out a separate family group record for your
own parents. Please note that if you are a parent yourself, you will put
your own name on the family record twice: once as the child of your
parents and then once as a parent with your spouse and children. If the
family has more than one marriage, you should fill out a separate family
group record for each marriage.

You can fill out this form for each branch of the family, or you may
choose only to fill in your immediate family's information.

Again, consider how much information and how far back to you
want to journey into your family history. It is your personal choice. Fill in
as much as you can at the beginning even if your goal is only to cover
your immediate family. You may find that you enjoy the search and want
to trace your roots farther back than you originally thought.

Just How Easy Did You Say This Was?

It may seem that modern technology has made genealogy a breeze with
the availability of user-friendly computer software and high-speed Internet search engines, but some old-fashioned pencil-and-paper research is
still needed to discover your family roots, as you'll realize when compiling

your pedigree chart and family group record. Some computer programs include both of these forms, and if you are comfortable with the computer, feel free to use this type of application. However, make sure you keep copies of your updated information on a backup system, and keep a hard copy in a secure, protected place like a safe or safe deposit box.

Other Tools

Additional handy forms you may want to copy from the back of the book include these:

✽ *Resources checklist:* This list provides the most up-to-date resources available to you to search for family information. It will help you keep a record of what resources you have tried during your search for information and which work best for you.

✽ *Research log:* This keeps a record of a specific search or, as the genealogists say, an objective. It keeps in one place or sheet all the ways you tried to find out where your great-grandmother was born, for example.

✽ *Research calendar:* This calendar will hold the research log information of the family, so at a glance you can see where each objective is being searched.

✽ *Correspondence record:* Handy for those old-fashioned searches done by correspondence, this record helps keep track of all the letters, e-mails, and calls going out and coming in.

✽ *Artifacts and heirlooms tracker:* This form has little to do with formal genealogy, but what a wonderful tool to keep track of who has what in the family!

✽ Before continuing with the next steps, make copies of the pedigree chart and family group record found at the end of the book. Find a quiet place where you can sit and relax, and start filling in the blanks. Don't get discouraged if you find that you can't complete all the responses. Chapters 2 and 3 will give you more information and ways to find the answers to questions of dates, places, and even names that are part of your family heritage.

Step 5: Narrow Your Search

What information are you looking for? Are you searching for the names of ancestors? Do you want to know when or where each was born? Are you interested in knowing whether they married, whom they married, or whether they had children? Do you want to find out whether a relative is living or has passed away?

Why bother with all this cut-and-dried information? Trees have roots, which give the tree stability and strength to stand tall. The ho-hum details like birth dates and marriages are important if you want to really find accurate and detailed information about your family. It's easy to overlook the details of a single tree when you are consumed by the forest. No detail is too small or insignificant to the long-term goal of researching your family's history.

Trees have roots, which give the tree stability and strength to stand tall.

You might be looking for deeper answers. Your curiosity might lead you to wonder what type of life the person had, how they felt when television was first available to the public, or what music they loved.

Take another small step and select one relative or ancestor you want to find out more about. Circle the blanks you want to fill in for this person on your pedigree chart or family group record. Make a few notes of information not listed on these two forms that you have questions about. You might wish to find a copy of a birth certificate, a

TIPS FOR BEGINNERS

These pointers from genealogy enthusiasts might come in handy as you begin your search for family history and heritage.

🌸 Keep copies of everything you find in your search. It may not seem important now, but it might be something that turns out to be very important in the future. Take special care in preserving the originals of documents and photos (see chapters 4 and 5).

🌸 Ask your family members whether there is a formal or informal genealogy book or other records within the family. This could give you a great head start! Don't forget to ask whether there is a family Bible that was handed down from parent to child, sometimes over many generations. Many families kept family events such as births, marriages, and deaths recorded in such a Bible.

🌸 Make sure that you keep in mind possible alternate spellings of your surname as you are researching. Difficult-to-read or illegible handwriting was often transferred incorrectly to official documents.

marriage certificate, a photo from this person's childhood, and a photo taken of the person as an adult. You may have a question or two you'd like to ask this person. Write those questions down. You may not get the chance to ask the person the questions, but you may discover another relative who can answer them or even a family friend who will give you insight.

Treasure what you find. . . . this information is part of your family history.

In your family research file you may want to make a note or two about your expectations. Make your goals realistic. You may not find all the answers. You may not get complete answers. Treasure what you do find. Positive or negative, this information is part of your family history.

Select and Search Available Records

There are two main types of genealogical records. The first is *compiled records*. These records have already been researched by others and appear in books, microfilm, microfiche, or computer databases. The second type is called *original records*. These are records established at or near the time of an event, such as a birth certificate, census report, or death certificate. Most professional genealogists recommend first searching in compiled records and then looking for original records, to save time and effort.

Ask Family Relatives

You may find you have easy access to original records by asking different relatives for the information. You may need to make contact with different relatives and compare everyone's recollections to average the time period or place.

I was pleasantly surprised when I contacted my cousin Jeff for information on my parents. It turns out Jeff is the "official" family historian. He had already done extensive research on my father's side of the family and was thrilled to share the information with me. Is there a family historian you don't know about in your family?

Search the Internet

The Internet has made access to many public records very easy. In many cases you can simply send off an E-mail request for a document. Keep in mind that you may still have to pay a fee for a copy of a document or record.

Also available are software packages that bring some indexes into your home without even needing Internet access. These wonderful new approaches to gathering information will be detailed in chapter 2.

Use Other Resources

Local libraries; Internet genealogy sites; and city, township, and county government record departments can also provide valuable data. Be aware that you might have to broaden the time period, consider spelling variations, or formally write for copies of documents.

Step 6: Evaluate the Information Gathered

You'll need to start evaluating the information you've gathered. Is the information complete? Does anything directly conflict with other information? Did you find the data you were looking for?

Take time to copy any applicable information to your pedigree chart(s) and family group record(s). Begin to organize your information with a filing, indexing, or organizational system that you are comfortable with. Finally, share what you've discovered with other interested family members and friends.

With your known facts organized, you are ready to start filling in as many blanks about your family history as you can. As you begin chapter

2, you'll find practical ways to get more information about your family. I'll start with the old-fashioned family interview of living relatives and round out your search with methods to access files via your computer.

Free Help!

You can receive a free pamphlet detailing how to access vital records (birth, marriage, and death certificates) by requesting Publication No. (PHS) 82-1142 from the U.S. Department of Health and Human Services, 200 Independence Avenue, SW, Washington, D.C. 20201. Or access the information at this government agency's Web site: www.os.dhhs.gov/.

2

Grassroots Research

You should have as much information as you know so far written into your pedigree chart and family group records. Your next step is to start researching and gathering information from family and local, county, state, federal, and, in some cases, international resources. A good search for family heritage will include some good old-fashioned detective work with family interviews and correspondence sent to agencies who can provide copies of documents. I also recommend you take advantage of the convenience of the home personal computer and Internet access (covered in the next chapter). However, don't for a second think that just because you can now send electronic mail (or E-mail, as it's more commonly called) or delve into government records online that you will not have to use the early "low-tech" tools of genealogy. Thousands of records and documents still can't be accessed with the click of your computer mouse; moreover, many of us haven't yet joined the global cyber community. For all these reasons, we've dedicated this chapter to grassroots, pencil-and-paper research.

 ## GETTING THE FAMILY SCOOP

Any family connections you can make, you should make. The information you can gather from living relatives is the most important information you can have. Just knowing an approximate time frame of birth, marriage, immigration to the United States, and deaths of relatives can save you hours, days, and even years of time when putting together a family history.

The information you can gather from living relatives is the most important information you can have.

You may find that relatives differ on exact facts of family experiences, but having such different options broadens your choices of resources to use. Even while writing this book, I made educated guesses on some of my oldest known family members, such as my great-great-grandfather who immigrated from Ireland and my mother's mother who was born, lived, and died in the same village in Germany. I was able to gather information on many of these relatives using only my time frame estimates. Later, I confirmed my finds with the Given family historian, my cousin Jeff, and my only known maternal cousin,

Ingrid. You can follow the same techniques even if you don't have a family historian or genealogy enthusiast to verify your discoveries.

☙ THE FAMILY INTERVIEW

The best way to get information from your relatives is to set up an interview with each one. Face-to-face meetings are preferable, but when that's not always possible, you might have to interview over the phone or via mail, E-mail, or fax, with at least one follow-up by telephone. Remember to address the same questions yourself and to interview close family friends, too.

The best way to get information from your relatives is to set up an interview with each one.

The questions suggested in this section and the answers you'll receive may at times seem obvious or simplistic, but any information you gather will help you record, document, and preserve your family history. Memories stored in only the human mind may fade, and details may be overlooked or even forgotten. It's never too late or too early to start asking questions and finding the answers about your family so that you can avoid such lost history.

The guidelines that follow for conducting a family interview are broken down into several subcategories so as not to overwhelm you with a superlong list of questions. Try small doses of questions—one or two of these smaller lists, for example—with plenty of positive, patient feedback and interaction between you and the interviewee. You may

(continues on page 36)

Where to Find What at a Glance

Newspapers

Visit the newspaper office or check for online archives for obituaries, engagement and wedding announcements, will readings, divorce and tax notices, births and fictitious name announcements, local histories, and criminal activities. These records might include family surnames, spouses, siblings, children and extended family, birth or death dates, and more.

Social Security Death Index (SSDI)

By writing the Social Security Administration, using software that includes the SSDI, or visiting the Web sites that include the SSDI, you will find the Social Security number and death date of a relative, and you might also find birth date, place of birth, and place of death.

United States Census Records

Census records vary by the year taken, but you can find them at public libraries and Web sites, on CD-ROM indexes, and in the National Archives in Washington, D.C. (check regional offices also), to locate birth dates, spouses, children, occupations, and locations.

Cemetery Records

Check with your local courthouse or go directly to a cemetery of known places within your family or ask relatives where family members are buried; you might find birth dates and places of birth along with dates and places of death. (See the later section in this chapter on visiting cemeteries.)

School Records

Check with specific school or county school administration offices and even your local public library for birth dates, addresses, grades, where any copies of school records were sent, teachers, yearbooks, school newspapers, programs, and more.

City or County Histories

The local library is your best bet for family histories as well as the names of residents and active volunteers who might be able to provide helpful interviews describing the feel of the town or county.

Telephone Directories

Local libraries and some online Web sites provide names and addresses of families or businesses, in addition to local addresses for city and county government offices that can lead you to land and tax records.

City and County Plat Maps

Located at the county recorder's office or a local genealogical society, these maps can help you locate the names of people who owned town or county lots and land.

Church or Religious Records

Find local churches, genealogical societies, regional church offices. You may be able to locate birth, marriage, and death dates; mention of your relatives in church programs or newspapers; plus records of baptism, christening, or confirmation dates and missionary assignments or positions held within the church.

Local Police

Not what most of us want to check, but the police department can lead to information about relatives who might have had some run-ins with the law; you might find information about birth, spouse, sibling, parents, children, addresses, and the record of the offender. Also note that in small towns the police chief might very well know most citizens—even those without records.

Military and Veteran's Records

Visit city hall, the public library, or your local genealogical society to locate militia members before the Civil War era. Contact the branch of the appropriate armed service—U.S. Army, Navy, Air Force, or Marines—directly, too.

(continued from page 33)

end up unearthing an extra treasured tidbit if you listen carefully to any side comments your relative may add to his or her answers. Don't hesitate to explore these surprises. You can always go back to your prepared questions later in the interview.

In addition, keep in mind that older generations may consider some of these questions as rather personal, giving you a well-intentioned lecture on minding your manners and own business. Some questions may also trigger truly painful or unpleasant memories for some individuals. Very real feelings of guilt, shame, or embarrassment may persist on certain topics such as divorce, mental and physical illnesses, run-ins with the law, or ancestors who were labeled the black sheep or even disowned entirely. Use good judgment and never force a relative to answer.

Me, Myself, and I

It is easiest to make yourself the first guinea pig of your interview skills. Answering some personal questions about yourself will also give you some insight on how certain questions may affect you emotionally and, as a result, other people, too.

Childhood

1. What is the name you were given at birth?

2. When were you born (month, day, year, and time)?

3. Where were you born? In a hospital or at home? Do you know the name of the hospital?

4. Where is your birth certificate?

5. Why was your name chosen? What is the meaning of your name?

FINDING FAMILY TREASURE

You never know where or how you might come across some valuable tidbit during your family heritage quest. My mother told me that my grandfather Given came to the U.S. from Ireland, so imagine my surprise when I found out this wasn't the case at all. During a phone interview with my cousin Jeff, I was asking several questions about my dad's mother, whose maiden name was Doty. I off-handedly mentioned a college professor who was positive that our great-great-grandfathers fought side by side during the Civil War. At the time, I blew off the professor's comments. I told my cousin how I could just kick myself now! In some strange way this remark reminded him that maybe he did have some information that dated that far back in U.S. history. It was becoming clear to me that the Given family arrived in America much earlier than I realized. This caused me to joke about how they probably would never end up in the Mayflower Society or the Daughters of the American Revolution. Which, in turn, led him to remember that he *did* notice the name Doty on the roster of passengers of the *Mayflower* while viewing a traveling exhibit of the Mayflower. Which led me to ask him—well, you get the picture!

I researched my cousin's comments and found that my grandmother Given was a direct descendant of Edward Doty who was an indentured servant on the Mayflower; my great-grandmother Given was a direct descendant of a Civil War soldier; and it was my great-great-grandfather Given who brought his family to the United States. And all I originally wanted to know was more about my dad's mother.

Keep your interviews to small doses of prepared questions as suggested, but also keep an open mind and open ears.

6. Have you ever had a nickname? Who gave it to you and why?

7. What were your favorite hobbies as a child?

8. Did you have a pet as a child?

9. Were you raised in a particular faith?

Family Reflections

1. What is your birth order?

2. Do or did your parents or siblings like to tell any funny stories about you?

3. What did you want to be when you grew up?

4. Did you have a favorite relative? Why was this person so special?

5. Do you remember your grandparents? What do you remember?

6. Do you remember a special vacation or family event?

7. Do you look more like your mom or your dad? What physical traits did you inherit from each?

8. What was your favorite meal?

9. If you had to pick only one, what special occasion would you celebrate? Birthday? New Year's Eve? A holiday or holy day?

10. Can you name any family or person that spent a lot of time with yours?

The World around Me

1. What schools did you attend? Did you ever have to be the new kid in school?

2. Any teachers or adults who had an important influence in your life?

3. First girlfriend? Boyfriend? First serious romance?

4. Who is your hero and why?

5. Any strong political or personal beliefs?

6. Do you vote? In local elections? National elections?

7. Favorite movie, song, or book?

8. Important milestones for you? First job? First home?

9. Favorite color?

10. Any goals or dreams still ahead to accomplish?

My Own Family

1. How did you meet your spouse or mate?

2. Does your spouse or mate have any physical or personality traits of your own family?

3. Did you pick up any traits, habits, or traditions from your mate's family?

4. Did you ever change political, personal, or religious beliefs for your mate?

5. Any very special occasion(s) with your own family?

6. Memories of your wedding?

7. Do you have any children (names, birth dates, adoptions)?

8. The one most important lesson you've learned from your mate or children?

9. What new traditions have you started within your own family?

On to the Rest of the Family

Once you have a solid foundation of how you fit into your world, it is time ask a few questions of those around you, including immediate and extended family members as well as close friends. Some questions can be asked casually, say, over breakfast or dinner or during a long car ride or phone conversation. For more detailed questions and in-depth background, you may want to have a quiet hour or so to hold an interview at a convenient time. Let your interviewee know what you are doing, why you want this information, and that you are willing to share any of the information you gather about the family's heritage with them. Get comfortable with the person by asking some less serious or silly, easy questions at the start.

Being able to hear loved ones' voices, especially if they live far away or have died, is a unique treasure for your family heritage scrapbook.

You may also wish to use a tape recorder if your interviewee is willing, which will give you an audio record for the future, too. Being able to hear loved ones' voices, especially if they live far away or have died, is a unique treasure for your family heritage scrapbook.

Another option is to select a few questions and send them in writing to the interviewee. Supply blank index cards or acid-free paper for the person to provide his or her answers. This approach allows for more detailed responses, at the subject's own pace. If the interviewee handwrites the reply, you have another more personlaized artifact for your scrapbook.

Finally, remember that the following lists are only guidelines. You do not need to ask every question suggested here; some may be more important to you personally, and some may be better avoided altogether out of courtesy or respect for privacy. Tailor each interview to each person individually. Be considerate, too, of the time needed to participate in your quest so your interviews don't last too long. Any material you're able to gather, no matter how small, is a valuable asset.

Warm-Up Questions: Favorites

1. What is your favorite candy?

2. What is your favorite cookie?

3. What is your favorite drink?

4. What is your favorite perfume?

5. What is your favorite restaurant?

6. What was your favorite vacation?

7. What is your favorite poem?

8. What is your favorite TV show?

(continues on page 44)

MISSION IMPOSSIBLE

In an article entitled "Impossible and Improbable" for Genealogy.com, Donna Przecha states that four situations may make it almost impossible to ever really get confirmation and information about a family member. The following problems are considered the extremes in family history research. They are not typical, but they do pop up. Przecha suggests that if you find these situations within your own family, keep an open mind and try to locate the missing relative through some of the newer indexed resources provided by city, county, and state agencies and organizations. Don't be disappointed, however, if you end up hitting a brick wall despite your best efforts. In some cases, not even a professional genealogist would be able to find solid information.

Disowned family members: Some parents have even gone as far as erecting a grave marker for children the family has disowned. Your best bet is to hope that the child is mentioned in a family Bible or a parent's will (which states that the child was disowned and can't lay claim to any assets of the family).

Bigamy: In this case, several wives might have filed paperwork on a deceased husband in different states. It can get very confusing since the husband in question might not have informed all family members that he indeed married more than one wife. In such a case, track the legal documents of marriage certificates, death certificates, obituaries, and wills, plus take a look at any court records.

Name changes: If someone wishes to disappear from a former life, that person just changes his or her name either by using a new name or by submitting false information to get new documents. This technique is usually done by people who were immigrants, war veterans, freed slaves, and even women who bore children out of wedlock. Try to consult as many legal or official documents as possible.

Duplicate names: Believe it or not, some families gave all female or male children the same first name with different middle names, or they may have named one son Jim and the second son James. You might also come across a family member who gave two children the same name, but research will indicate that one child died before the second child was born. Duplicate names can get confusing, but it is usually a rare case. When it does arise, simply try to dig as deep as you can into the family history lines.

Wrong sex or race: Sometimes information was just not recorded correctly, or a typo occurred. In addition, in the past some race classifications followed different rules. For example, if a person was a quarter black, he or she might have been classified as white in some parts of the country or by some officials or as black elsewhere.

(continued from page 41)

9. Who is your favorite news TV anchor?

10. Who is your favorite author?

11. What is your favorite book?

12. What is your favorite season?

13. What is your favorite scent?

14. What is your favorite word?

15. What is your favorite tree?

16. What is your favorite flower?

17. What is your favorite painting?

18. What is your favorite quote?

19. Who is your favorite poet?

20. What is your favorite color?

21. What is your favorite sport?

22. What is your favorite holiday?

23. What is your favorite style of music?

24. What is your favorite musical instrument?

25. Who is your favorite musical group?

26. What is your favorite song?

27. Who is your favorite singer?

28. Who is your favorite movie star?

29. What is your favorite movie?

30. What is your favorite amusement park ride?

31. Who is your favorite artist?

32. Who is your favorite athlete?

33. What is your favorite animal at the zoo?

34. What is your favorite animal on a farm?

35. What is your favorite meal?

36. What is your favorite fruit?

37. What is your favorite vegetable?

38. What is your favorite flavor of ice cream?

39. What is your favorite board game?

40. What is your favorite card game?

Background and Reference

1. What is your mother's name?

2. When and where was she born?

3. Is she still alive? When did she die?

4. What is your most vivid image of your mother?

5. What is your father's name?

6. When and where was he born?

7. Is he still alive? When did he die?

8. What is your most vivid image of your father?

9. Where did your parents meet?

10. When and where did they get married?

11. What are your brothers' and sisters' names?

12. What is the most enjoyable memory of time spent with your parents?

13. What are some of the most valuable lessons your parents taught you?

Childhood

1. What type of house did you live in as a child? Other buildings on the same property?

2. Did you move about during your childhood? Where and when? What can you remember of each house, the family circumstances, and the reason for the move?

3. How was your home heated?

4. Did you have a fireplace?

5. What kind of kitchen stove did your parents cook on? What fuel was used and did you have to buy the fuel, or was this a chore, such as cutting wood, with which you had to help?

6. Did you always have electricity? If not, when did you get it? Was it a big deal?

7. Did you ever use candles or kerosene lamps?

8. Did you always have a television set? If not, when did your family get one? Was it a big deal?

9. Did your family have a cellar? Where did you store food? Did your family can some foods?

10. Did your family always have a telephone? Was your home phone line shared with other neighbors in a party line? Was getting a telephone a big deal to your family?

11. Where did your family get water? Was it plentiful? What methods were used to conserve water?

12. What is your favorite childhood memory?

Learning Life's Lessons

1. What was your position in the family? Oldest? Youngest?

2. What were your duties as a small child? Did you have chores?

3. Who cooked the meals? Who did the ironing, cleaning, and such?

4. Did you buy or make your own clothing?

5. When did you learn to cook, and who taught you?

6. Did you ever learn to sew? crochet? knit? embroider? And who taught you?

7. Did you ever learn the mechanics of a car? Who taught you?

8. Did your family keep in touch with distant family? How did you stay in touch? Do you still keep in touch?

9. Did you visit relatives often?

10. How did you get your mail?

11. What do you remember about family pets?

12. Were you especially close to anyone in the family? Who?

13. How did the family spend its evenings?

14. Did you get an allowance? How much? What did you spend it on?

15. Do you remember your family discussing world events and politics? What were some of the topics?

Careers and Ambitions

1. What did your father do for a living?

2. Did your mother ever work outside the home? What did she do?

3. Did you contribute to the family income? How?

4. Did your family have a garden? Who did the work on it? What kinds of vegetables did you grow? Was anything canned?

5. Did you raise chickens or any other meat?

6. What kind of meat did you eat?

7. If you lived on a farm, what crops were planted? Who did the work? family? hired hands? Did you keep a cow for milk? Did you make your own butter and cheese? Did anyone in the family sell eggs or butter?

8. What was your first job? Do you remember how much your pay was?

9. Who influenced you most and helped you develop your skills?

10. What careers have you had? How long at each?

11. Would you choose the same career if you had it to do over?

Days, Seasons, and Special Occasions

1. What did Sunday mean to you: another day free of school or work, or perhaps a big family dinner?

2. Did you attend church on Sunday? Where?

3. Were there any other special days of the week?

4. How did you spend Christmas/Hanukkah?

5. What kinds of gifts did you receive at Christmas/Hanukkah?

6. Did your family observe Easter?

7. How and where did you observe the Fourth of July?

8. Other special holidays?

9. How was your birthday celebrated? What kinds of gifts did you receive? Best gift ever?

10. Did your family entertain often? When?

11. Did your family attend picnics? family reunions? What do you remember about them?

12. How did you keep cool in the summer? Swim in a lake? Visit the shore?

13. What did you wear in the winter to keep warm?

14. Do you remember any particular blizzards, tornadoes, floods, or other disasters?

Friends and Entertainment

1. Did you have a favorite toy?

2. What were your favorite foods? What did you hate?

3. What did you do for recreation?

4. What kind of books did you read?

5. Did you or your brothers or sisters have any hobbies?

6. Who is or was your best friend?

7. What did you and your friends do when you got together?

8. Did you and your playmates play any organized games or sports?

9. Did you ever learn to swim? Who taught you?

10. Did you participate in youth organizations?

11. What was the most mischievous thing you did as a youngster?

12. How did your parents punish you (spanking, no allowance, grounded, etc.)?

13. Whom did you admire most when you were young?

14. Who do you admire the most today?

15. Has there ever been anyone in your life that you considered to be your "soul mate" or kindred spirit? Who was it, and why did you feel that way?

School and Education

1. Where did you go to school? Did you ever attend a one-room schoolhouse?

2. What were your favorite subjects in school? least favorite?

3. Who was your favorite teacher and why?

4. Do you still know anyone that you went to grade school with? In what grade did you meet?

5. Do you still keep in touch with any high school, community college, or university buddies?

6. How did you get to school? If you walked, how far? What do you remember about these walks? Did you walk alone or with friends?

7. Did you ever miss a long stretch of school because of illness? What was the illness? What was done to help you heal or recover? How did you pass the time?

8. What did you do during summer vacations? Best summer vacation you ever went on?

9. In high school, were you involved in sports? What were some of the highlights?

10. Were you in the school band? What instrument(s)? Did you continue to play into adulthood?

11. What songs and dances were popular then?

12. What was some of the slang you used when you were a teenager?

13. What was your first date like? How old were you? What did you do?

14. What was your proudest achievement in school?

15. How old were you when you left home? Where to and why did you leave? How did it feel to be on your own?

16. How many years of school did you attend? Did you study in your adult years?

Transportation and Surroundings

1. Describe the size of the town where you grew up or lived as an adult.

2. Where did your parents shop? Stores? Mail-order catalogs?

3. How large or small were the stores? Family owned?

4. If you lived in a small town or on the farm, did you ever go into the city to shop?

5. What was the largest town you remember visiting when you were young?

6. Did you ever travel on a train while you were young?

7. Did you or your family own a horse and buggy?

8. When did your family acquire its first car? What make? How much did it cost?

9. When did you learn to drive a car? Did someone teach you?

10. Did you celebrate upon getting your driver's license?

11. Did you have to run errands for your parents or siblings once you could drive?

12. Was or is there a car you'd just die for?

13. Do you buckle up when in a car?

14. Did you ever own or ride on a motorcycle? Was your mother or father upset when you announced you wanted or bought a motorcycle? How (if you did) did you calm her or him down?

15. Have you ever traveled by plane? What kind of plane was it? Were you nervous on that first plane trip?

Traditions

1. What family traditions are still practiced in your family?

2. What are the origins of your family traditions?

3. Is there one tradition or ritual you wish your family did *not* have?

4. Can you briefly tell one or more of your family's best stories or "tall tales"?

5. Do you recall any family members that were eccentric? What earned them that reputation?

6. What's the best gift you've ever received, and who gave it to you?

7. What's the worst present you've ever unwrapped? How did you get rid of it?

8. Is there a song, book, poem, prayer, blessing, or quote that just seems created for your family or that your family could have inspired?

9. What personal traits or characteristics seemed to run in the family?

10. Is there an enduring piece of advice or wisdom that's been passed down from generation to generation in your family?

Marriage

1. When and where did you meet your husband, wife, or partner?

2. How and when did you get engaged? Who proposed? How long were you engaged?

3. When and where did you marry? How old were you and your spouse?

4. Did you go on a honeymoon? Where?

5. Where was your first home? Did you move around?

6. What is your spouse's occupation?

7. After living together for a time, what surprised you the most about your mate?

8. How would you describe your partner? What do you admire most about him or her?

9. What's your favorite story about your partner?

10. Where and when were your children born? What are their names?

11. Do any stories come to mind about their births?

12. What were some of the family hardships you faced?

13. What were some of the most enjoyable family activities you shared?

14. What were some of the family rules?

15. What's the most important lesson you hope your children learned from you?

16. What caused you to say, "Just wait until you have children of your own!"?

Other Aspects of Life

1. Did you or your mate go into military service?

2. If so, what did you do while he or she was away?

3. Did you experience the Great Depression? What are your memories of this time?

4. Did you ever have to see off a member of the family as he or she left for war? How did that feel?

5. Ever greet a family member returning from service during a war? How did you welcome him or her home?

6. What memories do you have of war years?

7. Do you like to write letters? Do you have any pen pals?

8. Do you own a computer? In what ways do you utilize the computer in your life? Games? Record keeping? Surfing the Web?

9. What magazines do you read each week or month?

10. To what organizations have you belonged?

11. Have you been politically active during your lifetime?

12. Which party affiliation do you take? Democrat? Republican? Independent? Why?

13. Which presidents have you voted for?

14. Which president do you remember or admire most?

15. Ever want to run for office? What office would you want to occupy?

Philosophy and Outlook

1. Do you have a philosophy of life to share with your descendants? What is it?

2. Do you have a favorite philosopher, teacher, or writer who best expresses your philosophy?

3. Do you have religious leanings or strong religious beliefs?

4. In your opinion, which have been the greatest advances or inventions during your lifetime?

5. What things have given you the most pleasure or satisfaction?

6. Is there anything that has caused you ongoing concern? What events or trends have disturbed you most in your lifetime?

7. What has been your experience in regard to the following: Answers to prayers? Necessity and power of love? Willpower as opposed to being ruled by one's feelings?

8. What do you consider to be your most important achievements? What one thing are you most proud of?

9. What would you say is the funniest thing that's ever happened to you?

10. What has been your favorite time of life?

11. Which person most influenced your life and why?

12. Did you travel? Which places were most interesting and why? Is there a place you've never visited that you would like to?

13. Have you ever made a sacrifice that's made a lasting impression on you?

14. What was your wisest decision?

15. What wasn't your wisest decision?

16. What makes your family truly unique?

17. What single piece of advice do you want to leave your children and grandchildren?

Questions Specifically for Grandparents

1. What were the names of your parent's parents? Do you know any relatives further back?

2. When and where were they born, and where did they live?

3. What did they do for a living?

4. Do you have personal memories of them? What were they like?

5. What was the most enjoyable time you spent with any or each of your grandparents?

6. What do you know about your grandparent's children, other than your own parents?

7. What do you remember hearing about your great-grandparents?

8. Did you ever meet them?

9. From what part of the country or world did your family emigrate? Any stories told in your family about the crossing? Did they become U.S. citizens?

10. Do you have any relatives who still live in foreign countries?

11. Where did your family settle in this country? Why?

12. Do you have any relatives who were famous or took part in well-known historical events?

13. How far back can you trace your family tree?

14. How have times changed from when you were a kid? a young adult?

Records, Documents, and Artifacts

1. Do you have any photographs of family members that are over ten, fifteen, twenty, or thirty years old? May I have copies made of these photos?

2. Do you have any newspaper clippings of birth, engagement, marriage, or death announcements of a family member? May I have copies made?

3. Do you have any legal documents like marriage certificates, land deeds, immigration or naturalization papers, death certificates, or wills of a family member? May I make copies?

FAMILY HISTORY LOST: MAIDEN NAMES

Too often vital family history is lost because we don't pay attention or document the female spouses of a family. The most interesting of my own family history came from my grandmother, Fannie Doty Given, who was the descendent of Edward Doty of the *Mayflower* and my great-grandmother Cynthia Johnson Given, whose ancestors fought in the American Revolution. For this reason, I suggest you keep a Maiden Name Log (provided in the back of this book) simply record the maiden name as the woman's middle name, and tuck this list into your family research files.

The following are places to find maiden names if they are currently missing in your pedigree chart:

- Marriage certificate
- Marriage license
- Marriage application
- Divorce records
- Census records
- Family Bible records
- Baptism papers
- Christening papers
- Military records (veteran's benefit records list spouse's name)
- Engagement announcements
- Wedding announcements
- Obituaries
- Diplomas

4. Do you have any other documents like diplomas, awards, military records, Social Security cards, or adoption papers of a relative? Do you know any relative who might have such documents?

5. Do you know of any family Bibles, diaries, journals, yearbooks, or other books owned or used by a family member?

6. Who was the family historian? Anyone in the family enjoy or research our family roots?

7. Do you know of any heirlooms passed from one generation to the next?

8. Do you have or know of any old family letters or correspondence kept by a family member?

9. Is there anyone, family member or family friend, who you think might be able to help me discover more information or documentation of our family?

 ## AFTER EACH INTERVIEW

While the experience is still fresh, sit down with your interview notes and read each response thoroughly. If possible, transcribe your notes into a typed or word-processed document. Most people use some kind of personal shorthand during an interview, and, if you are like me, that shorthand might not make much sense two weeks down the road. Note any follow-up questions or any clarification you might discover you need upon reviewing the interview, and then make an appointment as soon as possible with the person to ask any additional questions.

Make notes of any further research you might have to do about this person or about your family in general. Keep a "To Do" list of needed follow-ups in your family research files, additional people you should contact, requests that might need to be made in writing to a government agency, and other tasks you might forget to do while you continue to research. Don't forget to document where, when, how, and why this family interview was done. Add a few of your personal thoughts about the interview. Did a piece of information surprise you? Did the interview confirm something that up until the interview you weren't sure was accurate? Did any information contradict another relative's information or your own personal memories?

Send a note of thanks to the interviewee who gave you his or her time and shared with you some family history.

Send a note of thanks to the interviewee who gave you his or her time and shared with you some family history. Include a printed or typed copy of the interview for the relative to fact-check. Request that the individual contact you if any of the information was recorded incorrectly, especially any name spellings or important dates like birthdays or weddings.

Reasons to Document Your Research

Kory Meyerink, an accredited and professional genealogist in Salt Lake City, gives four distinct reasons for documentation:

1. **Saves time:** Taking time to document where you got your facts (or allegations) will save you time later in your research. Let's face it—most of us do our research a little bit at a time, as we have time and opportunities. Often you do some research on one family, only to set it aside for a couple years (or more) while other activities, and even other re-

search, take priority. Well, what happens when you sit down to work on that line you put off two or three years ago? Without writing down what you searched and where you found your information, you will likely look at some of the same sources again, only to find what you had already learned.

2. **Avoids duplication of research:** Most of us don't have time to do only "original research" on all of our families; after all, every person we find means there are two more (his or her parents) for us to find. We depend on quality previous research to speed up our search. Without documentation, we do not know what sources somebody has already used, which means we will likely use some of the same sources the earlier family historian used.

3. **Gives credit where credit is due:** Throughout the course of our research we are constantly using the research of others. It may be a published family history, a brief biographical sketch, or a computerized lineage from Ancestral File or the World Family Tree. As noted, our research moves forward much faster when we use such resources. Now, if we use such resources, aren't we obligated in some way to contribute (i.e., give back) to that growing pool of previously solved genealogical puzzles?

4. **It's not as difficult as you might think:** Perhaps the biggest objection to documentation is the dismay at the necessity of proper formatting when citing sources. Well, guess what? There are so many ways to cite sources that formatting your citations should not be a big hang-up or time commitment. Certainly if you are submitting an article for a scholarly journal you would be expected to follow their citation format. Lineage societies require a certain level of documentation to constitute proof of a connection. However, because in most cases you are working on a record for your family's own personal viewing alone, the good news is that you do *not* need to follow those standards in everything you document. You only need to record enough information so that another researcher (say, your children when they're older and want to continue your work) can determine what you have searched.

A Visit to the Cemetery

The answers we seek are often found within the peaceful resting sanctuary of our ancestors: cemeteries. Much information pertinent to your heritage quest can often be found at a cemetery or gravesite. My family's biggest family heritage discovery was that the paternal great-great-grandparents had not returned to Ireland, as family history stated, but were actually buried not ten minutes from the family homestead in the little town of New Harmony, Illinois. Without a visit to the cemetery, we still might be wondering where these ancestors might have ventured.

The answers we seek are often found within the peaceful resting sanctuary of our ancestors: cemeteries.

Finding the Cemetery

Finding the gravesite alone may still leave some questions unanswered as well as bring to the surface new ones. In my case, why did my dad's father not know where his great-grandparents were buried? Did he not keep in touch with his family who lived so close? Regard all such experiences as simply more leads to follow in your exciting family history detective work.

Considering Culture

All cultures have developed elaborate burial rituals through the ages. The dead have provided plenty of work for stonemasons and sculptors.

So tradesmen usually developed their own stone shapes and carving styles, but the use of specific graven images carved into the gravestone has become standard. In addition, surviving family erect markers and use icons to communicate information. For example, a weeping willow tree indicates mourning or natural grief. Clasped hands signify farewells said at death, while a hand pointing upward indicates the loved one's path to a heavenly reward. An urn represents immortality.

Clasped hands signify farewells said at death, while a hand pointing upward indicates the loved one's path to a heavenly reward.

Knowing What to Expect

Statuary in a cemetery is very common. Some of these sculptures or the images on them may seem self-explanatory, others may be more cryptic, but all serve to reveal something about the loved one buried there. Flowers represent the fragility of life, and plucked flowers indicate the person died young, while life was still in early bloom. A lion represents courage. A snake with its tail in its mouth indicates everlasting life in heaven, while a coiled snake indicates sin. Roosters are common in some cemeteries and represent resurrection. The pelican symbolizes redemption through Christ, while ants indicate Christian industriousness. Scales represent the weighing of justice for the judgment of the dead.

These carved icons or statuary, taken with tombstone epitaphs and other carvings, can often provide additional insight into the nature of the person or the family. Understanding what they represent not only enhances your appreciation of the cemetery but can help you read between the lines and perhaps learn more about the people interred there. Cemetery visits thus add another valuable dimension to your research.

RESEARCHING VIA LETTER WRITING

During your family history search, you will inevitably need to write a letter requesting information from a relative or to request a copy of a document or record from government or genealogical societies. Written correspondence can be an expeditious (rather than driving or flying across your state or the country) way of performing your genealogical research and certainly more economical. Your success may vary through the prolific writing of letters, but even if you are unable to accumulate much family data in this way, you'll glean other rewards. You may end up establishing new friendships or renewing old ones.

A few general rules to genealogical correspondence etiquette tend to bring more efficient and satisfying results (see sample letters in the back of this book for examples):

🖐 Type or word-process the letter, but if you don't have access to a type-writer or computer, print neatly.

🖐 Use standard business envelopes (no. 10) for your letters.

🖐 Be sure to use the correct postage.

🖐 Always include a self-addressed, stamped envelope (SASE) with all your correspondence unless you are told not to do so.

🖐 If you expect many pages of text to be returned to you, enclose a second stamp for your respondent to use, should it be necessary.

🖐 Send a note of thanks to anyone who helps you even if the individual was unable to locate the information you needed.

Your letter should state specifically what it is you need. The request should be sent to the appropriate person who can meet that request, if you are sending a letter to a government office, business, or organization. Make every attempt to find out whom you need to write, and spell this person's name correctly.

You don't have to be scholar to write an effective letter of request. Save the long-winded prose for your great American novel. When writing a letter of request, follow these guidelines for the best and quickest replies.

- Spell all names correctly; if in doubt, do more research.

- Get the address right, and address all letters correctly by U.S. Post Office guidelines.

- Discuss one topic per letter, and state it in the first sentence of the letter.

- Be courteous and respectful to those you seek assistance from.

- Highlight important words/points—using <u>underlining</u>, **boldface**, *italics*, larger font, or ALL CAPS—but with discretion.

- Use standard English with correct grammar and punctuation.

- Edit and rewrite.

- Avoid having all paragraphs the same length.

- Use short and varied sentences averaging between seven and seventeen words.

- Avoid jargon (terms that are highly technical and understood by only a few people) and flowery terms (e.g., *magnificent, exceptional*).

- Use active voice (e.g., "My father received an award" instead of "My father was given an award").

(continues on page 70)

GRAVESTONE OR MEMORIAL RUBBINGS

Creating gravestone or memorial rubbings is a very old technique practiced by professionals and enthusiasts over the years. They are another way to document an ancestor and, if done with skill and patience, create an interesting piece of art.

As interesting as the practice can be, however, some states and cemeteries have banned it. Connecticut has particular problems because many of its gravestones are made of sandstone that can erode internally, leaving the surface (which has hardened over the years due to environmental exposure) seemingly very stable for rubbing when in fact the stone is hollow beneath. The pressure of wax rubbing or even cleaning, therefore, can cause the stone to fracture or implode, causing irrevocable damage to an historic artifact.

Many cemeteries, if they allow rubbings at all, now require a permit before someone can do rubbings, so make sure you check this information out before visiting a cemetery to do a rubbing.

If rubbings are not allowed, then consider photographing the gravestone instead as a record for your family heritage scrapbook. Take several shots, including one that shows a large portion of the cemetery and one that includes the closest stones, to provide context. Photograph the whole gravestone so that inscription and carving are visible, and make sure to take at least one picture in which the inscription fills the camera frame.

If you are permitted to make a rubbing, follow these steps to create a wonderful keepsake of your cemetery visit:

1. Practice on a rock at home, or check with a local monuments/ gravestone service to see whether you can practice on one of their tombstones before going to the cemetery.

2. Be sure that the tombstone you have chosen is completely stable. If it is wobbly or the surface is crumbling, do not do a rubbing— take a photograph instead.

3. If needed, clean the stone with plain water and a soft-bristle (natural or nylon) brush. Scrub the stone from the bottom up to avoid further streaking and staining. Flush well with water when you are done.

4. Cut a piece of plain white paper, butcher paper, rice paper, or Pellon to a size slightly larger than the stone. (You can obtain rice paper from art supply stores and Pellon from craft and fabric shops.)

5. Tape the paper to the stone. Make sure it is secure so it won't slide as you are rubbing and cause a blurred image. It must cover the entire face of the stone so you won't get marks on the gravestone.

6. Using rubbing wax, a large crayon, charcoal, or chalk, gently start to rub along the outside edges of the paper to create a frame for your rubbing.

7. Rub lightly over the paper, then apply just a touch more pressure to darken in the image if that is what you desire. Be very careful and gentle. You can apply more "color" by going over and over the areas.

8. When the rubbing is done, carefully remove it from the tombstone and trim the edges to suit your liking.

9. If you used charcoal or chalk to create your rubbing, you will need to apply several light coats of a spray sealer to the paper to fix the charcoal or chalk before touching or rolling the rubbing.

10. Jot down in your journal the gravesite location (insert a map of the cemetery with the stones numbered), the date the rubbing was done, and a hand-written transcription of the epitaph.

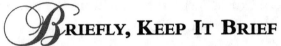

BRIEFLY, KEEP IT BRIEF

Follow the seven Cs of letter and memo writing:

Conversational

   Clear

      Concise

         Complete

            Concrete

               Constructive

                  Correct

(continued from page 67)

Steps to Assure Replies

When using correspondence to gather your family history, you want to make it as simple as possible for the recipient to meet your request. Formatting your initial letter in an easy-to-reply form can do this. For example, you might simply write a single question at the top left of one sheet, leaving the rest of the page blank so all the person has to do is write an answer and then pop it into the included SASE back to the sender.

You can also give the person the easy option of letting you know that he or she doesn't have the information you need. On the back of the SASE, write, "Please circle this sentence if you do not have the information I need, and send this envelope back to me. Thank you." This simple note of acknowledgment will help you know immediately that the recipient doesn't have the information. You will not wait endlessly for a reply, nor will the recipient end up feeling guilty that he or she can't help you. You acknowledge that might be the case right off the bat!

You'll need a bit of patience with this form of gathering family history, but savor every bit of information that lands in your mailbox (or fax machine or E-mail account). Enjoy your letters' replies as you would pieces of a jigsaw puzzle. Over time you'll be able to add more and more pieces to your overall family heritage image. At the same time, you need to consider more carefully how to organize your correspondence as well as the other ever-growing products of your grassroots research. Keep all your information organized as it is discovered or mailed to you. Use your family heritage files as described in chapter 1.

LOW-TECH RESEARCH MEETS THE HIGH-TECH WEB

We remain convinced that grassroots research as described in this chapter—family interviews, cemetery visits, and written correspondence—is the best way to truly understand our own families. Therefore, do not hesitate to contact your relatives and close family friends for help in collecting material. We've all been in the position of wondering why we didn't ask more questions of our parents or pay better attention when Grandma talked about the good ol' days. Time is always of the essence.

Because time is continually short when it comes to learning enough about our families, the World Wide Web, or Internet, can be a valuable, additional tool in your genealogy research. At the click of a mouse, you can visit distant loved ones via E-mail or tap into vast databases of information without even leaving your chair. The Web provides a convenient and economical means to learn an astonishing amount of family history that at one time seemed inaccessible.

$\mathcal{M}$ORE THAN JUST A BURIAL GROUND

In many early New England burying grounds the graves are positioned east/west. This east/west orientation is the most common orientation in other parts of the country and world as well. The earliest settlers had their feet pointing toward the east and the head of the coffin toward the west, ready to rise up and face the new day when "the trumpet shall sound and the dead shall be raised" or when Christ would appear and they would be reborn. Early graves were seldom in the neat rows that we are used to seeing. Burials were more haphazard, more medieval in their irregularity; families didn't own plots and burial spaces were often reused. The north side of the cemetery was considered less desirable and was often the last part of the burying ground to be used or you may find the north side set aside for slaves, servants, suicides, "unknowns" or John Does.

3

Internet Genealogy and Other Shortcuts

The creators of the information superhighway probably had no clue what an integral role the Internet would play for professional genealogists and amateur genealogy buffs all over the world. The Internet cannot replace the old-fashioned grassroots searches discussed in chapter 2, but it can speed up the process of gathering some types of information.

As irreplaceable as grassroots research is, however, the other side of the coin is that much research can be done with the aid of a computer and Internet access. This chapter will highlight some of the key sites, databases, and search engines that can help you in your own family history search, as well as some information about software that can make organizing and sharing your research much simpler.

Some Tips to Get You Started

Before you use the Internet, organize as much as you can about your family and your grassroots research. Here's where your family research file comes in handy yet again! Knowing a name, birth date, places/locations, and a death date can make searching the Web much easier. If you don't have the exact information you need, make some educated estimates and be prepared to canvas line after line in an online index.

Family heritage research can be done on the Internet in many ways. The numerous genealogy Web sites, for starters, are full of practical and specialized information about searching for a family surname and even a particular family member. You might get lucky and hit the jackpot after researching for a few hours, or you may end up having to keep very detailed research notes so you can go back to a specific Web site and spend more time there.

> *Family heritage research can be done on the Internet in many ways.*

Most genealogy experts and enthusiasts know that the Internet will never completely replace information searches at genealogy centers, courthouses, and libraries and such. However, those same folks will quickly admit that some information that was never easily accessible in the past is now as simple to find as clicking a button on your home computer! E-mails to a long-lost relative may be the opening needed to obtain copies of important family documents. A brief post on a mail list or newsgroup may bring news of a distant cousin who knows more than you ever imagined about one of your ancestors.

Some genealogy software packages come with a limited or free subscription to a coordinating genealogy Web site and also usually include basic research indexes such as the Social Security Death Index. Additional indexes can be included in the software package on CDs such as "Passenger and Immigration Lists of Boston 1821 to 1850" or "Selected U.S./International Marriage Records 1560 to 1900."

Some of the information stored on the indexes placed on CDs by software companies can be found online at various genealogy Web sites. Following is a partial listing of beneficial sites to your family heritage research. A complete listing would be impossible, because new sites launch daily and older sites can move or totally disappear from the Web:

New England Historic Genealogy Society: www.NewEnglandAncestors.org

US Genealogy Network: www.usgennet.org

Root Web: www.rootsweb.com/~ilissdsa/

International Internet Genealogical Society: www.iigs.org/

The American Society for Genealogy and Family History: users.erols.com/kingr/index.html

Lethbridge Family History Center: www.leth.net/fhc/index.htm

Federation of Genealogical Societies: www.fgs.org

National Genealogical Society: www.ngsgenealogy.org/

Gentech Resources: www.gentech.org

Society of Genealogists Resources: www.sog.org.uk/

The Newberry Library's Friends of Genealogy: www.newberry.org/nl/genealogy/L3gfriends.html

SURNAME SEARCHES

Your family name or surname is your best beginning clue to finding out more about your family heritage. The surname search is thus one of the most truly personal of all searches. Somehow our family name and

75

what we can find out about it directly lead us to the feeling of belonging to a family unit. Whether common or unusual, surname information abounds on the Internet.

The Internet has made researching your surname very easy. Much of the information already mentioned can now be found on the Web, including the Social Security Death Index and U.S. Census Indexes (both discussed later in this chapter). The following sections describe these additional surname tools: Web sites, newsgroups, personal Web site genealogies, bulletin boards, and online services and search sites.

Web Sites

Various Web sites have huge surname search engines that can help you locate information or even the e-mail address of a potential relative. Some of these search engines and their accompanying indexes will contain details of the family line and list a contact person to reach. You'll then be able to see whether you are actually related to the individual. Indexes vary as to ways to conduct a search—that is, by surname alone or by additional specific information such as time period or location.

Various Web sites have huge surname search engines that can help you locate information or even the e-mail address of a potential relative.

Very general indexes, such as Everton Publisher's (www.emh .everton.com/full-name.html), list where the surname can be found in other indexes and CDs. Very specialized surname indexes also are available, such as the one Dr. Rick R. Nash created called the Mississippi

𝒟ID JOHN SHOEMAKER MAKE SHOES?

Elsdon C. Smith, author of several name books, including *The Story of Our Names* and *Dictionary of American Family Names*, and cofounder of the American Name Society, states that almost every American family name can be classified on the basis of the surname's derivation in one or more of the four following groups:

🦋 From the father's name or other paternal relationships (patronymics; e.g., Johnson, or "son of John"; O'Connor, or "son of Connor"): 32%

🦋 From occupation or office (occupational names; e.g., Smith, Baker): 15%

🦋 From description of action or looks (nicknames; e.g., Schwarzkopf means "black head," or someone with black hair): 10%

🦋 From village names or landscape features (place names; e.g., Hill, Rivers): 43%

African-American Surname Index (www.members.tripod.com/ NashRR), which even allows you to add a new surname to the index. Be aware that some surname indexes are basically commercial enterprises that will try to sell you an item with your family surname or coat of arms. Some of these sites are very informative whether you purchase an item or not, while others are little more than an advertisement for the company.

Mail Lists

Internet mail lists, or *Newsgroups*, are set up to where all the subscribed members receive e-mail posts in an e-mail or digest (all e-mails during

(continues on page 80)

 HELPFUL MAIL LIST SITES

FindMail: www.findmail.com

> Similar to Deja News, only for mailing lists, FindMail allows you to search for mailing lists of interest or to read actual messages and post via an online interface.

Deja News: www.dejanews.com

> Deja News is devoted to searching newsgroup discussions, with archives stretching back to March 1995.

List of Lists: catalog.com/vivian/interest-group-search.html

> Search or browse for lists of interest.

Liszt: www.liszt.com

> Long a favorite for those looking for mailing lists.

Publicly Accessible Mailing Lists (PAML): www.neosoft.com/internet/paml/

> Other well-known places to find mailing lists.

Amnesi: www.amnesi.com

> Can't remember the exact URL of a Web site? Tell Amnesi what you remember, and it will provide of list of sites it thinks match. The Java interface is a bit clunky and slow, but the results are impressive.

Ask Jeeves: www.ask.com/

Ask Jeeves is a human-powered search service that aims to direct you to the exact page that answers your question. If it fails to find a match within its own database, then it will provide matching Web pages from various search engines.

Information Please: www.infoplease.com

Information Please almanacs are favorites among researchers who need trustworthy facts. This site allows searching across Information Please's various almanacs, encyclopedia, and dictionary.

When.com: www.when.com

An events directory and personal calendar Web site. Users can browse events listings, ranging from Internet chat sessions to upcoming trade shows. Events can then be linked to a Web-based personal calendar.

(continued from page 77)

one day) in their online mailbox. The majority of mail lists are free. They only request that you follow newsgroup protocol or the list rules that are sent to you when you subscribe.

Currently more than thirty newsgroups discuss various topics of genealogy, from general to surname-specific. To subscribe, you simply send an e-mail to the group, but since all newsgroups have different ways of subscribing and unsubscribing, you'll have to learn more about the newsgroup you wish to join through a newsgroup directory. See the sidebar, "Helpful Mail List Sites" on page 78 for several mail list directories, with a partial list of newsgroups available in genealogy. Mail lists are also available through different Web sites, such as www.groups.yahoo.com. At Yahoo! Groups, you can search for mail lists of your interest (e.g., a specific surname) and even start a mail list with your surname if you can't find one already organized!

Personal Web Site Genealogies

Many people have done extensive research on family surnames and have created personal Web sites that include much of their gathered information, from the meaning of the family surname to pedigree and family group charts. Finding such Web sites can give you a wealth of information about your own family heritage. People have been known to find missing relatives by finding them on a personal genealogy Web site!

You can access these sites by finding them in a general search engine (e.g., Yahoo!) or by using a search engine on a genealogy Web site. Most genealogy Web sites list such personal family histories under U.S. and International/World Indexes. Some sites will allow you to access the information or contact the originator without charge, while others require that you become a paying member of the site before you can access all the information. Most will allow you to upload or add your own family history without cost.

Bulletin Boards

Bulletin boards on Web sites allow you to post a message online for anyone else who may be visiting or viewing the site. These boards are often broken down into surnames. You'll find your surname board and post a message listing what you know of your family history. Keep track of any posting you make at a site in your family heritage journal, and check back to this site weekly or so to find out whether anyone has information to share.

Usually any response is posted back to the Web site so that the information is shared with everyone with that particular surname, but sometimes individuals will send you a personal e-mail to your private mailbox. For example, a previously unknown cousin of mine, Wayne Given, wrote me after spotting my general post, asking for information on my father, Claude Byrum Given, on the Given surname board at www.kindredspirits.com. It turns out this cousin is the oldest of my generation of cousins and he told me how my dad got his nickname, Bob. (Seems my uncle Opal gave him the nickname because my dad "bobbed" when he walked.) See the sidebar, "Internet Newsgroup Post Sample" for an example of an Internet newsgroup post.

Online Services and Search Sites

America Online, CompuServe, Prodigy, Net, and other online services, and local bulletin boards have genealogy sections where individuals submit these kinds of messages and hope for a reply. These sites also include files and articles on genealogy that can be very helpful in educating you on a specific topic, including vital records, adoption issues, slave genealogies, or surname histories. The major search engines such as Yahoo!, Alta Vista, and About.com have dedicated categories that include genealogy, surnames, family history searches, and history. Whether you use an online service or a search engine site, you'll find the smaller community inviting and a great starting place for family research. Each site maintains a library of forms, facts, family Web pages and more.

❧ INDEXES AND DATABASES FOR MEGA AMOUNTS OF INFORMATION

We've selected the most popular and easy-to-access sources of information for this section. As you use and learn more about each source of information, you'll very naturally be led to additional information sources. Appendix A lists many other sources to check out.

The sources discussed here can help fill in details of your immediate family and some extended family. That is the first step of a family heritage search. Without those details, it is almost impossible to search back more than one or two generations.

United States Census Indexes

A *census* is an official listing of citizens and specific information about them. In the United States the census is taken every ten years, beginning in August 1790. In 1989, the Bureau of the Census in Washington, D.C., published *200 Years of Census Taking: Population and Housing Questions, 1790–1990*. This book includes some wonderful facts and tidbits about the U.S. Census for interested readers.

The indexes for information gathered from a U.S. Census (www.census.gov./genealogy) are broken down to a county within a state; therefore, for starters you need to have some idea of which state and, even better, the county in which your relative may have resided.

According to experts, without indexes, census records researchers would have to search line by line to find an ancestor—an enormously time-consuming process, obviously. Few people, if any, have the time (or desire) to search the 1900 census for someone living in heavily populated New York City, for example. The standard format for census in-

*I*NTERNET NEWSGROUP POST SAMPLE

[Subject line]: RE: GIVEN surname

[Body of text]: Looking for anyone who might have information about members of the GIVEN family.

Specifically: Claude (Bob) Byrum Given, born 1920 in Illinois, died in 1966 in Illinois, lived in Illinois and Indiana.

Thanks for any responses. You may reply on board or privately.

[Signature]: Maria Given Nerius

Mnerius@aol.com

dexes published in book form or on CD-ROM includes only names, locality, county, and a page number. If you were looking for an ancestor name like Charles Smith in a standard 1860 census index, you'd stand a good chance of finding ten or more people listed by that name in one county. Without any other identifying information, it can be impossible to determine which of the ten is your ancestor, if any. Make sure when you examine entries that you try to match the information in the census index to what you already might know about the family member before deciding which Charles Smith is your ancestor.

Every index contains some errors and omissions. If you don't find your ancestor listed in an index but know the person lived in a specific place in a rural county, do a line-by-line search of the census for that place.

Besides being available online, the 1790, 1800, 1810, 1820, 1830, 1840, 1850, 1860, 1870, 1880, and fragments of the 1890, 1900, 1910, and 1920 census schedules have been microfilmed for each state. Microfilm copies can be used at the National Archives in Washington, D.C.; regional branches of the National Archives; the Family History Library (of the Church of Jesus Christ of Latter-Day Saints, discussed later in this chapter) in Salt Lake City; and at other public, private, and institutional libraries throughout the country.

If you don't find your ancestor listed in an index but know the person lived in a specific place in a rural county, do a line-by-line search of the census for that place.

Soundex

Census indexes for the 1880, 1900, 1910, and 1920 census schedules (as well as some other databases) have been indexed using a soundex system. A *soundex* is a phonetic index in which last names are grouped by how they sound rather than the way they are spelled. For example, Smit, Smith, Smyth, and Smythe share a common sound. Soundex cards are arranged by soundex code and then alphabetically by given names.

If you don't work easily with codes, numbers, or puzzles, just take a deep breath and focus on the following formula for creating a soundex code from your own family surname:

Soundex Formula for Coding Surnames

1. The letters *a, e, i, o, u* (except when these vowels are the first letter), *y, w,* and *h* are not coded.

2. The first letter of a surname is not coded, except for vowels.

3. When the first letter of the surname is a vowel, it becomes the soundex code.

4. Every soundex number must be a three-digit code.

5. Double consonants should be treated as one letter.

6. Names with two consecutive consonants that share the same code number should be treated as one letter.

7. The soundex coding system for a surname:

1 = *b, p, f, v*

2 = *c, s, k, g, j, q, x, z*

3 = *d, t*

4 = *l*

5 = *m, n*

6 = *r*

8. Write down the surname to be coded.

9. Rewrite the surname leaving out all vowels (except when the first letter of the surname is a vowel) and the letters *h, w,* and *y*.

10. Write down the first letter and the next three consonants of the letters remaining.

11. Write the first letter of the four remaining consonants, followed by the code number of the three letters remaining.

12. If fewer than three letters remain, enter the number 0 to make a three-digit number after the initial letter.

As an alternative, many genealogy software packages include a program within the system that will automatically convert your surname into its soundex code. Plug this soundex code into any index search engine or CD, and you should be able to find information on a relative.

It's not a sure bet by any means, but there is a good chance you can track down family information using the U.S. Census. Many original pages of the census ledgers are also available on www.genealogy.com.

Social Security Death Index

The Social Security Act of 1936 provided peace of mind for American workers and gave today's genealogists and family historians a valuable resource to find family information. The Social Security Death Index (SSDI) is one of the largest and most useful databases available (www.ancestry.com/search/rectype/vital/ssdi/main.htm). It contains names, birth dates, death dates, Social Security numbers, and other useful information about more than fifty-five million people.

Don't be surprised if you can't find a relative in the SSDI database.

Whenever a participant in the Social Security program dies, a death certificate must be filed with the Social Security Administration. The Social Security Administration maintains a computer database that is an index of these deceased persons, available to anyone. The implementation of the Social Security Act in 1937 stipulated that applicants fill out forms requiring data about their birth, family status, and employment. Not only were millions of files created for members of our families, the act forced many of our relatives, who until then had no recorded birth, to go to the local county clerks or state office of vital statistics to file a delayed birth certificate.

The SSDI Web site allows you to type in an ancestor's name and learn whether his or her death was reported to the Social Security Administration. If it was, your ancestor's entry will appear on the computer screen with his or her Social Security number, date and place of death, and date and place of issuance of his or her Social Security card. This information permits you to contact the Social Security Administration to obtain a copy of your ancestor's Social Security file. This file will contain more information about the relative and his or her family as well as material on employment and even military service.

Don't be surprised if you can't find a relative in the SSDI database even if you are positive that the person is deceased. Only individuals who paid into the system are on record, meaning that anyone who was self-employed or employed by railroad companies, the federal government, or the military may not be listed. Railroad workers and employees will be covered by the Railroad Retirement Act of 1935; the Railroad Retirement Board in Chicago has their records. Check with nearest National Archives regional office for guidance in finding military personnel records. The nearest federal personnel office will have information about government employees.

U.S. Geographical Names Information System

You'll quickly realize that you should have paid more attention to geography when you were in school, because knowing at least the geographic areas where your ancestors lived will help you narrow a search for family information. The U.S. Geographical Names Information System (GNIS) can help (www.mapping.usgs.gov). It contains a comprehensive list of important man-made features, such as cemeteries, churches and hospitals, and natural landmarks, such as rivers, forests, and peaks, throughout the United States. You might just find a cemetery where an ancestor was buried.

❦ To learn the exact location of a river, cemetery, hospital, forest, or other geographic feature, enter the name and select the feature type given. To narrow your results, also fill out any location information that you know.

❦ To learn the names of geographic features in a particular location, select the feature type, state, and/or county.

❦ You can also access the GNIS database at many of the larger genealogical Web sites.

The Family History Library: The Mother of All Genealogy Sources

The Genealogical Society of Utah founded the Family History Library (www.familysearch.org) in Salt Lake City in 1894. It houses the largest collection of genealogical material in the world, with an estimated two billion records on deceased persons alone! The library sends out specialist teams around the world to locate and copy existing records. Currently two hundred camera operators in forty-five countries are gathering more material for this huge genealogy resource. There are around 2,500 satellites or regional branches called Family History Centers located throughout the world.

Since 1938, the library has been using microfilm as the principal medium; in addition, more than 250,000 books are available. The approximately two million rolls of film at the Family History Library contain original records such as birth, marriage, and death certificates; censuses; probate records; passenger lists; wills; cemetery records; land grants and deeds; naturalization records; and many other document types. Hundreds of film readers are available in the building; the largest portion of these are in the U.S./Canadian section, but remember that this library houses records from all over the world.

When permitted, the library will photograph the original records. Master copies of the films are stored in the Granite Mountain Records Vault in the Wasatch Mountains southeast of Salt Lake City. This repository is not open to the public. With the use of new technology, more information can be stored in less space—a good thing since the collection is growing at a rate of more than 4,100 rolls of film a month.

Every library must have a catalog of its contents, or it would be close to impossible to find the library materials we need. All materials received by the Family History Library are thus described in a computer-based catalog simply called *The Family History Library Catalog.* This database is available to library users in Salt Lake City and in every LDS (Latter-Day Saints or Mormon) Family History Center. The catalog is available in three forms: microfiche, CD, and the Family History search engine. The microfiche version allows researchers to search under authors and titles, subjects, surnames, and localities. The *CD Family History Library Catalog* and site search engine provide a locality search, surname search, microfilm/fiche number search, and a computer number search. The author/title and subject searches are similar in many ways to catalog searches in most public and college libraries. The locality and surname searches are unique to the *Family History Library Catalog.*

The Family History Library adds thousands of published genealogies and family histories to its already large collection of this type of publication. The surname catalog permits you to type in any surname you desire and learn whether the library has family histories or genealogies that contain that particular surname. Often there will be hundreds of books with your surname mentioned in them. Adding key words such as localities where your family lived or other surnames found in your pedigree can narrow the search further.

Whether you go to Salt Lake City, visit online, or use one of the Family History Centers, you will find a very helpful volunteer staff to answer your questions and help you locate information.

The Ancestral File

The Ancestral File is a genealogical system developed by the Family History Department of the Church of Jesus Christ of Latter-Day Saints helping link individuals to ancestors in pedigree, family group, and descendant formats. Until recently, the only way to access the database was by visiting the Family History Department in Salt Lake City, Utah, or a regional office. Now, you can access many of the files via the Internet at the official Web site, Family Search Internet Genealogy Service (www.familysearch.com). The database is truly incredible, with a staff of volunteers who will help you start your family history search. The information (documents or books) you discover during a search is sent to a local Family History Center near you. You can then read the documents or publications during reading hours. It works like a huge lending library.

 ## PUTTING IT ALL TOGETHER

As mentioned at the onset, computer software such as My Family Tree Maker can be used to compose and organize your pedigree charts and other family records. If you decide to invest in a software program, read the packaging carefully. Make sure your computer system has all the requirements needed and that the software will record and report the information you need or want for your family heritage scrapbook. Not all software is compatible, and every manufacturer offers different features. It's up to you to figure out which one suits your needs the best.

Computer technology alone, however, won't be enough to compile and preserve all the artifacts you have now gathered through both grassroots and Internet research. Along the way you also likely have discovered other items for your family heritage scrapbook, from photographs to family movies to heirloom quilts. The next few chapters will describe how to best save such precious mementos.

4

The Art of Preserving Our Memories

All the family history to include in a family heritage scrapbook can begin to really stack up into piles and piles of facts and artifacts. It's important to preserve as much of it as we can. It gives a written and visual presentation to our history and future. This chapter will focus on organizing and preserving your information—whether in the form of family documents, a favorite book, an heirloom quilt, or a treasured rocking chair.

AVOIDING INFORMATION OVERLOAD

Our main focus for now is to get all your paper information organized and ready to place into the heritage scrapbook. Use acid-free folders and boxes rather than wooden or cardboard boxes for storing your family history information.

Start a file for every family group; otherwise, the number and various names of relatives can quickly overwhelm you. You might become tempted simply to declare everyone a third cousin twice removed on your mother's side of the family! Having the groups organized on the forms makes it much easier to see how members are related, and classifying by group facilitates locating information quickly.

This chapter presents various categories of what we're rather loosely calling "information" as well as suggested methods of organization. If you are more comfortable using your own system of organizing this information, use your own system. What matters is that you are able to locate specific information for your family heritage history and scrapbook in a logical, quick manner.

What matters is that you are able to locate specific information for your family heritage history and scrapbook in a logical, quick manner.

This is the time to get rid of any duplicate information you may have on your pedigree charts and family group records. Combine all the input from family and friends and from your searches. Double-check to make sure you don't accidentally overlook a name, date, or place. Once you've compiled the list of relatives and the relationships onto the pedigree charts and family group records, throw away any duplicate information.

PRESERVING AS YOU ORGANIZE

The ultimate goal of the family heritage project is to organize *and* preserve your family history. The methods of preserving records, documents, legal papers, photos, and memorabilia recommended in this book have been provided by experts and are proven methods. Don't get careless with your family's important memorabilia. When in doubt about any method of preserving or restoring an original family document or piece of paper memorabilia, please consult a professional expert. You don't need to hire the expert to do the preservation or repair, but the information an expert can provide may save you from damaging the item.

The concerns specific to family photographs are discussed in chapter 5. Chapter 5 will include how to preserve your photos in the best manner so that generations to come can enjoy the family photos as much as you did.

The First Rule of Genealogy

The first rule of genealogy is simple: *Do not do what can't be undone.* I highly recommend you write that sentence one hundred times and then paste it to your family research file. Joking aside, exactly what does this rule mean to you and me as amateur genealogists? Take a look at this list of don'ts:

1. Do not cut or crop any old photos that don't have a negative. Only cut or crop copies of a photograph.

2. Do not write on a photograph in dark permanent or water-based ink. Water-based inks can bleed or run if wet, harming the photograph.

3. Do not laminate any documents or original photographs. You can't undo lamination without harming or destroying paper or photographs. Make copies and laminate the copy.

4. Do not write or make notes on any paper documents. Even pencil marking that can be erased might harm the document.

5. Do not eat or drink near any documents, photographs, or memorabilia. Accidents happen and the result can be permanent damage to your family treasures.

 ## PRESERVATION CHALLENGES

Some situations pose common challenges to preserving family documents and other memorabilia: pollution and household pests, mold and mildew, and man-made disasters and acts of nature. The section suggests some ways to prevent these problems from originating in the first place and to combat them if they do occur.

Pollution and Pests

Air pollution is generated inside the home as well as outside. Its components include acidic gases, particulate material, and ozone. Both inorganic and organic materials can be damaged by exposure to pollutants. Indoor sources of air pollution include smoke, dust, paints, stains, cleaning agents, and new synthetic materials such as insulation or carpeting.

The effects of indoor pollutants, such as acidic gases from wood products or coatings, may be intensified when allowed to build up inside cabinets or other closed environments over long periods. You may want to air out your stored materials on occasion. Keep storage areas clean and ventilated as best you can.

Keep storage areas clean and
ventilated as best you can.

Pests found in the home vary widely, from insects to rodents. Wood, textiles, basketry, paper, photographs, books, leather, feathers, and especially organic substances with food residues are very attractive to pests. High relative humidity may encourage a population explosion of bugs. Low temperatures may make them dormant but probably will not kill them. Because so many types of pests are attracted to paper, you might want to contact your local agricultural extension service or an entomologist for accurate identification if you find any. Chemical treatment may permanently damage record materials. Instead, concentrate on the source of the infestation. Seal all possible entry points. Promptly remove or seal up pest lures, such as food or trash. Maintain a low temperature and relative humidity, and keep the area clean and dust-free. Get into the habit of checking all your storage areas biannually so you can catch any problem quickly.

Mold and Mildew

Mold and mildew grow in areas with high temperature, high relative humidity, and low air circulation. Isolate moldy record materials in a cool, dry location, with plenty of air circulation so they will not contaminate nearby items; do not return the records to their original location until the conditions causing the mold or mildew growth are addressed.

THE WHITE GLOVE TREATMENT

Using white cotton gloves is an essential aspect of artifact preservation. The oils and salts transferred from one's hands when handling items causes serious deterioration. Gloves help protect the artifacts from that kind of damage.

❧ Always wear gloves when handling paper, photographs, textiles, and wooden items. Metal artifacts are especially vulnerable.

❧ Some artifacts, however, should *not* be handled with gloves. These include items that can be slippery, such as glass and ceramics, and fragile or brittle items that could actually be at a greater risk if the handler is wearing gloves.

❧ Change gloves as they become soiled, and hand- or machine-wash them using a mild detergent. Do not use any liquid fabric softeners or dryer sheets. An automatic dryer can be used, but air drying may be preferable.

Once materials are placed in a better environment, the mold or mildew will become loose and powdery as the substrate dries and the mold or mildew turns dormant. It may then be gently brushed off the record materials. Because mold and mildew are merely dormant, if it remains on the record materials or is distributed throughout the space and onto other objects, it will grow whenever environmental conditions are favorable again. Therefore, mold or mildew should be removed either outdoors or into a vacuum cleaner equipped with a HEPA filter, not a regular vacuum cleaner that will merely exhaust and recirculate mold back into the room.

The faster record materials are dried, the better. However, some items may distort physically if dried too quickly. Contact a preservation professional for advice on how to handle moldy or mildewy record materials of high value.

When and How to Select a Professional Conservator

Before attempting to repair, clean, or mount any important family keepsake or heirloom, contact a professional conservator. Working with a conservator will help ensure that you can enjoy your objects for years to come. This person will examine the artifact and document its condition and any inherent problems. Taking into account your concerns and any relevant historical information, a treatment option will be proposed. Questions to consider when determining a course of action include the following:

- Is treatment necessary, or is it based on popular aesthetics?

- Is the object strong enough to be displayed?

- Do the risks of treatment outweigh the benefits?

- What treatment provides the most results with the least intervention?

A helpful brochure, *Guidelines for Selecting a Conservator,* available from the American Institute for Conservation of Historical and Artistic Works can help you make an informed choice if you need the help of a professional conservator. Contact:

American Institute for Conservation of Historic and Artistic
    Works (AIC)
1717 K St., NW, Ste. 200
Washington, D.C. 20006
Phone: (202) 452-9545
Fax: (202) 452-9328
E-mail: info@aic-faic.org
Web site: //aic.stanford.edu

Man-Made Disasters and Acts of Nature

The two most common forms of disaster damage are those caused by water and fire. Prompt attention to your important documents and family treasures immediately following a disaster will greatly reduce any permanent damage. In the case of wet objects, remember that most materials become weaker when wet and will need supports for transport. If handling is possible, separate all items to avoid bleeding from inks and dyes. Rinse any silt or debris off with clean, cool water. Then blot carefully with absorbent toweling to remove as much moisture as possible. Lay items flat to dry, covered with clean, thin, cotton sheets in a room with good air circulation. If there are too many pieces to dry immediately, contact a local conservator. It may be possible to freeze some items (to prevent mold growth) until they can be examined and dried. If pieces are already dry, soil may be removed with a soft brush.

> ### *The two most common forms of disaster damage are those caused by water and fire.*

In the case of fire, soot and smoke damage need to be addressed. Remove particulate matter as described for wet items, and call a conservator. Do not permit the use of ozone to remove smoky odors. It will accelerate the aging and breakdown of most items. Consult with a preservation or conservation expert if in doubt or when dealing with the most valuable of family items.

Books and Web sites are dedicated to specific disaster problems. Ask the reference librarian at your local library, or use a Web search engine with the key words *preservation* or *conservation of materials.* Or simply check out the genealogy Web sites listed in the back of the book; most of the larger sites do include disaster information.

SLIDES AND HOME MOVIES

At one time most family vacations and special events were photographed using slide film. Slide shows became famous as a long, boring event to be avoided at all costs! Today, however, many families no longer document their special occasions this way. The technology has not become totally obsolete, but it may be headed in that direction.

Similarly rare these days are family movies shot on 16mm or 8mm film, owing to the introduction of VHS tape and camcorders. Many of you may have the old rolls of family footage but no projector with which to view them. Transferring the film to videotape is one possibility (see the sidebar on page 101), yet, even with the convenience of VHS videotape, one has to wonder just how long even this technology will be viable.

Many people believe they are preserving their slides and home movies when they transfer them to videotape. This impression is false.

Many people believe they are preserving their slides and home movies when they transfer them to videotape. This impression is false. Video technology offers us ready-access viewing of our slides and home movies; however, VHS cassettes have a shelf life of less than ten years. This shelf life is significantly shorter than that for slides or movie film. Experts recommend transferring slide and old home movie images to videotape for easy viewing access, but they also suggest storing the slides and original movie footage in a secure, dark, dry, cool place to help postpone deterioration and prolong the life of the film. An air-conditioned, dehumidified room is ideal. If you don't have the ability to store the slides or film properly, storage businesses can provide this service for you at a reasonable fee.

𝒜RCHIVAL MIST SAVES BOOKS
AND OTHER PAPER MEMORABILIA

If you have lots of paper memorabilia, a product called Archival Mist may help you tremendously. Produced by the company that helped preserve books in the Library of Congress (Preservation Technologies), the product can be used to make all paper acid-free, extending the life of family archives and heirlooms. Archival Mist gently neutralizes the destructive acids in paper and deposits a safe, permanent alkaline buffer to protect against future acid attack. Safe and easy to use in a pump-spray bottle, Archival Mist effectively treats paper keepsakes, including newspaper clippings, certificates, documents, awards, children's artwork, and all other paper-based material. It is available nationwide at retail craft outlets.

Slides can also be used to make photographs. You'll have to take your slides to a store that specializes in photography or a photo developer who has the ability to make photos from slides. There's no one-hour service for such a task, but it is worth the week or two it will take for the shop make the photos. Having a photo made from a slide is a great way to incorporate the slide images into your scrapbook and allow you to store the original slides in a proper environment. You can also have photos created from film and video. This is not a typical request so you'll have to locate a company that specializes in this service.

❦ VIDEOCASSETTES

You may not be using any images from a videocassette in your family heritage scrapbook, but video is still a major way families preserve his-

TRANSFERRING 8MM FILM TO VHS TAPE

With a little practice and some luck, you may be able to transfer your old home movies to a VHS cassette on your own. If you don't have a projector, you can try to locate and borrow one. You will want to display the image onto a white piece of matte board. Place a camcorder on a tripod and tape the image. Some photography mail-order catalogs sell transfer boxes into which you put the lens of the projector and the film image is reflected past a mirror into the lens of your video camera.

tory and memories. Since the late 1950s, video has served as a powerful medium of artistic and visual documentation. Most weddings, for example, now include a person, either amateur or professional, to videotape the ceremony and reception.

As convenient and common as it is, videotape is even more fragile than color photographs. Plasticizers help keep the film supple so it is less likely to break or stretch. Lubricants serve a similar purpose by helping keep the tape moving smoothly through the mechanical transport system that moves the film from one spool, past the VCR (video-cassette recorder) head, which reads the tape, and on to the other spool.

Each of the component parts of the finished tape is subject to unique problems, and a failure of any one of them can make the tape unplayable. Because the mix of component parts is complex, even the best-quality tape can begin to degrade as quickly as within a year or two of being manufactured. Even under ideal conditions, the binder that holds together the mixture of chemicals that makes up the tape is very delicate, and it is usually quite easy to scrape off parts of the chemicals from the base. The image that is played back on the TV screen will become poorer until it can no longer be viewed.

Videotape tape is subject to harm from a variety of sources. Just as with paper and photographs, heat can speed the chemical reactions that cause the tape to fail, and humidity can encourage the growth of various biological agents that can destroy the tape. Binder breakdown is a frequent cause for tape failure. Like all adhesive agents, as the binder ages, it begins to lose its stick. When this happens microscopic pieces of oxide as well as the other chemicals embedded in the binder slowly fall away. As each bit of oxide is lost, a small piece of information is lost, too, creating various problems when the tape is played.

Since videotapes can only be viewed by playing them through a VCR unit, there is always a chance of additional damage from mechanical troubles within a VCR. Dirt and dust are the most frequent problem. Dirt, even microscopic particles, if located in strategic spots on the transport mechanism or VCR head, can cause continual scratching of the tape, which degrades the overall image quality.

Since videotapes can only be viewed by playing them through a VCR unit, there is always a chance of additional damage from mechanical troubles within a VCR.

Experts have not yet come up with a good long-term strategy for preserving videotape. Most tape will last only ten years. Within this short time span, it is possible to take steps that will keep the tape and the images preserved on the tape in good condition, enabling you to make copies of the original tape. Video experts offer the following practical suggestions for maintaining videotape in good condition:

1. Buy name-brand videotape. The chemicals used by various manufacturers, quality control practices, and other procedures vary dramatically among manufacturers.

2. Always use a clean, well-functioning VCR to play any family tape. Professional cleaning of a VCR, including demagnetization of the head, is always a good idea.

3. Make a preservation copy of the videotape as soon as it is shot. This can be done at home by connecting two VCRs or by having a video shop make the copy for you. Check the preservation copy once a year, but otherwise never play it. This copy will serve you well when the time comes to copy the tape onto a new tape.

4. Consider dubbing Beta tapes to VHS format. Beta systems have survived as a professional medium, and tapes and equipment are readily available from Sony and hobbyists.

Get Digital

You'll need to hire out for this job, but the results are awesome. Average transfer costs for 8mm film to a digital format runs around 15 cents a foot. Most shops that provide this service will also have a set-up fee that averages $50 per digital session, but several film rolls may be processed during the session. Digitized transfer can be used in many ways, including uploading to a Web site. With short home movies, you may even be able to e-mail the digital file to a loved one that he or she can open and play!

5. View and rewind your videotape annually. Annual viewing makes it possible to detect problems before they lead to the catastrophic failure of the tape. Annual rewinding helps avoid a number of problems that can occur as the tightly wound VCR tape rests up against itself.

6. Make sure the VCR has recently been serviced before playing the preservation copy of your tapes.

7. Assume videotape will have to be copied. The medium of tape is very fragile and subject to a variety of fatal harms. Plan on copying tape at least once every ten years.

Additional Important Tips

✿ When tapes are not in use, store them on end (like books on a library shelf) to prevent deformation. Do not store videotapes lying flat. When housed in a horizontal position, pressure from other tapes can cause distortions. Rewind tapes after recording or playback.

✿ Don't leave tapes threaded in the videocassette recorder for a long period. Leaving a tape in the playback machinery overnight, for example, is not desirable. Likewise, tapes should be inserted and ejected only at blank, unrecorded sections.

✿ Well protect videotapes from heat or water damage. Magnetic tape cannot tolerate high temperatures. Temperatures above 150 degrees Fahrenheit can cause permanent damage to videotape. In the unfortunate event of a disaster, experience, research, and testing have led to the development of highly effective restoration and remastering techniques that may preserve lost or damaged information.

✿ Never eject a tape in the middle of a recording. Pausing tapes for prolonged periods also results in degraded image quality. After recording, rewind the tape before ejecting it.

✿ Always return tapes to carefully labeled protective inert plastic containers when they are not in use. Cardboard boxes deteriorate and provide little protection from handling, environmental fluctuations, fire, or water.

❧ Always use a new, brand-name tape from a recognized manufacturer for important recordings. Avoid extended-play tapes because they use a thinner polyester tape base and therefore are less wear-resistant.

❧ Before recording, wind the tape from one hub to another and then back. This procedure will relieve stresses on the tape that could result in a slightly irregular passage of the tape through the recorder. Record at standard speed.

❧ Always break off the tab on a videocassette to prevent accidental re-recording. Keep your preservation copies in a separate location from the copies you will view on a regular basis or give to family or friends.

 ## BASICS OF PRESERVING PAPER

The common bond among many of your family heritage items is the fact that most will be made up of paper. The best way to minimize damage to your family records is to properly store your papers away from four hazards that measurably shorten paper's life span:

1. Heat. Heat speeds chemical reactions and causes paper to decay more quickly. The rate of change is dramatic, doubling with every ten degrees (Fahrenheit) increase in temperature.

2. Humidity. Humidity does its harm in two ways. Humidity levels above 70% will promote mold growth. Rapid changes in humidity can also damage paper. Wide variations in humidity causes paper to "cycle," expanding and contracting as water is drawn from and goes back into the paper fibers.

3. Light. Bright light, particularly sunlight and fluorescent light, will also deteriorate paper. Like heat, the ultra-violet radiation can speed chemical reactions that harm the paper. Damage from light usually shows up first in ink, you'll notice that the ink fades and will eventually disappear.

4. Careless handling. Careless handling by people is probably the number one cause of harm to paper. Particularly as paper ages and becomes brittle, it will easily rip if it is not handled with a very delicate touch. Never touch any paper you wish to preserve until you've thoroughly cleaned your hands.

Storing Paper

Storing loose papers properly is an important step in preserving your family records. Proper storage can lengthen the useful life of any piece of paper. Store family papers in a cool, dry place, where the humidity stays relatively constant. A bedroom closet is often a good choice particularly if the bedroom is air-conditioned. A room where the temperature remains between sixty-five and seventy degrees Fahrenheit with a constant relative humidity of about forty-five percent is the most ideal environment. Uninsulated attics or damp basements should never be used to store valuable family papers.

Uninsulated attics or damp basements should never be used to store valuable family papers.

If you desire to store a poor quality piece of paper, place it between two blank sheets of high quality paper. Acid will migrate into the blank paper, which can be thrown away, rather than into family letters or other heirlooms. Do not use glue, tape, or pressure sensitive tape directly on important family papers. Use Mylar photo/page protectors/holders and insert items in these. Segregate material by type. Do not place newspaper clippings, letters, and photos all in the same pocket. Rather put each in its own pocket, using the plastic sheets to buffer one item from the other.

Display Carefully

If you feel strongly that you must frame and display a particular document, mat it in acid-free material, leave a small gap between the item and the glass of the frame. It is a wise investment to spend a few extra dollars to purchase glass that filters out ultra-violet radiation. When hanging the item avoid a location where direct sunlight from a window or another source of light will reach it. Do not store particularly bad pieces of paper touching higher quality paper.

Records, Documents, and Other Legal Papers

Organize this information into the pedigree or family group it belongs. This category of history includes birth, marriage, and death certificates, baptism papers, immigration documents, wills, financial statements, deeds, military records, school report cards, diplomas, and certificates. These records and documents will back up your factual information. You can get copies of many public records by contacting the appropriate agencies or governmental offices (see chapter 2).

The general rule is to avoid overhandling this type of paper documentation. Always make sure your hands are clean or you wear gloves. Make copies of any records or documents you wish to include in your family heritage album. I highly recommend you spray any older documents with Archival Mist to remove any acid the paper may have picked up over the years. Then store the original. Keep a running list of where you are filing or storing the legal documents.

More Important Tips

✍ Do not repair documents with glue or pressure-sensitive tape since many such adhesives are highly acidic.

✍ Store documents flat when possible. Do not flatten tightly curled documents with force since fibers will break, weakening the paper.

✍ Do not wrap documents with a rubber band because the rubber will harden and bond to paper.

✍ Do not use paper clips, staples, straight pins, or other metal objects that will eventually rust.

Correspondence and Other Handwritten Items

Before organizing these paper objects, you may want to read each piece carefully. Some families are dedicated letter writers, while others might send out a holiday card once a year. This category can get quite out of control for the pack rat! It's not easy, but you may want to continue to save only the most important or special letters, postcards, greeting cards, and correspondence for your family heritage scrapbook. Set aside other pieces for a baby album, a child's album, or an album focused on general family memories. Keep only the historically vital correspondence for the heritage album.

It takes a little extra time to read through the handwritten papers, but the reward is worth it for your scrapbook.

Journals and diaries fall into this paper category, too. You'll want to read through any journal or diary (that you have permission to look in) and look for entries that will be of interest in your family heritage scrapbook. Make copies of these entries, and organize the copies with the appropriate family group.

Handwritten items really add a special touch to a scrapbook. Chapter 6 discusses the importance of handwriting the journaling in your scrapbook, and the same reasoning can be applied to handwritten correspondence and journal/diary entries. A person's handwriting style gives an additional insight into this family member. Many family heritage enthusiasts have even had handwriting analysis done on family members to get a better idea of personality and character.

Don't overlook this important aspect of your family heritage scrapbook. It takes a little extra time to read through the handwritten papers, but the reward is worth it for your scrapbook. A letter can be copied onto acid free, archival paper and used as a background paper for an individual page in your scrapbook. You may also use a copy of a handwritten note as a border for a page. Keep an open mind, and you'll be able to incorporate your family's handwritten words in many ways.

More Important Tips

🐜 Store letters, postcards, and greeting cards flat.

🐜 Place journals/diaries upright on a shelf, using bookends when the shelf is not full.

🐜 Remove all acidic materials from journals and diaries such as bookmarks, pressed flowers, and scraps of paper.

🐜 Attach postcards and greeting cards with archival photo corners. Avoid using tape or glue as much as possible since it will eventually cause yellowing and may "ooze" and cause items and pages to stick together.

Printed Memorabilia, Newspaper Clippings, Magazines, and Books

We all have memorabilia of some sort. And most of these keepsakes and treasures are simple bits of paper that hold important memories: a movie

PAPER RESTORATION IS FOR THE EXPERTS

It may be tempting, but don't try to repair any old documents or papers you may have found. Over the years, professional conservators have developed a sophisticated array of tools and techniques that can be used to clean, restore, and mend documents or books. Successfully using these procedures, however, frequently requires considerable skill, the use of toxic chemicals, and some good luck. Restoration of damaged paper is often expensive and risky, and sometimes it doesn't work, according to a majority of experts in the field. A professional conservator should do it.

Home remedies and fix-it attempts often not only fail to fix the problem but introduce new problems that are even more difficult to fix. It is better to store a partially damaged document under good conditions than to try to fix it without professional help. Perhaps the most destructive "home remedy" professional conservators face are repairs done with cellophane tape. This type of tape should never be used to repair torn or ripped paper or in an attempt to refasten a torn cover of a book. Most tape sticks for only five to ten years. Eventually the tape falls off, leaving behind a tear or rip embedded with a sticky adhesive mess that discolors the paper. Even a trained conservator who might have been able to fix the original rip or tear in a way that is permanent will find it difficult and probably impossible to remove the adhesive and the discoloration from the paper.

Experts also agree that close behind tape in its destructive effect is the practice of lamination. Lamination does not lengthen the natural life of paper, and its sticky plastic is virtually impossible to remove. Lamination should not be confused with the professional practice of encapsulation. Encapsulated documents are placed between two sheets of inert plastic. However, the "sandwich" that is created is sealed only around the edges, thus the document is not attached to the plastic in any way.

ticket stub from a first date, an airline ticket from a family vacation, a wedding invitation, a "Happy 29th Birthday Again" card. Life can be full of bits and pieces of paper that become precious mementos and souvenirs. Unfortunately, most of our memorabilia was not printed on acid-free, archival paper! Even if it was, handling and improper storage have led to acidity on the paper. It's best to keep this type of paper away from any photos in your heritage scrapbook. You can mat it, place it in a Mylar pocket, or spray it with Archival Mist. Or you can elect to make a copy of the item on an acid-free, archival paper for your scrapbook.

Books of any sort can be family treasures.

You may have found newspaper clippings of all sorts (e.g., wedding announcements, obituaries, news stories) as you went through the family Bible, storage, and personal papers. In most cases, it is a good idea to copy the clipping onto an acid-free, archival paper for use in your heritage scrapbook. Or attach the newspaper clipping to an acid-free archival paper and trim, giving you a matted clipping. Try to identify the origin of your clippings by providing a date, the source of the item, names, and place. If you find a complete newspaper or front page of a newspaper, you may want to make a note of the date. It might match up to a relative's birth or death. Also, national and historic events might have been why the paper was saved, so cherish that piece of history, too.

The practice is not so common today, but past generations did keep magazines and other periodicals. Throwing such luxuries out was considered wasteful, so the magazines were stored or passed on to other family members or friends. It can be very interesting in creating time lines to read some of the old magazines that might be stored in a relative's attic, basement, or hall closet. The topics and subjects covered will give you a better understanding of life during your relative's childhood and beyond. You might wish to include a cover or copy of an article within your scrapbook.

Books of any sort can be family treasures. I, for example, have some of my dad's school textbooks from his first year at college. The books are important to my family because he was the first member of the Given family ever to attend and graduate from college—a major event in the family history. In addition, my dad wrote notes to himself in the margins of the pages, so his handwriting is a very special part of these books. You might wish to make copies of pages out of favorite family member's books. These copies can be used as background papers or borders or placed in pockets of your family heritage scrapbook. My mother loved and studied floral arranging. She too made notes in her favorite books.

During family member interviews, remember to ask about the person's favorite reading materials. This is just another insight into your family's history.

More Important Tips

🐝 Avoid folding any of this printed material. Do your best to store it unfolded because the folds stress the paper. The folding and unfolding of paper causes it to break down.

🐝 Remove staples and other metal fasteners because the metal can rust from the paper. To remove staples or old paper clips, slide a very thin piece of stiff plastic under the fastener on both sides of the document. Slide the paper clip off the plastic, or use a pair of tweezers or a thin knife to bend the ends of the staple up and pry it out. The plastic will protect the paper from abrasion and your tools. Do not use staple pullers—they tear paper.

🐝 To remove the musty smell from old magazines or books, you'll first need to make sure the item is dry. Then place the item in an open container that you can place inside a large, closed container. Place an open box of baking soda inside the closed container. Do not allow the deodorizer to touch the books. Leave for a few days in a cool place, checking once a day to make sure no mold is growing.

The Ultimate Preservation Solution: Preservation Copying in a Nutshell

No matter how well any paper or photographic item is stored, eventually, the item will degrade to the point where it is either prohibitively expensive to repair it or where repair is no longer possible. When this point is reached, copying is the only practical way to preserve the material into the future. This process is termed *preservation copying*.

Although modern copying technology can preserve items otherwise destined to be lost, most copying technologies do not reproduce the original item with total accuracy. Small amounts of definition and clarity are lost each time an image is copied. This loss of clarity becomes more pronounced over several generations of copies, as you may have encountered when you've made a copy. It is not quite the same quality as the original.

Digital technology is the only current way to create an exact duplicate of the original; however, because digital technology is stored in electromagnetic media, such as videotape, it is susceptible to very rapid decay.

Despite its limitations, copying is the only practical way for the layperson to preserve many items. I strongly recommend that you copy your legal documents and place them in your heritage scrapbook. It's your choice, of course, but you might wish to do this with other pieces of memorabilia and older photographs, too. Any print shop can give you excellent copies of paper documents, and most photo developers have duplicate services for photos without a negative.

You may already have duplicates of some information. Put aside the original and keep the duplicates handy for organizing into your information base and to share with other family members. If you have a computer with a scanner, you can scan documents for preparing a computer-generated digital scrapbook. This is a great way to share copies with computer-savvy relatives.

More Important Tips

🦋 Paper items can be either photographed or copied using a photocopier. The image placed on paper by a photocopier is very stable; however, be sure to use good-quality paper. Acid-free paper is a must. Paper marketed as photocopier paper and loaded into most commercial coin-operated photocopiers is usually of poor quality.

🦋 When photographic copies of documents or photographs are made, take care to select a photographer experienced in copy work. Copy photography is as much an art as a science, and an experienced hand will obtain the best copy image.

🦋 Contemporary color photographs of significant importance to a family should be copied about twenty-five years after they are taken to preserve their original color hues.

🦋 Material that has been glued in scrapbooks is very difficult to copy. Usually the only solution is to destroy the scrapbook or the scrapbook page to make good copies of the items found within the volume.

ADDITIONAL FAMILY MEMORIES AND HEIRLOOMS

There are a number of other items that should be properly preserved. Though you don't think of these things regularly in relation to scrapbooking, they do help preserve memories—and that's what our scrapbooks are made of.

Grandpa's Rocking Chair and Other Furniture

When most of us think of furniture, we tend think of wood, but furniture can have many components: metal, bone, plastic, shell, leather, and fabric as well as paints and resins. You must take all these materials into account to care for any furniture heirloom properly.

Caring for historic furniture has changed dramatically. At one time furniture was viewed only for its functional characteristic, and it was considered acceptable to repair damaged or broken furniture with whatever means were available so it could be used again. If the paint or varnish was in poor condition, it was routinely removed and replaced with new paint or varnish or in some cases simply coated with a new layer of finish over existing layers. Today, the monetary, cultural, and artistic values of historic furniture demand that such amateur repair practices be reviewed. According to experts, stripping and refinishing furniture is no longer standard practice. An early finish is as important to historic furniture as are legs or any other element. The finish coating offers important data to researchers and is part of the history of the object. In addition, it is desirable to be able to observe on a piece of furniture patterns of wear that indicate the history of use. The removal and replacement of a surface finish, therefore, is considered a last-ditch effort after other conservation methods have failed. Proper care and maintenance is the only way to ensure furniture preservation for future generations to appreciate.

What Causes Furniture Damage?

The environment can have a profound effect on the preservation of furniture just as it has for all our family treasures.

Light

Light is very damaging to organic materials such as wood. Damage from light is cumulative and irreversible. A tabletop exposed to diffuse light for several years will suffer similar effects of light damage as a tabletop exposed to direct sunlight for a shorter time. Light provides the energy and increased temperature necessary to chemically degrade finishes and wood colorants; in severe cases, it causes the wood cell structure to break down. Clear finishes turn yellow or opaque in response to light, and the color of the wood itself can also change. The resulting damaged finishes and bleached wood cannot be restored to their original color without stripping and refinishing, a practice not recommended as loss of the patina or evidence of use can affect the furniture's monetary value. To limit the effects of light, move all furniture out of direct sunlight.

Moisture

Furniture is also affected by the amount of moisture in the air. Wood and other organic materials respond to changes in relative humidity by expanding or contracting as they try to maintain equilibrium with the moisture in the environment. Furniture finishes are also affected as differences between the response of wood and its coating to changes in humidity, eventually causing the varnish to detach. Remember, too, that moisture is the perfect environment for mold, mildew, and insects. Avoid storing unused family furniture in attics or basements or near heating or air conditioning vents and active fireplaces.

Cleaning Furniture

It was once thought that furniture needed to be cleaned and polished with various mixtures of oils and other materials to keep it from drying out. These mixtures enhance the appearance of wood temporarily but ultimately do not keep wood from drying out. It's more important to keep furniture in a stable environment.

Stop! Before You Use Oil . . .

Furniture oils are not recommended for maintenance as many of them contain linseed oil or other drying oils, and when used repeatedly they will create a gummy, insoluble surface coating that darkens and obscures the grain of the wood. Other furniture polishes contain nondrying oils such as lemon oil; although these do not harden or darken, they nevertheless attract and entrap dirt and grime. Silicone polishes are also not recommended as they leave a film that is difficult to remove and can interfere with future finish treatments.

Giving Wax the Go-Ahead

The best maintenance for clear varnished furniture is a coating of good paste wax. Wax is a very stable material that does not change chemically over time and provides protection from moisture and airborne pollutants. A thin coat applied following the directions on the can is all that is needed, no more than once a year. It may not be appropriate, however, to wax furniture that is gilded, painted, or lacquered or that has unstable veneers or flaking finish. Consult a conservator if any question about the appropriateness of waxing arises.

The best maintenance for clear varnished furniture is a coating of good paste wax.

Keeping It Dry

Dry dusting with a soft cloth is recommended for routine cleaning. Dust and dirt are harmful to finished surfaces and should be regularly removed as they can scratch or otherwise damage polished surfaces. A soft cotton cloth or artist's brush is best. Feather dusters are not recommended for dusting as the feathers tend to get caught in cracks and crevices and can cause detachment of fragile veneers and gilding. A clean cloth slightly dampened in water may help to remove more stubborn dirt.

When dusting, be cautious in areas with loose elements such as veneers, moldings, and metal mounts. Should an element become detached, place it in a plastic bag labeled with its original location on the piece and place it in a drawer or other accessible location until a conservator can reattach it.

Great Grandma's Quilt and Other Fabric Items

This category of textiles encompasses all kinds of materials, from hand-sewn clothing to tatted tablecloths to marvelous quilts. Textiles have played a significant role in family life over the years, blending traditions and varying cultures. Pieces such as quilts, tapestries, embroideries, samplers, flags, and christening gowns should be treasured for their artistic, technical, cultural, and sentimental value.

Fabric artifacts may be composed of a myriad of materials and techniques. Some were made from natural fibers such as cotton, flax, silk, or wool and, in more modern times, artificial fibers such as rayon, nylon, and polyester. Fabric and textile items can be simple in structure and composition or incorporate beads, pearls, metals, paints, dyes, stones, bones, shells, feathers, and leathers.

Handling Fabric

Proper handling is important. Keep hands and body free of jewelry when working with delicate fibers to avoid snagging a thread or yarn. Clean hands are vital when handling textiles. Skin oils, perspiration, and even the residue from skin creams that are readily absorbed by fibers, cause stains.

Textiles can be more fragile than they appear. Before attempting to move a piece, familiarize yourself with its weak areas. Support textiles in a manner that distributes the weight evenly. Sliding a piece of paper or cardboard underneath, for example, may support delicate embroidery, while heavier pieces such as carpets and tapestries may be rolled onto a carpet tube.

Avoiding Deterioration

The deterioration of textiles is largely chemical in nature. The specific factors affecting degradation are the same those for any family heirloom: handling, light, temperature, relative humidity, and pollutants.

Light

Light can fade color and cause a breakdown of textile fibers. Fabrics and finishes (sizing and starches) can turn yellow as a result of chemical breakdown. Both natural and artificial light sources can cause this photochemical degradation, with the effects being cumulative and irreversible. Limiting exposure to both factors will reduce damage. Rotating a collection displaying textiles for short periods at low light levels is highly recommended by experts in the preservation of textiles.

---

*Light can fade color and cause
a breakdown of textile fibers.*

High Temperatures

Storing or displaying textile items in areas of high temperatures and humidity can accelerate the rate of chemical reactions, speeding up the collapse and decay of fibers, dyes, and composition elements. Therefore, textiles should not be used or displayed near direct sources of heat such as fireplaces, spotlights, and windows. Try to keep textiles dry while in use, and be aware of any humidity in storage areas.

Dust and Particles

Textiles are also subject to physical abrasion and damage by dust and gritty particles. These particles in combination with air pollutants may accelerate the rate of breakdown. Household cleaners, particularly those containing chlorine, bleach, and ammonia, are considered sources of chemical pollution.

Cleaning Textiles

Use care when cleaning all textiles. Avoid the very American habit of overcleaning with harsh detergents. Vacuuming is the best primary way to clean textiles. It is effective in removing dust and other physical contaminants and discourages insects and molds as well. For many fragile or three-dimensional textiles, dusting the piece with a soft brush directly into the nozzle of a vacuum is recommended. For large or sturdy textiles, vacuuming with an up-and-down motion (lifting, not dragging, the nozzle) through a sheet of flexible plastic screening may work.

Keeping an item clean will reduce damage caused by insects, rodents, and microorganisms such as molds and fungi.

Keeping an item clean will reduce damage caused by insects, rodents, and microorganisms such as molds and fungi. Signs of infestation include small, irregularly shaped holes, the presence of casings, and excrement. Other indications of serious problems include an increase in discoloration, the tarnishing of metal, and a sweet, musty odor. Inspect your collections every six months to identify any problems early.

❧ PAINTED WORKS OF ART

Paintings may come into the family by way of a family member who has artistic talent or who collected the piece of art. Pictures are usually safest when hanging on a wall, provided that they are well framed, with the picture and hanging hardware adequately secured. Consider the following points when you display a painting:

🍃 Direct sunlight can cause fading of certain pigments, increased yellowing of varnish, and excessive heat on the painting surface. It is best to exhibit paintings on dividing walls within a building rather than on perimeter walls where temperature fluctuations will be greater and condensation can occur. If paintings are placed on uninsulated exterior walls, it may help to place small rubber spacers on the back of the frame to increase air circulation.

✣ Although a fireplace is often a focal spot for a room, a painting displayed above a mantel will be exposed to soot, heat, and environmental extremes. Hanging paintings above heating and air conditioning vents or in bathrooms with tubs or showers isn't a good idea, either, because the rapid environmental fluctuations will be harmful to the painting.

✣ When lighting paintings, use indirect lighting. Lights that attach to the top of the frame and hang over the picture are not a wise choice. These lights also cast a harsh glare, illuminate and heat the painting unevenly, and can fall into the artwork, causing burns or tears. Instead, indirect sunlight, recessed lighting, or ceiling-mounted spotlights are best for home installations. Halogen lamps are increasingly popular, but halogen bulbs emit high levels of ultraviolet light (the part of the spectrum that is damaging to artwork) and should be fitted with an ultraviolet filter when used near light-sensitive materials. These bulbs also have been known to explode and may pose a fire hazard. Tungsten lamps may be preferable for home lighting.

Storing Paintings

If you must store a painting, avoid damp basements or garages, where pictures can mold, and attics, which are very hot in the summer. A good storage method is to place the paintings in a closet with a stiff board protecting the image side of each artwork and a backing board attached to the reverse. Here again, a backing board attached to the reverse can protect your painting.

DISPLAYING TEXTILE ITEMS

Carefully select materials used in exhibition cases, frames, or other display units to ensure environmental stability. Wood, cardboard, and many plastics and metals are unsatisfactory because they emit volatile acids or chemicals. Consider these other display tips as well:

- If these less recommended materials are the only ones available, place a barrier of stable material, such as heavy-duty aluminum foil, between the object and the support.

- Avoid tightly sealed cases, plastic bags, or frames because they can trap damaging vapors and provide an environment associated with high-humidity problems.

- Be careful never to use any type of display that will stretch or tear fibers.

Archival materials, such as barrier films, acid-free unbuffered board, rolling tubes, and display boxes, are available through art supply stores and conservation supply catalogs. Often a local museum can provide information on sources for display items near you. You can also find display help from most fabric and textile retailers.

Framing Your Painting

If you intend to buy a new frame for a painting or have a painting treated by a conservator, take the opportunity to have it properly framed. Ideally, a painting should be held in the frame with mending plates that are attached to the frame with screws. Brass mending plates can be bent and adjusted so there is light pressure on the back of the stretcher or strainer. Sometimes nails are used to frame paintings, but nails can rust, fall out, or protrude through the canvas. Ask the framer or conservator to pad the rabbet, the part of the frame that touches the face of the painting, with felt or another suitable material to protect the image.

If you intend to buy a new frame for a painting or have a painting treated by a conservator, take the opportunity to have it properly framed.

 ## KEEPING KEEPSAKES SAFE

This chapter has covered a range of memorabilia from your family heritage search, describing the best ways to organize and preserve paper artifacts, film media, furniture, textiles, and even paintings. Photographs, too, play such a vital role in most people's lives and thus can comprise such a substantial part of your family heritage scrapbook that I devote the entire next chapter to them.

5

Photos

Picturing Your Family
Through the Years

Photographs need not be the only essential tool used in tracing and tracking your family roots, but a well-documented photo can give real emotion and meaning to your understanding of your family members. Photos put a "face" to the names of the relatives you have gathered to shape your family tree. The photographs found hidden away in an attic or basement, in shoeboxes or old cigar boxes, or in a family Bible or scrapbook hold tremendous value because they can visually aid you in your search for family roots. Old photos can prove invaluable, yet it is just important that you continue to add to the family history by taking new photographs to add to your growing family album.

You need to become aware of how to preserve older photographs correctly so that relatives can continue to enjoy them. Equally important, you need to know how to correctly preserve your own more current photographs so that future generations will not have to dig and search for the details of your life. Chapter 4 touched on this topic, but now we'll go into far more detail. You'll learn how to type the older photos and how to document the photos you take in your own lifetime. Plus, we've added several tips for taking interesting photos, including the techniques of how to color black-and-white photos to recapture the spirit of the past.

> *You need to become aware of how to preserve older photographs correctly so that relatives can continue to enjoy them.*

 ## FINDING OLD PHOTOGRAPHS

Relatives will obviously be your best bet for finding old family photographs. Just like when you started to trace your family tree, you will need to contact family members who might have or know who has the older family formal portraits and casual family photos. Remember to ask about photos during your family interviews. Don't assume only one member of the family will have all the copies. Every family member may end up playing an essential role in gathering, copying, and identifying the family's visual treasures.

Communicate with as many family members as you can. Make attempts to contact more distant relatives on the family tree and ask them whether they have any items they will allow you to copy. A distant cousin may have a photograph of an ancestor, but you'd never know unless you contacted him or her. Keep the communication open to all the possibilities. Ask in your phone calls or letters whether anyone knows of a family member who is keeping track of the family roots or is known to keep family photos or memorabilia. Also let it be known that if a relative dies and there is no immediate family interest in old photographs, you would like to be contacted. Offer to pay the shipping costs, and let others know you are willing to provide copies of old photographs in the future.

> *A distant cousin may have a photograph of an ancestor, but you'd never know unless you contacted him or her.*

Don't forget to ask family members if they remember any neighbors, family friends, or military buddies who might have your family members in their own photographs. It is commonplace for good friends to take vacations or attend big events together. It may be that the friend was the official photographer at such occasions. While visiting my father's family in rural Illinois, for example, I met a kind gentleman at my uncle's house who brought an incredible gift. He was held at the same POW camp in Germany as my father during World War II. The Red Cross had given journals for the American POWs. Inside this man's journal were several pictures of my father, and even better, my dad had written several passages in his friend's journal. In his own hand, he held what my father wrote about being on the POW farm. He wrote about meeting and falling in love with my mother, who just happened to be the farmer's daughter!

ℭLEANING A PHOTO

Most cleaning and stabilizing are done by blowing, dusting, washing, erasing, scraping, removing mounts and adhesives, mounting, applying adhesive, and doing a pencil touch-up. If the emulsion (photographic coating) or substrate (paper backing) is soft, crumbling, or flaking away, then any cleaning at all (even blowing with canned air) could damage the image in the affected area. Consult a restoration expert.

Canned air blowing is the safest and most widely used photographic cleaning technique. It is good practice to blow off photographic media prior to returning it to its archival storage sleeve. Dusting with a soft brush (a photo brush of camel hair or equivalent) is the next safest technique. The only situation in which brushing would be less safe than blowing is when abrasive dust could be pushed across the face of the photograph, scratching the emulsion. Brushing can be more effective than blowing for stubborn problems.

HANDLING AND PROTECTING PHOTOS OLD AND NEW

Photos can be preserved for generations with the right care and proper handling. You should understand several key points before you even begin to sort and organize your family photos:

❀ **Handling.** No matter how careful you are when looking at or working with your photographs, some amount of damage can still occur just because you handle them. Nevertheless, you want to enjoy them. Your best bet is to mount them on album pages in such a way that the pages are handled but the actual photographs are not. Using page protectors is your best defense for keeping fingers, body oils, dust, and objects from damaging your photos placed on album pages.

- ✻ **Dust.** Dust may seem soft, but it is really made up of minute abrasive particles. If your photographs are exposed to dust, the dust can leave tiny scratches on the photo surface. Choose a storage environment that minimizes dust exposure.

- ✻ **Heat.** Your photographs like a moderate cool environment. Heat speeds up chemical processes and causes paper to decay more quickly. You will not want to store them in hot places such as the attic. They'll appreciate your air conditioning just like you do.

- ✻ **Light.** Exposure to light for extended periods of time will cause photographs to fade. Like heat, ultraviolet radiation can speed up chemical reactions that harm paper and photographs. Because photographs are printed on light-sensitive materials, the photos will never be completely stable. You can minimize light exposure by choosing a storage location for your albums away from windows. Some albums contain album sleeves, which are boxes that the entire album fits inside. This eliminates the ability of light to seep in.

- ✻ **Moisture and humidity.** Humidity causes harm in a couple of ways. First, humidity levels above 70 percent promote the growth of mold. Second, rapid changes in humidity can also damage paper. Such fluctuations in humidity cause paper to expand and contract as water is drawn from and goes back into the paper fibers.

- ✻ **Acid.** Acid causes paper to slowly turn brown and become brittle. In time, all acidic paper will disintegrate and fall apart.

- ✻ **Vinyl.** You can tell vinyl from other, safer plastics by its smell. Vinyl puts off an odor. The smelly fumes are harmful to your photographs.

- ✻ **Adhesives.** You'll want to choose an adhesive that is both *acid-free* and *permanent:* acid-free because you don't want it to damage your photographs and permanent because you want your photographs to stay where you put them. Adhesives come in a variety of formats: liquid, double-sided sticky squares, and double-sided tape. You'll want to pick the safe adhesive(s) that best suit your style.

(continues on page 132)

YPES OF OLDER PHOTOGRAPHS

Several kinds of photographic processing have been used through history. Here's a brief guide to typing your photographs.

Daguerreotype

One of the most recognizable images in the history of photographic processes, the daguerreotype is made on highly polished metal plate with an image that has a reflective, mirrorlike appearance. The image is often compared to one of the small holograms you might see affixed to a credit card. Like the hologram, the daguerreotype image is only visible from certain angles; it is a mirror image (reversed left to right) of the original photographed scene.

Ambrotype

Most ambrotypes are not tinted and will have a low-contrast, whitish gray tone, similar in appearance to the tintype. An ambrotype consists of a glass plate supporting a collodion image, which is very similar to its cousin, the tintype (ferrotype process). The process was discovered by the sculptor Frederick Scott Archer in 1855 and quickly became an inexpensive alternative to the daguerreotype, almost completely supplanting it by 1860. Its use began to wane in 1862 with the introduction of the carte de visite.

Tintype

The tintype is relatively easy to identify because its image is made on an iron plate, thus the tintype will attract a magnet—a helpful tip in identification. Also, by removing the image from its case, you should be able to see the metal plate. The tintype plate is also very light compared to the heavy glass ambrotype plate.

Carte de Visite

The carte de visite is easily recognized by the small commercially produced card on which the photograph is mounted and by the imprint or backmark, giving the photographer's name and location. Cartes were introduced in 1859 by the French photographer Disderi. These early images are extremely rare and are unlikely to be encountered outside museums. Later carte de visites are not as rare since millions were produced as the nineteenth century wore on. The height of the "carte craze" was 1860–1866, which included the photography boom during the Civil War (what a difference a year makes!) and the first commercial photographic albums (the carte album), which began to grace ordinary middle-class parlors. Carte production waned from 1870 to the late 1880s, when they all but disappeared.

Cabinet Card

The cabinet card is a larger version of the carte de visite (about 4½ by 6½ inches), retaining the photographer's imprint and exhibiting similar styles of decorative artwork on the card face or back. Like the carte de visite, it consists of a paper photographic print mounted on a commercially produced mounting card. Some images from 1890s look like a black-and-white photograph; these were likely produced on a matte collodion, gelatin, or gelatin bromide paper. Sometimes the image can have a greenish cast. The cabinet card and the card photograph album were gradually replaced in the 1890s by the snapshot (an unmounted paper print) and the scrapbook album. A variety of other large card styles of various names and dimensions came about for professional portraits in the 1880s and 1890s. After 1900, card photographs generally had a much larger area surrounding the print. The last cabinet cards were produced in the twenties, perhaps as late as 1924.

(continued from page 129)

❋ **Inks.** Never write directly on the front or back of a photograph. The inks you choose for your album, whether for pens/markers to journal with or ink from stamp pads to decorate with, should be *acid-free, fade-proof, waterproof, pigment inks.*

❋ **Decorative items.** Decorative items may include mounting paper, die cuts, and stickers. All should be acid-free. Again, never place any of these items directly on the front or back of a photograph. Where stickers are concerned, not only should the paper be acid-free, but the adhesive should be as well.

❋ **Memorabilia.** Keepsakes (ticket stubs, engraved napkins, brochures, etc.) most often are not acid-free. You can still include these items in your album safely if you isolate them from your photographs. There are several ways to do this. One is to put the memorabilia on a page with no photographs and use page protectors to protect facing pages. You can "encapsulate" the acid-containing memorabilia in a sleeve and place it on the same page with your photographs. The sleeve provides an effective barrier between the acid-containing item and the other photographs and acid-free items on your album page. A final solution is to use a product like Archival Mist, which removes the acid from the items. You simply spray the item and allow it to dry completely before mounting.

Each one of these key concerns can cause serious and uncorrectable problems for your photographs. If you're like most people, you will have a limited number of older photographs, so caring for them properly is crucial. At the same time, you probably have an overwhelming number of more current photos to care for and organize, too. Keep in mind you will want to select only the most important or particularly special photos for your family heritage scrapbook. You will need only one or two photos of each family member you are going to include plus a variety of group shots of a family branch or group.

Know that you'll want to keep individual photos of family members temporarily stored within your pedigree or family group files.

Safeguard the photos there with a sleeve or page protector until the photos are placed into the family heritage scrapbook.

You will need only one or two photos of each family member you are going to include plus a variety of group shots of a family branch or group.

You'll be reminded several times in this book that you will want to seriously consider having copies made of your older photographs. The copy will be placed in your scrapbook, and the original will be stored in an acid-free, archival storage system.

Additional Important Tips

🌟 Keep in mind that color photos are more delicate than black-and-white photos.

🌟 If you want to record a special occasion or event for your grandchildren and great-grandchildren, ask the photographer to take a roll or two of black-and-white film. Video, color slides, and most color prints have a limited life expectancy.

🌟 Ideally, photographs should be stored in an extremely cool environment, with color film lasting longest at a temperature of about 40 degrees Fahrenheit, so store photographs in the coolest place in a home that is not subject to high or rapid changes in humidity.

🌟 Always handle photographic prints and particularly negatives by the edges.

(continues on page 137)

COMMON PROBLEMS WITH FAMILY PHOTOGRAPHS

Several common concerns arise when finding, sorting, and organizing your family photos. I have addressed here the top five concerns of most family genealogists and scrapbook enthusiasts:

1. **Broken, torn, or cracked photographs:** If the primary support of a photograph sustains serious damage, place it carefully in a polyester sleeve with an archival board support. If a photograph has a flaking binder layer or friable surface treatments, such as the pastel coloring often seen on crayon enlargements, place it in a shallow box, not a polyester sleeve. Do not use pressure-sensitive adhesive tapes to repair torn photographs. Consult a photographic materials conservator to perform repairs.

2. **Soiled photographs or negatives:** Brush soiled photographs carefully with a clean, soft brush. Proceed from the center of the photograph outward toward the edges. Do not attempt to clean photographs with water- or solvent-based cleaners, such as window cleaner or film cleaner. Improper cleaning of photographic materials can cause serious and often irreversible damage, such as permanent staining, abrasion, alteration, or loss of binder and image.

3. **Photographs or negatives adhered to enclosures:** High-humidity environments or direct exposure to liquids can cause photographs to adhere to frame glass or enclosure materials. This is a very difficult problem to resolve, and great care must be taken to reduce the possibility of further damage. If a photograph becomes attached to adjacent materials, consult a photographic materials conservator before attempting to remove them.

4. **Deteriorated negatives:** Chemical instability is a major factor in the deterioration of early film-based materials. If film-based negatives are brittle, discolored, or sticky or appear wavy and full of air bubbles, separate the negatives from the rest of the collection, and consult a photographic materials conservator. A conservator will be able to help identify these materials and make recommendations for their safe storage and/or duplication.

5. **Broken glass negatives or ambrotypes:** Place broken glass carefully in archival paper enclosures. Use a separate, clearly marked enclosure for each piece to reduce the possibility of scratching or further damage. For long-term storage, construct a custom sink mat that holds the pieces of broken glass, separated by mat-board shims, in one enclosure. Consult a photographic materials conservator for assistance.

THE MAGIC OF HAND COLORING A BLACK-AND-WHITE PHOTO

Coloring a black-and-white photo can add a special treasure and feel to your book. It is not as hard as it looks, and the effect is nostalgic and romantic. You may find some original hand-colored photos among your family heritage photos. These photos were hand-colored by professional photographers using oil paints. Modern products have taken much of the guesswork and mystery out of this technique. You no longer have to be a professional or even have any artistic ability to hand-color photos. Simply follow these steps:

1. Never hand-color an original black-and-white photo. Have a copy made. *Any* negative can be developed into a black-and-white photo, even your color negatives. Once the film has been developed, just ask your developer to make some copies in black and white. Most shops will not be able to do this process in-house, but it's worth the extra day or two it takes to get the black-and-white prints to hand-color.

2. There are three basic methods to hand coloring. The first involves an oil paint applied by brush or paint pen and takes some practice. The second uses acrylic paint or tints applied in the same fashion. The final method and the easiest is to use a marking pen specifically designed to hand-color black-and-white photos. SpotPen, Inc. and EK Success manufacture these pens.

3. Some methods require a solution to be sponge-applied to the photo to soften the top layer of the photo. You'll then apply the color. Depending on the method used, you'll have to use a finish on the photo once completed.

4. The hand-coloring markers are the most foolproof. You add color with the marker in a small area at a time, and the color is very faint. Work in a circular motion as you apply layer upon layer of color until the shade of color desired is reached.

5. Experiment with the different colors available. Many manufacturers carry stock colors that are close to the original hues used by professionals in the old days as well as more modern colors.

(continued from page 133)

❀ Store photographic materials in unbuffered paper enclosures. Alkaline buffering is added to archival storage papers to absorb acidity from the stored material or the environment surrounding it. However, some photographs may be altered by the buffering in alkaline papers, so un-buffered paper is recommended.

❀ Place film-based negatives, which can produce acidic gases as they age, in archival, buffered enclosures and store separately from other photographic materials.

❀ Store cased objects, such as daguerreotypes and ambrotypes, in their original cases or frames with the addition of custom-made, four-flap paper enclosures to reduce wear and tear on fragile cases.

❀ Place individually housed prints, negatives, and cased objects in acid-free, durable boxes that will afford further protection from light, dust, and potential environmental fluctuations.

❀ MIND THE DETAILS

With your research still fresh in your mind, make as many notes as possible about each older photograph that you can. When was the photo taken? Who is in it? How did you obtain it? Try to avoid writing on the back of a photo, but rather give the photo some type of indexing or code where it can be cross-referenced in your genealogy journal. Make any marks on the back of the photo along the edge in pencil and *very lightly* so as not to damage the photo. All of this information can be transferred to the scrapbook page when you mount the photo. Keep all these steps in mind as you begin to add new photographs of your family.

Once you have identified the types of old photos that you have, you'll want to document them in your family research files with as much detail as you can. Your files will be your handy reference to the photos, as it is for so many other parts of your quest. You will also want to take the photographs to a qualified, well-established photography studio and have several copies of the originals made.

---

*Make any marks on the back of the photo along the edge in pencil and **very** lightly so as not to damage the photo.*

Because older photographs are delicate and vulnerable to several dangers, they need to be preserved as effectively as possible. The next section offers tips applicable not just to old photographs but to the newer, equally precious ones of your collection, too.

❦ ORGANIZING YOUR PHOTOS, SORTING YOUR MEMORIES

Pop quiz: Do you know where most of your family photos are right now? Are your childhood and family photos spread out among the family members? Do you have your photos in a few old shoeboxes in the hall closet because someday you are going to have time to sort and organize them? The time is now. Don't delay starting this organization project. Be warned, however: It may end up being more time-consuming than you originally thought, and too often in our haste to finish the task, we don't properly store photos, which can cause damage that may or may not be correctable.

You can easily become overwhelmed by the volume of photographs and memorabilia collected over the years. When you feel this way, try to remember why you are undertaking this task—to relive special occasions and remember loved ones—and have fun viewing your memories. Take this organizational task in small steps, even if it's sorting just a single packet of vacation photos at a time.

You can organize the photos in several ways or combine different methods:

1. **By time:** Put the photos in order as to the dates the photos were taken. Try to find a start date and then follow this time frame from past to present or current date. Most experts will state the opposite: start with your most current photos and work back in time. Both ways work in the long run, but beginning with the oldest photos may better motivate you to keep at it until you reach the more current ones.

2. **By occasion:** Sort your photos by events or celebrations. Place all the holiday photos together in one box, file, or envelope; all the birthday photos in another.

3. **By relative:** Organize by family member, placing all the Dad photos in one envelope and all the different children and other relatives in separate envelopes.

4. **By size or type:** Keep photos of about the same size together, or separate black-and-whites from color photos.

Whatever way you organize, keep in mind what type of themes are developing and how you can use your thoughts to put together a heritage scrapbook. For your first heritage scrapbook, you might want to consider starting the scrapbook off with a family tree, and then let pages follow with photos of these names on the tree, with one relative per page at various life stages.

Preservation as Part of Organization

Keep your organization simple and easy to remember, but remember that an important accompaniment to this task is also to preserve your

WRITING ON THE BACK OF PHOTOGRAPHS—IF YOU MUST

I strongly recommend you do not write on any photograph, but many do as a way to document and keep track of the photo information. If you are going to write on a photo, you must only write on its back or the paper backing. When writing on the back of photos, you need to avoid the following:

❋ Dents that will show on the front

❋ Acid that will eventually damage the photo

❋ Dyes that will bleed through the photo

The following writing utensils are popular for writing on the back of photos because they do not cause permanent damage:

❋ Soft-leaded pencil (minimal pressure to avoid dents)

❋ Blue Stabilo pencil

❋ Zig or Sakura acid-free marker-style pens using only the lighter colors such as brown photos for your family heritage scrapbook and for enjoyment for years to come. Here are some suggestions:

✳ Keep negatives in a sleeve, and use acid-free labels to document your negatives with dates and subject matter. Store negatives with photos or in a separate, well-labeled filing system.

✳ Store photographs in acid-free sleeves, envelopes, or file in a dry, cool, dark place, but never in an attic or basement.

✳ Use acid-free strips of paper and an acid-free permanent pen to document your photographs, including the basics of who, what, where, when, why, and how. Wrap these strips around a group of photographs.

Saving Photos from Magnetic Album Pages

If you have an old magnetic photo album that has photos stuck to the pages like bubble gum in a child's hair, you may have a chance to save these photos with little or no damage done to the photo itself. Enter *un-du*.

Just a few drops of un-du Adhesive Remover will easily and safely remove any self-sticking adhesive.

Just a few drops of un-du Adhesive Remover will easily and safely remove any self-sticking adhesive. It comes with a nylon tool attached to the bottle, eliminating the need for razor blades, knives, and scrapers. This valuable tool instantly neutralizes all self-sticking adhesives and then quickly evaporates. It will not bleed inks and leaves behind no oily residues or lingering odors, and it's acid-free and photo-safe. You can use it for any of the following:

❋ Removing photos from old magnetic albums

❋ Removing and *reusing* scrapbook stickers

❋ Removing spray-mount adhesives and double-sided tapes

❋ Cleaning adhesive residue from punches and scissors

❋ Removing masking stickers for rubberstamping

❋ Separating lamination from scrapbook pages

To assure your success with un-du, follow these steps:

1. Make sure it's a magnetic album and not an album in which the photos were glued to the page. The product un-du cannot remove water-based glues such as Elmer's glue.

2. Understand that photos have two distinct parts: a film top and a paper backing. You must tip the bottle of un-du and the bottle's tool (attached to the bottle throat and looks like a spoon around the bottle tip) almost straight up so you can slide the tool underneath the paper backing. You want the liquid to flow between the paper backing and the magnetic album page. This product works so well that it is capable of removing a film top from the paper backing of a photo—although that is not something you want to do in the aim of preservation!

3. Start on one side of the photo working near a corner. Then work the opposite side of this corner. Once you get the corner of the photo to start lifting, you'll slowly work your way under this lifted corner. Continue until the photo is off.

4. Don't use an abundance of the liquid. If you feel too much is coming out of the bottle tip, just place a fingertip over the tip opening.

5. If you discover that an adhesive residue is on back of the paper, apply a small amount of un-du to this adhesive to loosen it. Then you will wipe up and off with a paper towel. This product temporarily neutralizes the adhesives; however, once it has evaporated the adhesive will become sticky again.

TAKING MEMORABLE PHOTOS

A big part of the family heritage scrapbooking is discovering and preserving the past. Keep in mind that today will turn into tomorrow, and tomorrow will someday be the past! That said, don't forget to record your family's current lives by taking photos. Some families have always understood the importance of keeping track of the family through documents, journals, diaries, and photographs, but others don't realize the value of family photos immediately. Hopefully, you are beginning to understand just what a role photographs play in family heritage. It's never too late to take a good picture!

Keep in mind that today will turn into tomorrow, and tomorrow will someday be the past!

Even professionals will admit that often it takes a dozen or more photos—and a lot of time, patience, and forethought—to get the perfect image. Family photos don't have to be perfect, but it is great when they at least are in focus and capture the moment. We've compiled some of the leading tips from professionals and hobbyists in this section of the book.

ALTERNATIVE PHOTO STORAGE SYSTEMS

Technology has changed the way we can preserve and store our photographs and other film images. More and more methods are becoming user-friendly, and once again your computer may be your best storage friend. You may seek a professional to explore these alternative methods (refer back to chapter 4, too), but keep in mind that technology comes down in price almost as fast as new techniques are developed. Check out some of these alternatives:

* Place photos on a VHS videotape cassette

* Transfer photos onto a DVD disk

* Place photos on microfiche

* Scan photos onto a 3.5-inch floppy disk or a zip computer disk

In addition, several formats are available to digitize photos to place them onto a computer disk. The main differences between the various formats is how much the scanned information can be compressed.

Know Your Camera

Sometimes it is very easy to blame the equipment rather than the person behind the camera for bad photos. In most cases, however, the equipment is just fine, and it is the photographer's lack of knowledge that lies behind a lost opportunity to capture family history in the making.

To start, simply read your camera's manual. You need to have a good understanding of what each button, whistle, and switch is doing when you take a picture. Learn what the symbols mean when they pop up in the viewfinder or display panel of your camera. Before you begin snapping, take this quiz:

❀ When is the flash ready?

❀ Is the focus automatic?

❀ Is there a self-timer?

❀ When will you know the battery is low?

❀ Can you zoom in on a subject?

❀ Is there an auto time/date stamp?

❀ Do you have red eye reducer?

❀ Why do some symbols flash on and off?

❀ Is there film in the camera?

The next step is to check your camera batteries and film. Always try to keep a fresh spare battery in your camera case. Many "broken" cameras simply need new batteries. Camera batteries often supply the energy for the flash, auto wind, auto focus (AF), and indicator display (ID) of your camera.

Loading the Camera and Film Speed

Now, on to the film. It has happened to most of us, but finding out that you didn't load the film properly in your camera is absolutely frustrating. It's a good idea to practice loading film in your camera. Many newer cameras will display a film-loading error indicator, but most of the older models don't have this wonderful alarm system. It's better to practice this simple step several times than to find out that you were clicking away on an empty camera at your son's wedding!

Be aware of the type of film you are loading into your camera. Different speeds of film are best for different photography needs. The film speed indicates relative sensitivity to light expressed as an ISO-speed number. The higher the number, the more sensitive or "faster" the film; the lower the number, the less sensitive or "slower" the film. A fast film requires less light for proper exposure than low-speed film.

Be aware of the type of film you are loading into your camera.

Graininess and sharpness are generally best with low-speed films. Graininess is the sandlike, granular appearance given to an image by the structure of the film's light-sensitive emulsion. As film speed increases, graininess increases. ISO 25-speed film is extremely fine-grained and ideal for big enlargements. Toward the other end of the scale, ISO 1,000-speed film allows for pictures in low-light situations, extended flash range, and stopping fast action using adjustable cameras. For general all-purpose family photography, a film speed of 200 is best.

Focusing

You miss the whole point of picture taking if your photo is out of focus. It's easy to rely on today's sophisticated camera automation. But how does the camera really know what you want it to focus on? Most simply assume that your subject is dead center in the image area. While this will often work, sometimes the AF system will literally fall through the cracks. For example, if you're taking a picture of two people standing next to each other, the camera might focus on the background between the two subjects.

Some cameras may have a separate button for focus lock or multiple auto focus zone systems, so read the manual before you start shooting.

Most cameras let you point the camera at one subject then hold the shutter release button halfway to lock focus. You can then recompose the shot as long as you don't let go of that button. Some cameras may have a separate button for focus lock or multiple auto focus zone systems, so read the manual before you start shooting. Some AF cameras send out a beam of near-infrared light to detect focus. These cameras can be fooled if you're shooting through glass (e.g., a museum display or a train window). Again, many point-and-shoot cameras have an infinity focus button that lets you override the AF in those circumstances.

Lighting

Good lighting is essential to a great photograph. Take some time and study the difference between backlight and frontlight. You'll need to know whether your camera has any way to adjust the lighting conditions.

Have you ever tried to take a picture of someone who was standing in front of a window or other brightly lit area only to find the subject comes out too dark in the final picture? The light coming from the rear fooled the camera, which adjusted the exposure down automatically—and incorrectly—for the bright background. Likewise, a brightly lit subject standing in front of a dark background (as often happens with a spot-lit performer) can trick the AF system and come back too light—again by auto-exposing for the dark background.

Some cameras automatically adjust, while many others offer override buttons. With a little familiarization, pushing the proper override should become second nature.

Finally, don't assume that just because the subject is too dark or too light that you blew the shot. Just as the camera's AF system can be fooled, so can the machine your lab uses to make the prints. If in doubt, carefully hold the negative (by the edges) in front of a brightly lit piece of white paper and see whether you can find more detail. If you do, go back to the lab and ask them to reprint the picture(s). The lab should do this for free. If not, consider looking for another lab.

Know Your Subject

Understanding and knowing your subject is important to taking a good photograph.

Ask yourself these questions before you start photographing:

✽ Why do you want to take photography of the person?

✽ Are you trying to capture this person on film to share with family or friends?

✽ Do you have a specific album page in mind and you want this person to be a part of that special scrapbook page?

✽ Why do you want to capture the moment or event?

✽ Are you celebrating a family get together?

✽ Are you recording a milestone in life like a birth, wedding, or anniversary?

✽ Is it the people in the photograph or maybe the entire setting you are trying to capture?

Make a list of shots or photos you are trying to capture. Take a deep breath and relax as you start taking the photos. Some photos will be

CROPPING BEGINS WHEN YOU FOCUS YOUR CAMERA

Cropping will be discussed in detail in chapters 7 and 8, but it's important to know what cropping is as you take the photograph. Cropping removes any unwanted or busy background details that take away from the main focus of the photograph. For example, when you take a photograph of your child in the Christmas play, what is it that you want to capture? Your child's beaming face? The costume your child is wearing? The stage with live animals and a baby doll Jesus? Grandfather's proud smile as he watches? Make a mental note of the moments you want to capture. And don't forget to take a few close-up, candid shots.

There are two ways to "crop" with your camera before pressing the button. The first is to have the lens zoom in to cut out distracting backgrounds; the second is for you to move physically closer to the subject you want a photo of. Using your viewfinder as your cropping tool in this way will make things much easier as you prepare your more current photos for your family heritage scrapbook.

spur of the moment, but others can be framed and thought out. Look into your viewfinder, and really *look* at what you are seeing. Look at the background. Look at the foreground. Look at the subject you are focusing on. Would this photo look better enlarged? Use your camera lens to zoom in, or physically step closer to the subject. Should you shoot this photo head-on? Or would you get a better view from a side angle? Maybe you should look down onto the subject or lie on the ground and let the camera lens look up onto the subject. Step out of the same old, same old photo box. Consider some of these great ideas and variations for our most common occasions and celebrations:

> ## Don't Crop Polaroids!
>
> Cutting a Polaroid photograph releases harmful chemicals from inside the image. As an alternative, you can place a frame made of acid-free paper over the top of the photograph, hiding the "ugly white part."

❋ **Try a new angle to traditional family or group photo.** If you have all the family around, nothing is wrong with everyone posing for a big group photo, but how about smaller groups? Consider taking a photo with only the grandchildren (or cousins, uncles, etc.) in it or maybe all of the women (or the men) in the family. The possibilities are endless and the photos are truly special.

❋ **Take "before," "during," and "after" photos.** These are great to use in a heritage album layout because everyone just loves to look at them. Consider taking before, during, and after photos of changes to your home such as a remodeled room or an addition to the house, haircuts, a garden, Thanksgiving dinner, Christmas before and after gifts are opened, a new home being built, or a child getting braces.

❋ **Try out black-and-white film.** It gives your everyday photos a classic look that can't be beat. What's really fun is to color your black and white photos.

❋ **Photograph the everyday traditions in your life.** Every family has them, so make sure that those traditions will live on for years through your heritage album. Does the family go to pick out the Christmas tree together? Does every day end with a bubble bath? Does Dad read the newspaper every morning as he eats breakfast? Is Friday Mom and Dad's date night? Is there an annual family picnic? Take pictures! Be sure to remember to explain the everyday tradition in detail in your journaling.

DID YOU KNOW?

People immediately look at another human in a photo even if the person is very small in the frame. Our attention will go to anything alive as opposed to something inanimate. The hierarchy of attention is humans over animals, animals over plants.

Colors draw our attention, and the warm shades of red, yellow, and orange will jump out of a background of cool tone colors such as blue and green. Even a small subject will dominate if it's different from its surroundings. It could be its color, brightness, or the direction it's facing. Anything that's isolated from everything else will draw attention to itself.

No matter what else is in the scene, the eye is irresistibly drawn to the lightest, brightest area. That's why any bright blob of light or bit of paper in the background is distracting. All other things being equal, the eye will go to the area of highest contrast. The eye will go to the subject that's in sharpest focus.

🎋 **Keep your camera loaded.** Try always to keep film and good batteries ready in your camera at all times. You never know when you will take that "perfect" photo! Take your camera everywhere. If you really want to be sure to capture great photos of your loved ones, always bring your camera.

Why, When, and Where to Take Photos

Everyday is an opportunity to obtain and preserve a little bit of your life and family. Not all moments need to be monumental, but special events and occasions do top the list of moments we want to remember and pass along to family, friends, and future generations. Keep an open mind and a loaded camera with you at all times. You never know when the perfect opportunity will arise.

It's important to photograph some of those moments that may be special only to your own family. Your child in the summer garden picking ripe tomatoes will not make the national news, but it is a tender moment in your family. Somehow my family, for instance, got into the habit of taking pictures of the official driver of a vacation. Silly pictures, but each has a special memory.

---

*Keep an open mind and a loaded camera
with you at all times. You never know
when the perfect opportunity will arise.*

Don't become overwhelmed with the responsibility of being the "picture taker" in your family. Pass the responsibility around, and you'll be happily surprised with the results from the different personalities that are part of every family unit.

Just in case you get photographer's block, the following section lists some ideas related to two ever-popular subjects: the holidays and vacations.

People Shots

❀ Take advantage of the gathering of friends and family to get some more or less planned group shots. A wide-angle lens is useful if you want to get a lot of people in a shot, but be careful—one that's wider than 28mm will distort the faces at the edges of the frame. It's better to stand back and use a longer lens.

❀ For those rather formal shots, shoot early, when kids are not fussy, grownups are not tired, and everyone looks their best.

- Arrange people so their eyes are at different levels, rather than in a straight line, which means some should sit, some stand, and some sprawl on the floor.

- Hand your camera to someone else and let him or her take your picture.

COMBINING WORDS AND PICTURES

This chapter has helped you identify older photographs, sort and organize all of your photographs, and we've given you lots of advice on how to add to your collection with great new photographs. All of this will take longer than the time it took you to read this chapter, but this process is so important to rounding out your knowledge of your family.

As you've been sorting and organizing, you've inevitably also been making notes and remembering special moments. To your photos you need to add those words—the facts and fun behind each photo; the dates, the places, the people who were framed so carefully in your viewfinder. This step is called *journaling*. You'll be an expert by the time you finish the next chapter on that topic, as well as the literal author of your family heritage!

6

Journaling

Words from the Heart

Journaling has come to mean the written word or text used on any type of memory album or scrapbook page to explain, describe, and add the little details about the photos or memorabilia. Today, the term *journaling* is usually used for personal writing that explores the inner world of the self.

In the broadest sense, journaling can be done with or without photos. Journals (rather than a heritage scrapbook) are a very valid form of heritage craft and will be discussed later in this chapter with other journaling methods such as calendars, diaries, personal essays, and unsent letters. Keep in mind that some wonderful heritage album pages have been created using mainly an individual's thoughts and feelings with a bit of memorabilia for interest on a page—an amusement park ticket stub, a playbill, an airline ticket, or even confetti from a parade.

I hope you don't just journal in your family heritage scrapbook but consider adding to your family history with a personal journal, which is nothing more than an updated version of a diary. All types of journaling and journals can become part of your legacy to your children, family, and friends.

 ## OBSERVE, THEN WRITE YOUR HEART OUT

Experts agree that the best journaling comes from people who make an effort to be an observer of their lives as well as a participant. Write about events that are happening to you or around you, in a way that helps put the events into perspective. This is especially effective when writing about life changes, job or career, relationships, or illness.

The best journaling comes from people who make an effort to be an observer of their lives as well as a participant.

Let yourself describe the event in detail, using as many of your senses as possible. What were the sounds, smells, sights, feelings, and emotions that you were experiencing at the time? Write about the event as though you were observing yourself.

Use third person—that is, *she* and *he*—rather than *I* in your sentences. Describe the activities as an outside observer. Frequently this helps give perspective to an otherwise very personal experience. You can later go back and replace the *he* or *she* pronouns with *I* when you begin to transfer these words onto your heritage album pages.

✿ WHO, WHAT, WHERE, WHEN, AND WHY: PUT THE ANSWERS IN YOUR SCRAPBOOK

To begin, and hopefully to make it less confusing, I will focus on journaling as it is applied to a family heritage scrapbook. Journaling can serve many purposes. In a few years you won't remember every detail of every picture or piece of memorabilia. Imagine the puzzlement for your descendants a hundred years from now! It's important to write the who, what, where, when, and why of each photograph and piece of memorabilia because each piece of information is what helps explain and define our lives. Photos come with a lot of feelings and stories. There was a reason the photograph was taken. And since photos can't talk, you need to write down those stories and the feelings and reasons behind them.

It's important to write the who, what, where, when, and why of each photograph and piece of memorabilia because each piece of information is what helps explain and define our lives.

Penmanship Problems?

Many people use the excuse that they don't have good handwriting so they don't want to include much journaling on their pages—they don't

(continues on page 160)

TIPS FOR JOURNALING YOUR FAMILY STORIES

Not everyone feels they have the gift of being able to write interesting words for family heritage journaling. It takes practice and some patience with yourself. Here are some great hints from the experts that might help you relax and gain confidence in family journaling:

- Write thoughts and ideas down soon after they come to you. Keep a small notebook handy, and make notes in a permanent heritage journal. For most of us, memory can be a haphazard game of roulette. Always write your ideas down!

- Write down names, dates, places, and anything else that strikes your fancy. All stories need a plot, characters, some dialogue, and a few background facts. You can edit later.

- Keep your thoughts and ideas on a calendar. It's one of the easiest ways to remember important dates.

- Use index cards or sticky notes to write down different parts of your story. Use one for the introduction, several for the body of the story, and then a final one for the closing or conclusion of the story.

- Keep in mind who is writing the story and who may read the story. Are you creating a page for the birth of your child and writing the story as you think your child would tell it or do you wish to write it from your point of view? Regardless of whose point of view you choose to use, identify the author.

There is a time and place for journaling by hand and journaling with a computer (discussed later). If your child is retelling a story and can write, then have your child write the story. If you are writing about an event when a child was younger, then a computer-typed story may be easier for a child to read as he or she grows older. If you are telling a long story, a computer-typed story will more easily fit onto your page. However, a personal story about yourself should be handwritten, if possible.

The lettering (done by hand or using a template) or font (generated by computer) you choose if using a template or the computer can be a very clear character of the story. Wonderful childish fonts are available for a child's story. There are dramatic fonts for a story about a vacation or milestone. Elegant fonts are suitable for wedding tales. Experiment with the fonts and find one that complements your story.

Draw a shape such as a fish, a ball, or a star on the page lightly in pencil. Write the journaling within the shape, filling up all of the shape. Erase the pencil line. The journaling remains behind in the shape of the original pencil drawing.

(continued from page 157)

want to ruin a beautiful heritage page with their messy penmanship. But that excuse doesn't hold as long as your writing is legible. Your wife or husband, son or daughter, and grandchildren or cousin will not open up your heritage album and think how terrible your handwriting is! They will appreciate the personal touch you added to the photographs with your handwriting. If you are still worried about it, you can always use your computer or typewriter for *some* your heritage album pages. Someday, a member of your family will look upon your typewritten or computer generated journaling and marvel that such an old-fashioned and obsolete machine was used!

THE KEY ELEMENTS

As you sort through generations of family photographs, as discussed in the previous chapter, you're likely at some point to be totally clueless as to how you are related to the people in the pictures. In many cases, no one may be left to help you with names, dates, or places. As families, we can make sure this type of situation doesn't arise. Journaling on a heritage page should include the following most significant items in your family heritage scrapbook:

- *Who* is in the photograph, including how this person is related to the family

- *What* they were doing at the time of the photo

- *Where* the photo was taken

- *When* was the photo taken (date)

- *Why* the photo was taken

Also include anything funny or meaningful that was said or done at the time. The idea is to include any information that will complete the story told in the photo and on the page.

I keep telling you to make sure you relate the "whole story," but what exactly is the whole story? For special moments and events captured in a photograph, you might want to include more than just the who, what, where, when, and why. What happened right before the photo was taken? What happened right after? So many details can get lost along the way, details that will mean so much to your family a few years down the road. A heritage scrapbook with no journaling may be fun and interesting to look at now, but it will lose much of its meaning in the years to come.

The family interviews (from chapter 2) will come in very handy for your journaling.

You've got facts and quotes from many family members that can fill in the blanks on the family heritage pages. Genealogy deals with the facts: dates, places, names, legal connections, and so forth. Journaling takes this information a step further, making the emotional connections. It can give other and just as important specifics, such as the weather or world events happening at the same time. It describes the places, with the colors found in the garden and the architecture of the buildings. It puts the human touches on those names of relatives by letting us know that Grandma Rodriguez was at her grandson's first birthday party on September 5, 1989, and she had a wonderful time holding him and watching him play with the birthday cake she made from scratch.

🌺 PIECES AND PARTS OF JOURNALING ON A PAGE

Everything is easier to understand when it can be broken down into separate elements that will build the whole. In this case, the whole will be each family heritage scrapbook page you create. Within a page, journaling can be broken down into several parts:

🌺 A *page title,* also called the *header*

🐝 *A caption,* which is a line or sentence placed under, above, or to the side of the photo

🐝 A paragraph or two of story or explanation of the page and photos on it

The journaling can be done by hand, with a stencil, using alphabet stickers, by your computer, using a letter template, or with die-cut letters. Your choice will depend on your personal style, level of creative comfort, or the supplies you have available. You may keep a journaling style throughout an entire heritage album or vary the style from page to page. Most experts recommend keeping a similar or complementary style throughout a heritage album. The basic heritage album is more about the journaling, record keeping, documenting, and describing of the family than the artsy-crafty expression you can use to have fun with your photos. As you begin to create your own heritage album, you'll know better the feel or tone you are trying to set for the album that will become a family heirloom. You may wind up creating several family heritage albums, allowing you to stretch your creativity a little differently with each one.

CAREFUL WITH THE WHOS

Hawaii is such a close-knit group of islands that often residents of a community there are indeed real family members. However, Hawaiian natives as a whole are very warm and friendly people. To show hospitality and welcome new people, they will often respectfully call new friends "cousins."

When journaling in your family heritage album, however, be careful when saying who the "who" is. Is Uncle John a bona fide uncle, or is he really a family friend? Somewhere you need to state that John was such a dear family friend that he was given official family status. Make sure the most distant relative in your family's future will be able to figure out who's really related to whom.

PELLING IT OUT

You may write one way in your everyday life, but you will probably find that you take more care when you are writing on your album pages. Still worried about your poor penmanship? A great way to make your handwriting look better is to use one of the many tools on the market to help you get your writing or lettering straight.

- *Template.* Many different kinds of templates are available that help you write creatively, but with an even straight flow.

- *Ruler.* Use a ruler to mark faint pencil lines to follow; after you allow the ink to dry, you can erase these lines.

- *Light box.* Place a lined sheet of paper onto a light box, then place your acid-free paper on top of it. The light from the box will allow you to see the lines so you can write in straight lines.

- *Computer.* If you are still uncomfortable with your handwriting, you can always use your computer and its printer. Choose from the multitude of fonts available with most software.

The Page Title

Get out your press badge and write some headlines! That's basically what you're doing when trying to come up with an appropriate page title. The page title can be one word, a phrase, a quote, or a complete sentence. You can be grammatically correct or throw punctuation out the window. Your title should reflect what your page is all about. If you can't think of anything, feel free to get inspiration from quotes, verses, song lyrics, bumper stickers, and T-shirts. Keep your family's unique style and sayings in mind, too. Perhaps you always call out, "Dinner's on! Get it while it's hot!" Then make that the title of a page depicting mealtimes.

As you assemble the parts of your page, you may come up with a title as you work. The title is usually placed at the top, bottom, or along the side of the page. Keep in mind the print size or font size should be larger than any other journaling you will do on the page. The title should catch the reader's eye but not be so big as to distract from the photos.

Elements of design are important but should not be your only focus.

Elements of design are important but should not be your only focus. A design can be *symmetrical,* meaning it is equally balanced from top to bottom or side to side (see figure 6.1). An *asymmetrical* design has the top, bottom, or a side "heavier," or containing more elements (see figure 6.2). Your title will play a critical role in the balance of the overall design. In general, the human eye prefers symmetrical and balanced design, so you may wish to use an asymmetrical design sparingly.

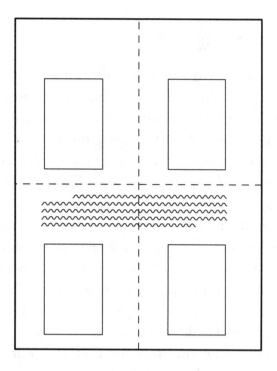

Figure 6.1. Example of a symmetrical design.

The Captions

This part of your heritage page is the perfect place for some of the more dry information such as names, dates, and places. Or you may just want to jot down something funny said while the photo was being taken. A caption should be sized so it is readable by all age groups, including those of us who do not have 20/20 vision!

There are exciting ways to use captions other than under the photograph. You can write around the edge or border of a photograph (remember: on the paper matting only, *not* on the actual photo). A charming effect is created when you write around the edge of the entire page, which will frame a grouping of photographs. Keep in mind that if using acid-free ink pens or markers, you can complement or contrast the caption ink with the background or matting papers.

Descriptive Body Journaling

Not all pages need extensive journaling or storytelling. You may find that a set of photos and memorabilia need more than one page in your heritage album. This is referred to in journalism terms as a two- or three-page spread. You'll be laying out two or three pages with feature photos from the same event or milestone. The best result is a two-page spread on two facing pages, so the viewer can appreciate the full effect. If possible, take the third page of photos and work it into a single separate page, or add more journaling to make it another two-page spread.

This body of text can be a single paragraph or many paragraphs. It's the story you want to tell the reader. Many heritage enthusiasts love to make a poem out of this descriptive passage. You'll find the more you write, the more you will enjoy writing, and your journaling will become easier and easier to compose.

Finally, as with your title and captions, your descriptive body can be done in your own handwriting, by lettering, or printed from a computer.

OTHER TYPES OF JOURNALING

Journaling can take many forms, including the traditional format of writing in a special blank notebook or diary that becomes your personal journal. Calendars can serve as journal sites, and oral histories are another valuable way to document your life. We'll look at all these options in the following sections.

The Journal or Diary

In the classic sense, a journal or diary is a book of observations, thoughts, feelings, commentary, and personal reflections. What is the difference between a journal and a diary? If anything, most diarists make daily entries into their diaries, while a journal is used frequently,

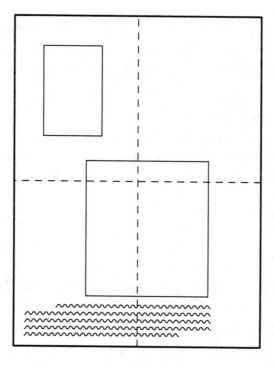

Figure 6.2. Example of an asymmetrical design.

but not necessarily on a daily basis. Blank journals can be purchased at most bookstores or office supply stores. Many active journal enthusiasts also use spiral notebooks, loose-leaf binders, or index cards.

*Many active journal enthusiasts
also use spiral notebooks, loose-leaf
binders, or index cards.*

Again, dating each entry is important. It helps keep a time line. In many cases, the writer of the journal will be the only reader, but history proves that journals are often discovered and treasured by family members and historians. There need be no rhyme or reason to the entries. Some people commit to making daily entries even if only to jot down a few sentences or phrases. Others keep a journal for a few months, during times of tragedy, or for a year, writing only occasionally on the pages.

Many personal journals and diaries have ended up being published by family members or the individual who wrote it. Ask your local librarian to help you find a few of these published treasures.

Calendars

One of my most precious keepsakes of my mother is the calendar notebook she kept the year I went off to college. I treasure this calendar filled with her handwriting about her everyday activities. It offered me insight to her life. Calendars can serve as journals and keep a wonderful yearly record for a family. They come in all sizes and styles, with plenty of room to jot down information. Notes can be made on the date as an event happens, before you forget. Hang a calendar in your kitchen area and invite members of the family to write down their thoughts on it. Give each family member a different color pen or marker. You'll enjoy reading the messages peppered with doctor's appointments, swim meets, baseball games, party reminders, and all those other activities that make up our years.

Calendars can serve as journals and keep a wonderful yearly record for a family.

Take advantage of the software and online services that provide another method of keeping track of your days. This is a less personal

OUT OF THE MOUTHS OF BABES

Kids can say really incredible things. You think you will remember all the wonderful things that your children say, but the reality is that as time passes you probably won't. Take time to write these cute quotes and stories down, and then use them in your family heritage scrapbooks.

Don't underestimate your child. He or she may want to start working on family heritage roots right beside you! Remember that children can begin to journal as soon as they learn to write. Teach and share the traditions of keeping a journal or diary, writing letters, and creating scrapbook pages. Here are some additional ideas:

- Create a page each year for all the cute things your child has said.

- Have your child draw the family, and place this with a more formal family portrait.

- Create a child's words of wisdom journal.

- Help your child make a nature journal for a year as you both watch the seasons.

- Put your child's artwork into a memory album or make a hand binding for the art.

- Jot down your child's promises, hopes, and dreams each year.

- Let your child help you select the photos for the family scrapbook.

- Let your child pick out background and matting papers.

- Keep those letters to Santa. Present them to your child when he or she is an adult.

- Create a font with your child's handwriting.

- Create a page comparing Daddy's or Mommy's hand outline with the child's.

touch, but in the long run it might be the organization method best suited to your lifestyle.

Personal Essays

Personal essays can be found as part of journals or done separately. This is a more stylized version of what you've been doing all along when you've been recording family stories and history. This form of journaling allows you to get creative in expressing the thoughts, dreams, and hopes you have for your family. The personal essay is like a short story about a specific event, emotion, or belief the writer has.

Essays have a general theme, with a beginning, middle, and end. Keep in mind that you may write the rough draft or outline of the essay in your journal or on a computer word-processing program before creating the final version for your family heritage scrapbook. Usually at least one or two rewrites are necessary before the final essay is completed. Many hobbyists have taken their personal essays to another level by submitting them for publication in books and magazines.

Poems and Little Ditties

Creative writing tends to send most people into a frantic frenzy. Most claim they aren't creative and not likely harboring a poet within. Rubbish! Some forms of poetry are highly formulized: You follow a formula and write a poem. You don't need to be brilliant, and you don't need to be William Shakespeare.

If you aren't in the mood to write your own poetry, then pick your favorite poet or songwriter and borrow a few lines. Who you enjoy will tell your family a little more about you. Don't rely heavily on the words of others, and remember to give credit where it is due. You might like to find a writer with the same family heritage to add interest to your family heritage scrapbook. The humanities and arts tell a story throughout our history, and it's a good idea to include some of that creativity with your own.

Welcome to Donegal
Dún na nGall

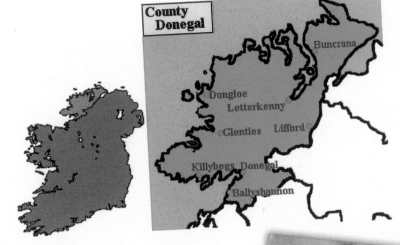

County Donegal

County Donegal

Buncrana

Dungloe
Letterkenny

Glenties · Lifford

Killybegs · Donegal

Ballyshannon

COUNTY DONEGAL

""Donegal county, Republic of Ireland), Donegal, county
northernmost in the country, in Ulster Province, bounded
Atlantic Ocean. It is mountainous and boggy and has ma
Numerous islands lie off the long and deeply indented sh
not fertile; small crops of barley and wheat are grown in
percent of the land is in pasture, and cattle, sheep, and
chief manufactures are linens, muslins, and woolens, in
homespun. The county has sandstone and granite quar
salmon fisheries. Donegal in ancient times was called
O'Donnell's country, after the family that ruled much
Along the coast are many ruins of castles, including t
at the head of Lough Swilly, and Kilbarron Castle, ne
Lifford. Area, 4830 sq km (1865 sq mi); population
*(county, Republic of Ireland)," Microsoft(R) Encart
Microsoft Corporation. All rights reserved.]*

JOHN GIVEN, SR. came
1830 to settle in White
wife Margaret and chil
travel from County Done
all farmers growing

GIVEN Surname Distribution

1850

Copyright © 1999 Hamrick Software

http://www.hamrick.com/names/

One in:
100
1,000
10,000

The color of each state indicates how frequently you will find someone
with this surname in each state. For instance, if a state is colored red,
then 1 in 100 people (or more) in that state have the surname. Similarly,
yellow means approximately 1 in 300 have the surname, green means 1
in 1000, and blue means 1 in 10,000 (or less).

I WAS TOLD AS A CHILD... that my grandfather, Harry Emmet
Given was the first ancestor to come to America from Ireland. In
my family history search I discovered that the Given Family really
came to American two generations before Grandpa Harry. This
opened up a huge world of many, many relatives. Although I was
never bothered by the fact I seemed to have a very small family
compared to my husband Ken's ostensibly massive family...it was a
joy to discover my Irish roots. This is the distribution of the Given
surname in the United States from early 1800 to 1990.
I wonder just how many of these people might be related to me!

WELCOME TO DONEGAL
(LEFT) is an example of an
opening page to a family
heritage scrapbook.
Family can easily learn
more about the homeland
or area where an ancestor
was born or raised.

SURNAME DISTRIBUTION (RIGHT) shows
how a family surname is distributed in the
United States. It can be interesting to
explore whether your surname is a popular
one and the regions in which your relatives
might have settled.

FAMILY COAT OF ARMS is another great opening page to your scrapbook. If you lift the coat of arms at the center of the page you will find a three-generation family tree.

There is no set rule for how you create a family heritage page. Here you can see the same family wedding photo done in **Classic Black-and-White** (large below) as well as two different color schemes (small right).

Xavier and Zenta Muller
Great Great Grandparents

Xavier and Zenta Muller
Great Great Grandparents

Xavier and Zenta Muller
1830

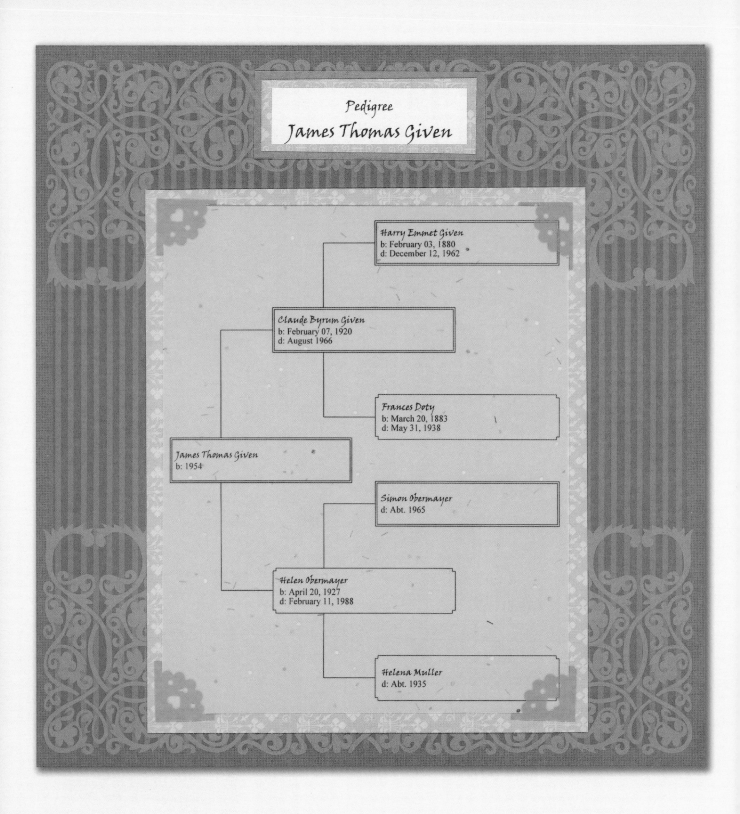

Pedigree
James Thomas Given

Harry Emmet Given
b: February 03, 1880
d: December 12, 1962

Claude Byrum Given
b: February 07, 1920
d: August 1966

Frances Doty
b: March 20, 1883
d: May 31, 1938

James Thomas Given
b: 1954

Simon Obermayer
d: Abt. 1965

Helen Obermayer
b: April 20, 1927
d: February 11, 1988

Helena Muller
d: Abt. 1935

PEDIGREE OF JAMES THOMAS GIVEN is an example of a formal pedigree chart. This chart was created with the aid of The Family Tree software and printed out on vellum paper. Slot corners were used to make the pedigree removable.

Family trees can take all shapes and forms from computer generated to free form. **THE GIVEN FAMILY TREE** was created by purchasing an acid free decorative paper that had the artwork preprinted on it. All that needed to be done was to fill in the family member names.

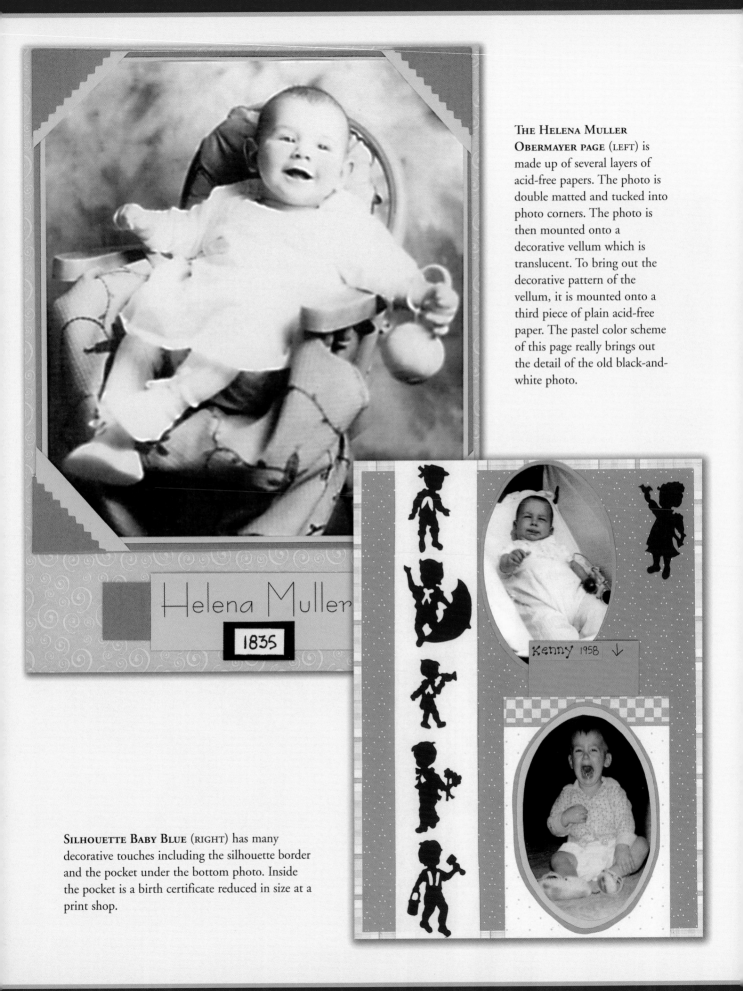

THE HELENA MULLER OBERMAYER PAGE (LEFT) is made up of several layers of acid-free papers. The photo is double matted and tucked into photo corners. The photo is then mounted onto a decorative vellum which is translucent. To bring out the decorative pattern of the vellum, it is mounted onto a third piece of plain acid-free paper. The pastel color scheme of this page really brings out the detail of the old black-and-white photo.

Helena Muller

1835

Kenny 1958 ↓

SILHOUETTE BABY BLUE (RIGHT) has many decorative touches including the silhouette border and the pocket under the bottom photo. Inside the pocket is a birth certificate reduced in size at a print shop.

STEPHANIE JO GIVEN FRIDAY (RIGHT). Coloring a black-and-white photo is easy and adds a wonderful delicate and romantic touch to a family heritage page. Keep in mind you can have any of your color photographs reprinted as black-and-white photos at most photo developers.

Stephanie Jo Given Friday
1970

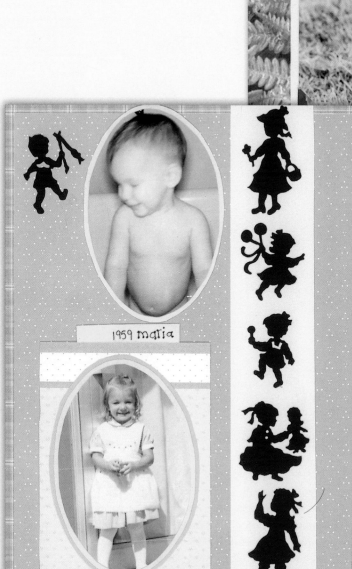

1959 maria

The second page of the **SILHOUETTE BABY PINK** (LEFT) shows how the two-page spread was designed in a mirror image format. The pastel color scheme is perfect for the black-and-white photos.

Fathers and Sons
Brothers and Friends

The men of my family are as diverse while sharing many common bonds and traits. I wanted to create a page that included all of them, side by side. All are tall with smiles that bring warmth to one's soul. When times are tough, they stick together and when times are good, they celebrate as one. They are fathers and sons. They are brothers and friends. Each has a profession and a dedication to work. Each has goals and dreams and wishes. How did I ever get so blessed as to be a part of this glorious family? How did I ever get so blessed as to love these special family men?

1999

1987

Three generations and five branches of family are shown in this **FATHERS AND SONS, BROTHERS AND FRIENDS** two-page spread. By using color coordinated photo corners, the reader can easily figure out who is related to whom and how!

Given Clan 1988

A Clan of Irish Folk Smile

A Clan of Irish Folk Smile

Top Left: Maria Nerius, James Given, Ronald Given and William Given. Top Right: See enlargement
Enlargement: Back: Dennis Given, Pud Williams, Stephanie Friday, Ken Nerius, William Given Charles
Given; Front: Virgina Given, Tollee Given,

When a group of family members gets together, take the opportuniy to capture it with a few photos. **A Clan of Irish Folk Smile** looks like a title to the page, but it is actually a sheet of paper that can be pulled from a pocket and lists all the family members in the photos.

HOME

Maria's Childhood Home

Ken's Childhood Home

A Place Called Home is a two-page spread. The first page (ABOVE) shows the homes of the grandparents and parents. The second page (RIGHT) shows the homes of the children. If you lift the photos of Maria's and Ken's childhood homes, you will find journaling that includes memories and the address of each home shown on the two pages.

IMRO REUNION 2000
(LEFT) demonstrates
how to incorporate a
family reunion into
your family heritage
scrapbook. The
enlarged group photo
was placed on a flap
that, when lifted,
shows journaling of
who is in the photo
and how each person
is related.

MOTHERS AND DAUGHTERS (RIGHT)
illustrates how to show off different
family relationships. The photos
selected for this page show a mother
and daughter at the same age (30
years young!). You can also see the
dramatic effect of mixing a black-and-
white photo on the same page as a
color photo.

Mothers and Daughters
Daughters and Mothers

There are no words to express how I love you.
Friends say we have the same smile and I know we
share the same heart. We both have a talent with
people, flowers, and chocolate chip cookies. Images of
our shared moments cross my mind each day.
Memories of laughter, tears, and love. I may not have
the words to express it, but you are the sweetest
reflection of me.

A family heritage scrapbook should capture some of life's small, but very special moments: the memories of one family member to another family member. **GRANDMOTHER'S GIFT BY THE SEA** is a great example of a special moment passed from one generation to the next.

Grandma and baby love the shore.

"No finer music than the ocean's roar."

A visit to feed the gulls. Just us, having fun!

Look closely at the picture here. In your hand, Heather, dear is a seashell that caught your eye this sunny California day. Grandma saved it and the memories of this day just for you.

3/82

Durango Memories is a 65" × 50" quilt designed and made by Vivian Ritter of Evergreen, Colorado. Photographs and newspaper articles were photocopied and heat transferred to commemorate her daughter and son-in-law's life together in Colorado. The center panel is machine pieced and appliquéd.

REMEMBERING DAD is a 33" × 41" quilt made by Vivian Ritter of Evergreen, Colorado. She used photocopy heat transfers of photos dating from the 1920s to the present. The label under each photo was computer generated, then transferred to fabric.

It is important to remember all members of a family. **ALWAYS IN MY HEART** is an example of a page dedicated to a loved one who has passed away. Some of the elements that can be included are a photo of the loved one or his or her parents, a photo of the grave site, and the funeral card. Corners were used so that any of the elements can be removed from the page for a closer look.

In Memory

Kenneth Nerius
1931-1977

CLAUDE BYRUM GIVEN
1920-1966

CHILD OF
Harry and Fannie
BROTHER OF
John, Opal, Wilma, Wanda, Clyde, Ronny
HUSBAND OF
Helen Obermayier
FATHER OF
William, Ronald, James, Maria
FRIEND TO ALL

CLAUDE BYRUM GIVEN (LEFT) is another example of how to dedicate a page to an individual family member. Slot corners were used to protect the older photograph and journaling explains the family members' relationships in a written form of a family tree.

GIVEN

CYNTHIA
1859~1928

CHARLES
1850~1938

IN MEMORIAM (RIGHT) shows three generations of family member grave markers. The bottom photo was placed on a flap that, when lifted, gives exact locations of the grave.

Letters, Sent and Unsent

Once upon a time letters were the main way a family got news, not just about family members but the world itself. Many of our ancestors were letter writers. And the letters weren't just read and discarded. They were read over and over and often passed around for all to enjoy. Full of family gossip and hometown updates, letters were a source of information. Many recipients have carefully kept their letters tied in small bundles placed inside a box for safe keeping in a bedroom closet or desk drawer. Have you been lucky to find such treasures?

A great example of the power of a letter is to write a letter to your child when he or she is still a baby.

Bill's family held annual family reunions, and between the reunions the family always kept in touch with a "round robin"–style letter that began with one of the siblings writing a newsy letter and sending it off to the next sibling's family. The family members would write about what was happening in his or her family's lives and send it on to the next sibling. That person would add his or her own news and stories and in turn send the entire writings on to the next. By the time it got back to the originator, that person would remove his or her pages, and write and update, and continue the circle. The letters were handwritten, and the envelope in which it arrived was bursting at the seams. This is a timeless style of letter writing that you might want to add to your own family's traditions.

Another great example of the power of a letter is to write a letter to your child when he or she is still a baby, and then give it to your "baby" much later, such as on his or her twenty-first birthday or wedding day.

Journals for Every Family Subject

Journals can be kept for specific times or events within the family. These mini-family heritage heirlooms are great ways to express your interests and hobbies—your artistic or creative side. Fill the journal with your own stories, funny jokes, happy endings, trials and tribulations, or ask all members of the family to join in. This can also be a bonding project for a mother and daughter, sister and brother, grandparent and grandchild, father and daughter, or mother and son. Think about starting one of the following special journals:

Garden Journal

Travel Journal

Cooking Journal

Dream Journal

Kids Say the Darndest Things Journal

Craft or Art Journal

Sports Journal

Collection Journal

Nature Journal

Camp Journal

School Journal

Home Remedies Journal

Mom's Best Advice Journal

Dad Knows Best Journal

Pet Journal

Career Journal

Letters can serve as a variation of a personal essay, with your private thoughts about someone directed to that person. Or you might write about a unique experience the two of you shared together that you want to explore in the emotionally meaningful way writing can allow. You need not send such letters (unless you want to) but rather use them as yet another special tool to document your own family heritage.

ORAL JOURNALING

When most of us think of journaling, we imagine only the written word. Thoughts and feelings are important to our family heritage scrapbook; however, the written word is in a way very limiting to our family history. For the most part, oral histories are used by historians to gather information about a time and place, such as eyewitness accounts of life during wartime. But you can use them, too, to add more dimension to your family heritage scrapbook, providing sounds—tone of voice, laughter, verbal habits—and even moving pictures, if videotape is used to create the oral journal.

To complete an oral history, take the family interview questions from chapter 2, and record on either audiotape or videotape the conversation. Through such recordings a family can capture the relative's inflection and, if on videotape, even gestures and facial subtleties. The effect of an oral history is raw and powerful commentary. Imagine your children's children being able to see and hear their great-great-grandpa talking about his love of fly fishing or what it was like to be a soldier.

For historians, the oral history provides an effective tool that allows a society to preserve oral traditions, skills, and crafts. The full cultural or individual significance of quilting or the making of a musical instrument can only be obtained through the nuance and subtlety of oral language. Thus, we can learn much from a personal history that we could never obtain from a textbook. But for a family, the oral history can be a way to see, hear, and feel the presence of a family member. It will take no more time to interview someone with a tape recorder or video camera. Yet, the result of an oral history is priceless and timeless.

BEYOND JOURNALING

I know you might be suffering a little hand fatigue with all this journaling you are doing, but I hope you are also enjoying this special process in creating your family heritage scrapbook. Discovering just how much your family—past, present, and future—means to you is a wonderful present you are giving yourself. It's time to gather up all the pieces and parts of your family history and scrapbook and put the whole thing together in a pretty package. Chapter 7 will start helping you gather the other items needed to complete this adventure: the album, the papers and protectors, and the exciting tools to crop, embellish, and lay out your pages. For now, you can lay down your pencil and pen. Just keep them safe—you'll need them again soon.

Discovering just how much your family—past, present, and future— means to you is a wonderful present you are giving yourself.

7

Tools of the Trade

You've gathered and organized your photos. You've gathered and organized your family history and memorabilia. You've got lots of great ideas for pages and just can't wait to get started on your family album. Now it's time to gather the supplies you need to create and present that family heritage into an organized package that will preserve your family's treasures into the future.

Dozens of products are available to help you. You'll see words such as *archival*, *photo safe*, *acid-free*, *lignin-free*, and more on the labeling of these products. It can get quite confusing. Other chapters have discussed the key criteria for your supplies, but let's review a few important words before you start purchasing your supplies:

Acid-free: Acids can be introduced into materials during manufacturing or after manufacturing, with an overall harmful effect of deteriorating the material. Materials with a pH value of 7.0 or higher are therefore a must. Your supplies should all be labeled acid-free.

Lignin-free: Lignin is a natural substance that exists in wood. When wood is broken down into paper, lignin is a residue that can be left in the paper. Large amounts of lignin make paper very acidic, causing it to break down. All papers you use should be lignin-free.

PVC-free: PVC is an unstable plastic, generally called vinyl or Naugahyde, that may exude oily plasticizers or corrosive and acidic hydrogen-chloride gas. It's best to avoid any PVC touching your photos or memorabilia. Any item that comes into direct contact with your photos (e.g., page protectors and photo corners) should be PVC-free. Some recent research states that a small amount of PVC is safe, but why take the risk?

 ## FIVE MUST-HAVE SUPPLIES

You only need five important ingredients besides your family heritage notes and photos to get started on your family heritage scrapbook. More supplies and tools may be useful as well; you can add more supplies as needed or wanted, and I describe some of these later. Without the following five necessities, however, you'll never get your heritage scrapbook off to a good start:

1. Album

2. Pages with or without protectors

3. Acid-free adhesive

4. Acid-free pen or marker

5. Utility or craft knife with a ruler *or* sharp scissors

Albums

Memory and scrapbook albums come in two standard sizes: 8½ by 11 inches and 12 by 12 inches. Many prefer the smaller album, because a wider variety of decorative papers are also available in this size, and it is easier to copy pages to share with family members. The larger option has the obvious advantage of allowing more photos and memorabilia per page. Your own needs and budget will help guide you to the best choice.

TIPS FOR SELECTING AN ALBUM

Keep this list handy when you go to purchase your album. If there is anything specific you are looking for, add it to this list.

❋ Avoid magnetic albums. Paper and adhesives in most magnetic albums can be highly acidic, which accelerates deterioration of your photographs.

❋ Choose a sturdy album if it will be handled frequently.

❋ Select a family color, if you have one.

❋ Check the manufacturer's warranties and guarantees.

❋ A slip case for the album provides extra protection.

❋ Will the album allow for additional pages if you want to augment your scrapbook in the future? Are the pages and page protectors included?

Albums can be found in photo supply stores and arts and craft stores, by mail order, and at various Web sites. The album itself may be as simple as a three-ring binder or as elaborate as a leather-bound spiral. The most popular album in scrapbooking is the three-ring binder. However, since several alternatives are possible, we've taken a look at the advantages and disadvantages of the most popular choices.

Three-Ring Binders

Every art and craft shop and office supply store carries this versatile and easy-to-use type of album. You will also find many to select from at stationery and photography shops. Choose a binder that is oversized to accommodate sheet protectors. Many enthusiasts will recommend D-rings to keep pages flat, but the O-rings will make page turning easier. Some binders are acid-free; others are not. Since pages are stored in acid-free page protectors, you will need to decide whether the binder must also be acid-free. See figure 7.1 for an example of a three-ring binder.

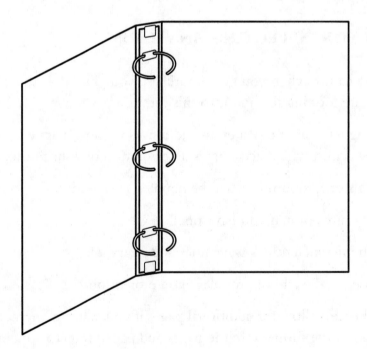

Figure 7.1. Three-ring binder.

✿ow Many Pages Will the Binder Hold?

The size of the binder rings determines how many pages can be inserted. A good rule of thumb for how many pages a binder will hold, as presented here, is that one page represents one sheet protector with two heritage pages back to back.

❄ 1-inch ring: approximately thirty-five pages

❄ 1½-inch ring: approximately fifty pages

❄ 2½-inch ring: approximately seventy pages

Advantages

❄ The album can be expanded

❄ Pages lie flat when opened

❄ Pages can be removed and moved around very easily

❄ Since page protectors are used, holes are not punched on scrapbook pages

❄ These albums are highly available in different cover styles

Disadvantages

❄ Two-page spread has a binder ring in the middle

❄ Pages can fall out if the binder is dropped hard enough to pop the rings

❄ Care must be taken to close rings securely if rings are opened to add or remove pages

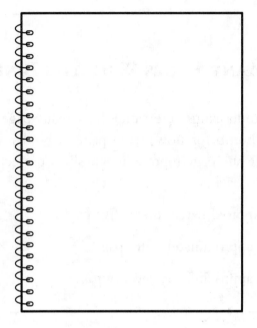

Figure 7.2.   Spiral.

Spirals

This style of binder or album comes in many sizes and is often found at art supply or stationery shops. This is a wonderful album for single themes such as gardening, Grandma's brag book, or vacation memories. Not all spirals are acid-free, so make sure you select carefully. You'll want to consider the larger spirals because you'll be adding photos and memorabilia to the album, and it must be able to accommodate the newer material. See figure 7.2 for an example of a spiral.

Advantages

❋ You can decorate the cover with your own creativity

❋ This is a self-contained album (binder and pages combined)

❋ Pages lie flat when opened

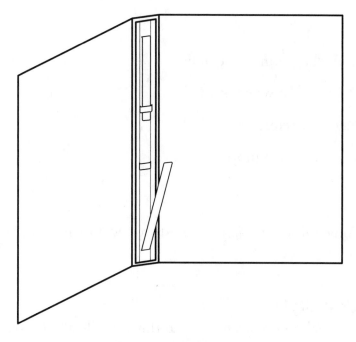

Figure 7.3.　Flex hinge.

Disadvantages

❀ Pages can easily wear near the spiral and be ripped out

❀ Additional pages can't be added over time

Flex Hinge

A plastic strap binding allows your albums to expand. These binders are great because pages lie flat and side by side. Look for pages that are heavyweight, acid-free, and lignin-free. Some pages have reinforced edges to protect against wear and tear. Photographs and memorabilia are mounted on both sides of a scrapbook page. Page protectors are sealed at the top and bottom and slip easily over your scrapbook page. These albums are durable and available in a variety of colors. Your best bet to find this type of album is at an office supply store. See figure 7.3 for an example of a flex hinge.

Advantages

- ✸ The album can be expanded

- ✸ Pages lie flat when opened

- ✸ Page protectors are available

- ✸ Pages can be removed or moved

Disadvantages

- ✸ Although pages can be moved around, moving a page affects both sides of the sheet

Post Style

A metal post holds pages into this versatile album, keeping pages tightly bound like a book. Look for pages that are heavyweight, acid-free, and lignin-free. Pages should have reinforced edges and hole punches. Some

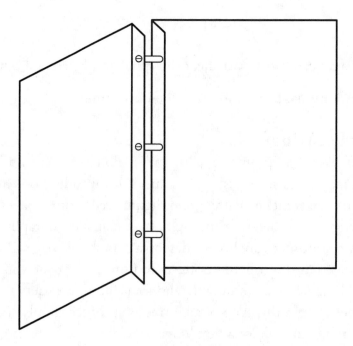

Figure 7.4. Post style.

albums offer plastic, hinged paper edges to allow the pages to lie flat. Page protectors are sealed at the top and bottom and slip easily over your scrapbook page. A variety of stores carry this type of binder, but try an office supply store first. See figure 7.4 for an example of post style.

Advantages

- ❋ The album is expandable by adding post extensions.
- ❋ Two-page spread pages are displayed side by side.

Disadvantages

- ❋ Pages do not totally lie flat when opened.
- ❋ Holes are punched on scrapbook pages that could be pulled out of the album.

Paper and Page Protectors

Once you've decided on the album, you'll need to start exploring all the paper possibilities. A majority of family heritage photos will be black-and-white ones, and so one popular theory is that one should stick with black-and-white or muted colors for the pages as well. This decision is truly personal taste. My own family is far too colorful to limit myself to black, white, or neutral shades. The artist in me wants color to be bright and bold. You'll need to think about your own preferences. It helps to take a photo or two to your local paper suppliers and see how they look against various background colors.

Paper

Paper selection doesn't need to be rushed. Spend some time learning about the papers and really seeing what is available to you. Papers can be found at most art, craft, rubberstamp, scrapbooking, stationery, and office supply stores.

More than once I've been inspired by the papers I see. The decorative paper may remind me of a photograph I have or bring back a childhood memory. A pleasing decorative or patterned sheet of paper may end up supporting your theme or motif throughout your heritage album. You may find a metallic lace paper that is perfect as a border to your pages or an old-fashioned print that is just the right touch to highlight the photos of your grandparents. Perhaps a faux handmade paper with rose petals will remind you of an aunt's garden. Or you may wish to start very simply and select a few shades of green to create a heritage album of your Irish folk.

A pleasing decorative or patterned sheet of paper may end up supporting your theme or motif throughout your heritage album.

As tempting as such variety may be, you don't need to buy out the store when you start picking your papers. I recommend you select six to a dozen papers you like and purchase these to play with. Keep in mind you will want solid-colored papers to coordinate with any decorative papers you have selected. You'll need the solids as backgrounds for matting your photos and in some cases your memorabilia and captions, too. (Matting and the details of cropping photos are described under "Basic Techniques" later in this chapter.)

You will also find "books" of papers available from several publishers. These books are often designed around themes such as seasons, holidays, or celebrations. Several publishers have also put together decorative and plain papers that correspond with time lines, including separating out the decades of the twentieth century. The books will contain decorative or patterned papers as well as coordinating plain papers. This type of book is often very helpful if you lack confidence in color theory or coordination. Keep the papers stored in protective sleeves until you have time to sit down and begin your project.

Keep the papers stored in protective sleeves until you have time to sit down and begin your project.

Page Protectors

And just what is that protective sleeve? Page or sheet protectors are sealed on three sides, and your heritage scrapbook page slides into the protector from the one open side. They safeguard your photos and memorabilia from dirt, dust, body oils, and other liquids that might spill and harm the page. They also help hold the scrapbook page.

Not all page protectors are created equal. Choose only those that do not contain any PVCs. You should be able to choose from nonglare or clear. You might consider the slight additional cost of heavyweight protectors over the standard protectors for your heritage pages. The extra support will reduce bending on the pages and your photos.

Not all albums require or use page protectors. Most experts agree, however, that page protectors should be used in all heritage scrapbook albums to ensure the safety and protection of precious heirlooms and family photos.

Adhesives

Your next supply will be the adhesive for your heritage scrapbook. There is no doubt in anyone's mind that the adhesive used in the last few generations has led to some of the most extensive damage to our photos. The worst case in the past was that the adhesive harmed the photo. Less permanent but often just as annoying, the old adhesives also simply didn't hold up over time. One of the biggest advances the art, craft, and photo industries have made is in the wide variety of safer, longer-lasting adhesives now available.

As with your other supplies, your adhesives must be acid-free and photo-safe.

As with your other supplies, your adhesives must be acid-free and photo-safe. There are numerous manufacturers and brands of archival-quality adhesives, but make sure the one you pick is clearly marked as archival, acid-free, and photo safe. If this wording is not on the adhesive, please contact the manufacturer before using this adhesive on your photos, journaling, acid-free papers, or memorabilia.

Adhesives can be found at almost any general merchandise store. The more user-friendly types (e.g., photo tape and photo squares) will be found at art, craft, scrapbooking, and photography retailers.

The key to selection may be how you prefer to apply the adhesive. The most common are as follows:

Double-stick tape: Comes with a tape dispenser; both sides of tape have adhesive.

Photo tape: Double-sided tape usually in a box dispenser; depending on the manufacturer, this tape will have backing only on one side or on both sides.

Photo squares: Little squares of double-sided tape that come as a sheet of squares or in a dispenser with paper backing on the top and bottom. Some "squares" may actually be circles of adhesive.

Glue sticks: Glue in solid form that ranges in stick diameter from ¼ to 1 inch; this type is not as messy as liquid glues and is very easy to control where glue is applied.

Liquid paper glues: Containers and the tips vary, but most control the flow of glue to avoid blobs of glue squirting out.

Most of us use a combination of these types of adhesives when working on a heritage album. Photo tape is perfect for large photos, while smaller pieces of memorabilia can be securely adhered to a page with a glue stick. Practice using your adhesive selections on scraps of paper before using them on your photos and memorabilia.

Photo Corners: The Alternatives

One alternative to applying any adhesive directly onto the photo or memorabilia is to use photo corners. The corners of photo or memorabilia will slip into the slot corners. The photo corner may have adhesive that is activated when a paper backing is removed, or you may have to dampen a dry gum or glue on the corner. Be aware that some photo corners may contain PVCs, so read the product labeling carefully. Photo corners are usually white, black, or clear, but there are many decorative corners that can be laser cut to look like lace or have designs at the center (e.g., baseballs, roses, fall leaves). You can also use rubber-stamps to create an image and cut out the design for your corners. Finally, try making your own photo corners from leftover scraps of acid-free paper. You'll have to apply your own adhesive, but creating your own photo corners is easy and fun (see the sidebar on page 192).

Pens, Markers, and Ink

Archival, acid-free, and photo-safe pens or markers are very important to your heritage scrapbook. You'll use the pens and markers for your journaling. You need to look for writing instruments that have permanent, fadeproof, and waterproof ink. The ballpoint pens used by most

SAFELY USING MEMORABILIA IN YOUR FAMILY HERITAGE SCRAPBOOK

❋ The safest way to incorporate items into your scrapbook that you aren't sure are acid-free and photo-safe is to encapsulate them in a clear Mylar pocket like the ones manufactured by 3L. These pockets will separate the memorabilia from the rest of your heritage page and prevent any acid from migrating to your photographs.

❋ Another good approach is to keep the acid-containing item as far from your photographs as possible on the page or create a separate page that will hold the memorabilia. Simply put the item on a page by itself with a page protector. You may want to mat or mount the acid-containing item on acid-free, buffered paper to provide a place for the acid to migrate to before it would make it to the photographs.

❋ You can also create an acid-free paper pocket for the item. You'll find instructions for making a page pocket in chapter 8.

for everyday correspondence are not permanent and tend to bleed, which leads to the possibility of damaging photos and memorabilia.

Archival, acid-free, and photo-safe pens or markers are very important to your heritage scrapbook.

A huge spectrum of these pens and markers is available, from sophisticated tones of gold and silver to shocking neons of lime and yellow. Again, some heritage album enthusiasts maintain that only black ink, with an occasional sentence or two in gold, should be used. The thought behind this strictly black-and-white or subdued color scheme is that only this set of hues will remain true to the dignity of our heritage. Keeping the color out of the heritage scrapbook might also keep it separate from your other types of memory albums and scrapbooks. However, most families are far too colorful to limit to a black and white palette.

My philosophy is not to limit your creativity. Keep your tools acid-free, lignin-free, and archival, but after that there are no rules. I believe the content of your heritage scrapbooks will differentiate them from the rest of the albums you might choose to create. Only you can be the judge of how to respect and represent your family's heritage.

Utility Knife and Ruler or Sharp Scissors

The reason you are given a choice for the tool you'll use to cut your papers and crop your photos is because you'll be using it often when creating a heritage scrapbook. On scrap paper try both tools. Which are you most comfortable with? Which tool gives you the best control over the cutting? Each of us is different. One person may have great precision with scissors; another might have trouble getting an even edge with scissors, even when using marking lines, and so prefer the utility knife with a ruler.

A friendly reminder: *never,* ever cut any of your older photos. Never cut or crop an original photo that doesn't have a matching negative (in case you need to make copies later), which rules out most of our older photographs of grandparents and great-grandparents. Remember the first rule of genealogy: Never do anything that can't be undone to an old photograph or document. Always make copies of your older photographs. Just take the photos to a reliable photographer or photo developer. Originals should be stored properly and kept whole.

Never do anything that can't be undone to an old photograph or document.

Keeping your cutting tool sharp is essential. Change the blades in your craft knives, personal trimmers, rotary cutters, and cropping tools as soon as you notice any dragging or ragged cuts. You don't want to damage a photo with a dull blade. You'll need to devote a pair of scissors for paper cutting and photo cropping only, versus those you might use for sewing projects, because cutting paper dulls a blade quicker than cutting fabric. Tie a bright piece of yarn around the handle of the scissors to help remind you of which to use for what household project. You don't need expensive scissors, just ones that are sturdy and fit your handgrip comfortably.

If you chose to use a utility knife and ruler, select a utility or craft knife that has a comfortable grip along with a metal ruler, because the straight edge lasts much longer than a plastic or wood one. You'll find all kinds of utility knives available. Some have a locked, stationary blade; others have a swivel blade. Try both. The swivel is best for decorative cutting like rounded corners and very tight corners. When using a util-

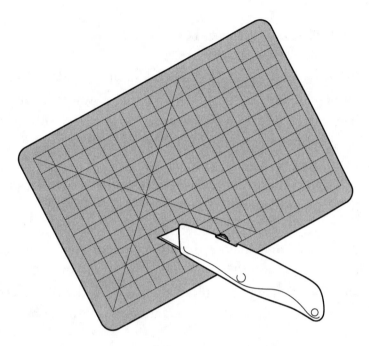

Figure 7.5. Utility knife and self-healing mat.

ity knife, it's best to use a self-healing mat underneath. This allows you to cut through something with the knife, but the mat is made of material that will "heal itself" when cut, rather than become ruined. This also keeps you from slicing into counters, tabletops, or other work surfaces. See figure 7.5 for an example of a utility knife and self-healing mat.

You'll also notice that several different types of blades are available for most utility knives. Each has a function and purpose. For paper cutting and photo cropping, the simple sharp-pointed blade works fine. As your designs for heritage pages grow more complex, you may want to invest in different styles of blades. The real key is to change blades often.

 ## MORE TOOLS TO CONSIDER

Tools such as those described in this section are not necessary for creating your family heritage scrapbook, but many are great time and effort savers, not to mention just plain fun. In the broadest sense of the word

(continues on page 194)

MAKE YOUR OWN PHOTO CORNERS

Photo corners can be helpful for photographs that you might want to remove at some future date. You might want to have copies made, or there might be handwritten notes on the back. Photo corners are great for securing memorabilia such as playbills or report cards to pages so that the whole page coordinates nicely.

Have you ever thought of making your own? It's really not hard. To make the corner itself, simply follow these steps:

1. Cut a piece of acid-free, lignin-free decorative paper or card stock in a rectangular shape twice as long as it is wide (see figure 7.6). You will need four rectangles of the same size to make photo corners for all four corners of a square or rectangular photograph.

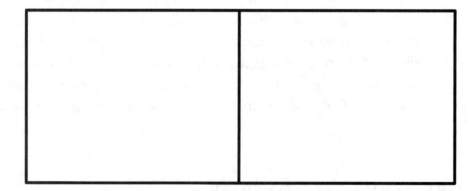

Figure 7.6. Paper cut into rectangular shape to make photo corners.

2. After you've cut four identical rectangles, fold them carefully from the center of one edge to the opposite corners (see figure 7.7). This will leave you with a right triangle. When you turn it over, you'll see the two corners that you folded, joined at the center.

3. Just add a photo square or piece of photo tape to the back across the "seam." That will hold the seam together, plus give you the adhesive you need to attach it to the page.

You can make your photo corners out of any solid color or decorative paper or card stock that might be appropriate for your photographs. You can also embellish them with pens, stickers, or punches. Also, remember that you can make them in any size that will go well with the size of your photographs.

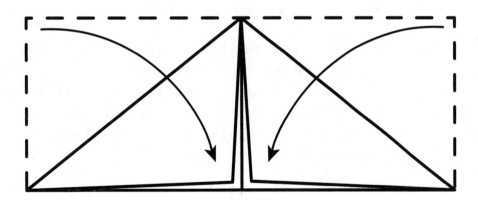

Figure 7.7. Directions for folding paper to make photo corners.

(continued from page 191)

A Scrapbooker's Wish List

The following tools were recommended by a sample group of twelve active members of a scrapbooking mail list:

Fiskar's Personal Trimmer: Helps save time while cropping photos and making mount mats

A software library of fonts and clip art: Reduces the need for endless searches on the Web for art for scrapbooks focused on family heritage. The group named D.J. Inkers and Dogbyte software by brand.

Tombow Adhesive Applicators: The preferred adhesive for most scrapbookers on the mailing list

Clearsnap Pigment Stamp Pads: The favored pigment ink for rubberstamping

Ranger's Vintage Inks: Available in wonderful vintage colors

McGill's Slot Corner Punches: No more having to cut your own plain slot corners; comes in a wide variety of fancy motifs that meet heritage needs

tool, the following items are great to add to your scrapbooking supplies. Several add to the creativity of your page designs. Is there an artist lurking in you? Some of the tools take the guesswork out of creating lines, curves, corners, and other decorative elements to your pages. If you have the budget for expanding your toolbox, you'll really enjoy considering any of the following wonders.

Paper Cutter or Personal Trimmer

This is my personal number one tool needed in scrapbooking of any kind. The paper cutter is for large cutting projects, while the smaller personal trimmer cuts papers for headline, caption, photo, and memorabilia matting and crops photos with clean, accurate edges. These are much easier on the hands than scissors and utility knives. Most have measurements and sizing guides incorporated into the overall design of the instrument.

Many different brands are offered at your local art, craft, scrapbooking, and office supply retailers. Keep in mind that you'll still want to keep your basic cutting tools of scissors, utility knife, and metal ruler in addition to a paper cutter or trimmer. See figures 7.8 and 7.9 for examples of personal trimmers.

Decorative Scissors

Dozens of interesting and beautiful decorative edges are available by using this type of scissors. These are great for cropping photographs and cutting paper borders and mats for your pages. The heritage scrapbook really only needs one or two different styles used within the album—too many different edges would be too distracting on a page. You can find these at most craft and scrapbooking stores as well as at many Web sites that sell scrapbooking supplies.

The cut is not as easy as with decorative scissors as with scallop and pinking shears, but with practice you'll love the results. Always practice on scrap papers until you understand how to keep the decorative edge pattern consistent over long lengths.

Circle, Oval, and Assorted Shaped Croppers

This tool allows you to crop a photo or cut a mat for the photo in a perfect circle, oval, or other shape. It has a cutting blade and adjustable cutting path. You'll need to read the cropper's instructions carefully because each brand varies. The tool is a good investment if you plan to make several heritage scrapbooks for gifts or decide you just love scrapbooking and continue to create scrapbooks with all your photos. You'll need to practice with duplicate or copies of photos before attempting on photos you wish to use in your scrapbook. You can't get the true feel of the tool by practicing on scrap paper.

Practice with duplicate or copies of photos before attempting on photos you wish to use in your scrapbook.

In this family of tools you'll also find a drafting compass, circle ruler, and circle cutting ruler. Again, these tools are a great investment if you plan to make many scrapbooks.

Templates

Templates can be used as a cropping guide or as a page layout guide. You'll use a pencil to lightly trace the template onto your photo and use it as a guide to crop the photo. Shapes include circles, ovals, squares, and novelty shapes.

Templates are also available for patterns that can be used in creating the family heritage scrapbook pages. The template gives placement of photos, headlines, captions, and more. Most templates are made from clear or see-through plastics.

Paper, Craft, and Corner Punches

You may be familiar with paper punches that punch out small holes, but did you know that paper punches come in dozens of designs, including stars, hearts, teardrops, squares, diamonds, and teddy bears? A paper punch is a hand held tool with a handle similar to a pair of scis-

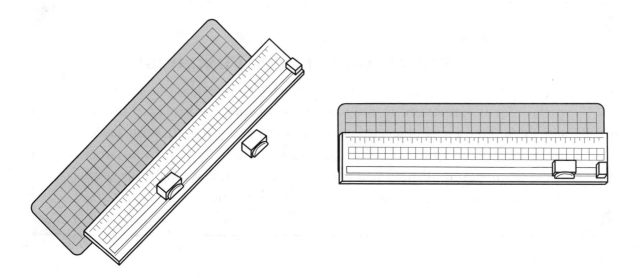

Figure 7.8. Example of personal trimmer.   **Figure 7.9.** Example of personal trimmer.

sors, while the craft punch is a solid mechanism that is placed on a hard surface with paper inserted and a top button is pressed down to "punch" the paper. A border can be created by craft-punching a strip of paper in a repeating fashion. In many cases you can use the punched-out paper within your page design, too. Several craft booklets have been written on how to use all the punch shapes to create delightful designs. See figures 7.10 and 7.11 for examples of punches.

The corner punch is a craft punch designed to round corners of paper or photographs. Some corner rounders are simple curves, but some very intricate designs are available that add a Victorian or old-fashioned look to papers, mats, and photographs. There are also slot punches that create beautiful photo corners with a simple punch out. Heritage experts highly recommend slot corners because no adhesive is needed. The slot created by the punch will hold the photo in place on a page. See figure 7.12 for an example of a corner punch.

You'll find paper, craft, and corner punches at most craft and scrap-booking stores. There are also many scrapbooking Web sites that offer a large variety for sale.

KEEP THOSE PUNCHES PUNCHING!

Paper punches add great die cuts to our scrapbook pages, but as for any metal tool, it's important to use some basic maintenance to keep the die cut sharp. Take a small piece of aluminum foil and punch the foil several times with your punch to keep the edges sharp. If you find the punch isn't punching smoothly, all you need to do is punch it several times using wax paper. The wax paper helps smooth out the punch.

Lettering Books

Lettering is needed for page headers and captions. If you want something extra special, take a look at books that feature decorative and unique lettering alphabets. The lettering can be done freehand by tracing the lettering onto your page, with a light box, or with a reflections instrument. Keep in mind that any letter should be done with acid-free and photo-safe pens and markers.

Clip Art Books

A wide variety of clip art books are available at art, craft, and book stores. If you have Web access, you can find free clip art to print or download. Perfect for using with your light box or for cutting out and gluing to a heritage scrapbook page, clip art comes in any theme, motif, and image. If your heritage is Irish, you might want to include some Celtic designs; or if your family enjoys nature and gardening, check out a floral motif. You can also find clip art books specifically designed for scrapbooking with interesting borders and mats.

Figure 7.10.   Example of paper punch.

Figure 7.11.   Example of paper punch.

If your heritage is Irish, you might want to include some Celtic designs; or if your family enjoys nature and gardening, check out a floral motif.

Clip art software is also available. You can print out elements of a page or the entire page. Most of the software will be found at computer stores or retail shops that sell computer software. Keep in mind you can also print the clip art onto paper and then cut out the design desired for your heritage page. Or you may decide to print and then trace this design onto your page.

Figure 7.12 Example of corner punch.

Computer Software

This category of scrapbooking tool has really become extensive. You can now find software for lettering, clip art, templates, and journaling. Some software programs even allow you to put together an entire virtual family heritage scrapbook. The most exciting thing about being able to place a family heritage scrapbook in a digital format is that you can easily share your work with family and friends by e-mailing pages or the entire scrapbook. You can also design your own family heritage Web site.

Software has become very user-friendly, and although I don't feel that virtual scrapbooks will ever replace a handmade family heritage album, I do feel that any help you can get from a software program makes the entire process easier to organize.

Light Box

Light boxes are used to trace designs, images, and patterns onto a piece of paper. You'll place the design onto the top of the light box, then place a blank sheet of paper over the design. Once you turn on the light box, the light will allow you to see the design through the top paper. You'll take a pencil, pen, or marker and trace the design.

Light boxes come in all shapes and sizes and have many uses. Try viewing slides and negatives using one. You can lay a lined paper down onto the light box, place your blank sheet onto it, and then write captions. This way you will not need lines on your actual heritage page or have to erase any pencil lines necessary to keep your writing straight. Light boxes can be found at most art, craft, office supply, and photography stores.

Reflections Instrument

This tool is one of the most amazing devices I've ever used. Like a light box, it helps you draw, trace, and write. The tool reflects any traceable image onto the surface of your project, and it doesn't even use electricity! The reflections instrument comes in two sizes: small and large. Although more craft and scrapbooking retailers are carrying this tool, you can find more information about the tool and ordering at www.nucentury.net.

Decorative Rulers

Made of flexible plastic or metal, decorative rulers add creativity to your heritage pages. You can use them to create unique borders, drawing with the ruler directly onto your family heritage page or use it to draw unique shapes to cut out and adhere to your pages. The rulers are fun and festive. Look for rulers with old-fashioned patterns if you want to keep the heritage integrity of your album. Often you can find rulers that match the patterns of decorative scissors.

Additional Specialty Pens

The pH tester pen almost deserves to be one of the must-have basic tools. This pen is handy to check the acid-free quality of handmade or

Downloading Clip Art from the Web

Here are the basic steps to downloading and saving free clip art you may find on the Internet. Most Web sites will include some helpful hints to downloading and opening the clip art files.

Netscape Windows Users

❀ Click with the right mouse button on the image, and select "Save this Image as . . ." from the menu.

Netscape Macintosh Users

❀ Click and hold the mouse button, and select "Save this Image as . . ." from the menu.

Microsoft Internet Explorer Users

❀ Click with the right mouse button on the image, and select "Save Picture as . . ." from the menu.

specialty papers you might find. You can also check the pH of any of your paper memorabilia. Please keep in mind that this pen does leave a color mark on the paper you are testing! Always test on the back side of the paper. These pens are usually found at a store with scrapbooking supplies.

Red eye remover and pet eye remover pens are wonderful to remove that zombie look people and pets get when the camera flash can be seen reflected in the eyes. You may not have noticed, but people and animals don't have the same type of look: people get a red reflection, while animals get a greenish reflection. It's important to get the right remover pen. Do not use regular markers to remove red eye or pet eye. You'll apply the pen lightly and in a circular motion to the eye reflection area you wish to tone down. Remember, as always, to use only acid-free, photo-safe pens.

Gel and milky pens are fun to include in your toolbox.

Gel and milky pens are fun to include in your toolbox. Gel pens use thick-bodied ink that has a shimmer to it. A milky pen can write clearly over most dark papers. Most gel and milky pens are acid-free and photo-safe, but always check out the product information. Inks are available in a wide variety of colors, including some awesome metallics.

Die Cuts and Stickers

Die cuts are well known to any scrapbooker, but you might not be familiar with this decorative touch. The die cut is an acid-free, photo-safe paper design that has been made with a die-cut machine into uniform

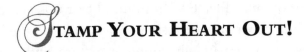 STAMP YOUR HEART OUT!

Rubberstamping is a great way to decorate family heritage scrapbooks. Find one or two designs that you can incorporate throughout your scrapbook. You can add additional interest by embossing stamped images. You can stamp directly onto your page or stamp the image on acid-free, photo-safe paper and cut the image out to adhere to a page. Most embossing powders are acid-free, so you don't have to worry about harming your photos. Never stamp directly onto a photo, and never emboss near a photo. Embossing needs to be melted with a heat tool, and this extreme heat will damage photos.

You do need to take special care in selecting inks that will not harm your photos or memorabilia. Here's what to look for:

* Acid-free

* Pigment ink

* Fadeproof

* Waterproof

images. The shapes available range from birthday cakes to dolls that can be dressed to letters and numbers. Although not widely used in family heritage albums, die cuts can be great for embellishing a child's page or for lettering. Many scrapbooking stores have the die-cut machine and will provide die cuts using your selection of paper. You'll also find die cuts packaged in coordinating colors.

Precut mats and frames for photos fall into the die-cut category. Most mats and frames will be found precut and packaged at craft and scrapbooking stores. Some of the mats and frames include embossing, which is a design or pattern that is raised on the paper surface. You can find embossers with small designs at most craft, rubberstamping, and scrapbooking retailers, or you can order them online.

Decorative stickers were once thought only to be of interest to children, but when scrapbooking became more popular, manufacturers began to print beautiful designs onto acid-free paper with acid-free inks, using acid-free, permanent adhesives. You can find silly fun stickers and stickers with detailed artwork. Most don't think that stickers are appropriate for a heritage quality scrapbook, but use your own judgement.

YOUR FAMILY HISTORY AND YOUR CREATIVITY

You've gathered your final supplies, and it is time to put everything together and create your family heritage scrapbook. The next chapter will include step-by-step instructions for the family heritage pages shown in the color insert in the center of this book. Chapter 8 will cover the basic techniques needed to crop and mat your photos and then describe more about how to theme and lay out each page of your scrapbook. Although most of us enjoy the thrill of tracking down information needed about our family heritage, the real fun is putting all the pieces and parts you've gathered into a delightful visual record for your family to enjoy for years to come. Flip the page and give your creativity and imagination a healthy workout!

8

Designing Your Heritage Scrapbook

Themes and Techniques

Before you even crop your first photo or write your first journaling caption, you should have an idea of what pages you want to create to complete your family heritage album. What will your cover pages look like? Will you create a page featuring each family member? Do you want a page or two with a holiday celebration? Do you want a page that only contains the family tree or a family member's pedigree chart?

Planning ahead can help you keep your focus and have a better idea of how to keep your research organized. One solution on how to plan out a family heritage scrapbook comes from a technique used in advertising called a *storyboard*. A storyboard is made up of a series of sketches or illustrations to visually explain how an advertisement can develop a "story." You can apply this principle to family heritage scrapbooking by creating a storyboard outline sheet. This technique works well when designing a heritage scrapbook because it is more visual that just outlining the pages you want with words as in a formal outline. You'll begin to get a feel of working within a rectangle (8½ by 11 scrapbook pages) or square (12 by 12 scrapbook pages). See figures 8.1 through 8.4 for an example of a storyboard outline.

❧ PLANNING THE LAYOUT OF YOUR SCRAPBOOK

First, make a list of everything you want to include in your family heritage book, from photos to memorabilia to documents. You can then begin to fill in your storybook outline and check off the items you've listed. Briefly note on each page what you would like to include on the page. Do you want to start your family heritage scrapbook with the family tree or prefer to end it that way? Do you want the first page to be photos of each family member? Using this type of outline will help you organize your thoughts before committing to a specific page. In the end, you might end up changing your original thoughts, but at least you'll have a starting point using this type of outline.

Once you have a working storyboard outline of your scrapbook, you'll want to concentrate on one page at a time. You can do this in two ways; both work well. Use your own judgment as to which method works best with your schedule and organization.

Method 1: Using an acid-free, lignin-free folder for each page, place all the information, photos, and memorabilia you need to create that

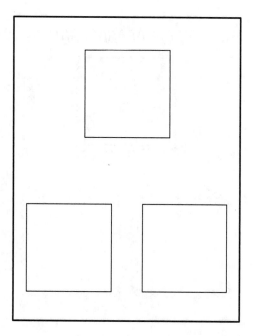

Figure 8.1. Scrapbook page with photo placement. Experiment with different photo placements.

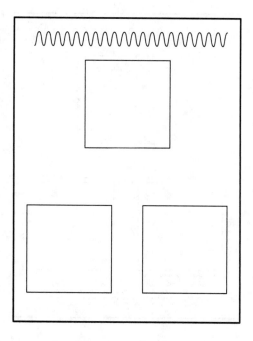

Figure 8.2. Scrapbook page with photos; title placement added.

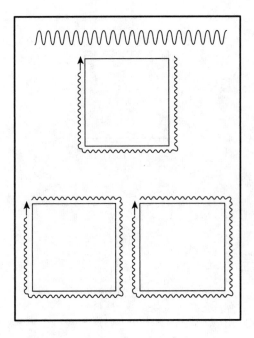

Figure 8.3. Scrapbook page with photos and title placement; caption placement added.

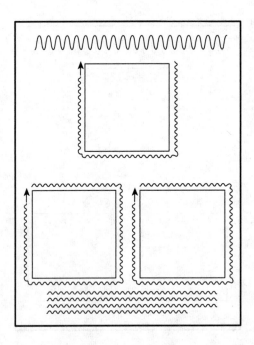

Figure 8.4. Scrapbook page with photos, title placement,
and caption placement; body journaling added.

MINIMIZE MEMORABILIA AND DOCUMENTS

Are you finding that your documents and memorabilia are bulking up your family heritage scrapbook, making it difficult to handle? Try reducing the size of your documents or memorabilia on a copying machine. By reducing documents into smaller, more manageable sizes, you can include more of your family heritage documentation. Most commercial print shops have the ability to reduce items, or, if you have a scanner, you should be able to reduce and print documents/memorabilia on your own. The smaller documents can be matted and tucked into a page pocket or matted onto or into a scrapbook page flap.

page into the folder at once. Create a folder for every page and place any decorative or background archival paper you plan to use in this folder, too.

Method 2: Working one page at a time, gather everything you need into a folder. Rather than organizing everything at once like in method 1, you'll only gather what you need for a specific page.

It's important to make notes of changes as the changes occur.

Keep a running updated outline. If you make changes in what information, memorabilia, or photo is on a page or the order of the pages within your scrapbook, simply correct it on your master storyboard outline. It's important to make notes of changes as the changes occur. You'll keep a copy of your master outline for your family research files.

The completed, updated master storyboard outline will help you quickly find any document, information, memorabilia, or photo you have placed into your finished heritage scrapbook if you need to in the future. You may also wish to create a table of contents once you finished your family heritage scrapbook.

EXAMPLES OF PAGE ORDER ORGANIZATION

No two family heritage scrapbooks are alike. And that's really one of the most exciting aspects of this art and craft. You know your family and your own likes and dislikes better than anyone. Your family heritage scrapbook is truly a celebration of the uniqueness of your family.

There is no way you can mess up or make a mistake in a family heritage scrapbook. The only way you can fail is if you don't create it!

You may think you aren't creative, but somewhere in that family tree you've been exploring are bound to be some creative genes. My mother used to encourage me to attempt any dream or goal as if I was positive that I would succeed. I am offering you the same advice. There is no way you can mess up or make a mistake in a family heritage scrapbook. The only way you can fail is if you don't create it! Yet, it helps to have some type of guide when deciding on the order of your pages within your own scrapbook. It also helps to have some guidance as to what to include within the pages. Here are ideas for ordering the pages of family heritage scrapbooks with four different themes.

Our Family

This is a great outline format, especially for smaller families. You can do this to include only your immediate family or several generations.

Page 1: Pedigree chart

Pages 2–3: Two-page spread for family group 1 to include photos, relationships, and journaling

Pages 4–5: Two-page spread of documents and memorabilia for each member of this family group

Pages 6–7: Allow any member of the family group to journal memories or thoughts of family.

Repeat for each family group.

Last page: From the heart, tell what it was like to create this heritage. Tell a funny story that might have happened during your family heritage research or what it was like selecting the photos you included in the scrapbook. As the creator of the family heritage scrapbook, you should sign this page and date it. You might want to include an oral history on audiotape or videotape to accompany the heritage album.

My Life Story

The focus of this style of heritage album is you. There is no greater gift you could give your child and their children than your own life story from your point of view. This can be great fun! Don't be shy or afraid to reveal the real you—it's not everyday you get the freedom to write history, so enjoy creating something that future generations will read.

Keep in mind that this is a general outline. Each individual obviously has a different time line of events—and different events themselves—in his or her life. For example, I'm including "your children" in both early adulthood and adulthood. The fact is a birth of a child may come in late teens to later adulthood. And that doesn't even consider adoption or foster parenting or those of us who choose not to have children. Adjust the time line categories as well as what each contains to your own life patterns. You may also need more pages for certain times in your life, while others times might not fill up a whole page. Again, adjust page numbers to fit your own needs.

Page 1: a formal or favorite photo of yourself with your journaling thoughts of this project or life in general.

There is no greater gift you could give your child and their children than your own life story from your point of view.

Pages 2–3: birth: A baby photo, birth announcement, godparents, memories of your own parents about your birth, a time line of other events happening on that day or year, and all documents about your birth. Page 3 might be a pocket page.

Pages 4–5: childhood: Your childhood photos, report cards, favorite activities, first day of school, favorite food, favorite toy, time line of events taking place in the world during your childhood, memories of relatives during childhood, your childhood friends, where you grew up, and memories of your childhood.

Pages 6–7: teenage years: Photos of you as a teenager, what the fads and favorites of that time period were, school memories, hopes and goals for adulthood, time line of historical events, your memories of your parents during this time, memorabilia such as movie tickets or school events, boyfriends or girlfriends, best friend, sports, favorite music or song, problems or worries during your teens, time spent driving or getting a driver's license, and other thoughts that apply to the teens.

VIRTUAL SCRAPBOOK

Several software programs are now available to help you create a totally virtual family heritage scrapbook. Although I hope the virtual heritage album will never totally replace the real thing, a computer-generated family heritage album makes a fantastic gift. You'll have to scan your photos and memorabilia or have them digitally converted (the most common format is jpg). You'll be able to select from a variety of templates for your individual scrapbook pages or create your own format in some of the software packages. Your next step will be to import the photos and memorabilia into the virtual scrapbook and add your journaling. The virtual scrapbook is then stored on your computer and backed up on a zip drive or burned onto a CD. It can be printed out, allowing you to make a real family book.

Pages 8–9: early adulthood: Photos, college or first job memories, memorabilia, where you lived if you moved out of your parent's home, dating or marriage, first apartment or home, time line of historical events including your thoughts on the events, happiest and saddest memories of this time, awards, community involvement, church or religious activities, memories of relatives or family reunions, your children, hobbies and interests, sports, career ups and downs, and any other memories from this time in your life.

Pages10–11: adulthood (midlife): Photos, major events or celebrations, your children, career or work, home and hobbies, historical events, church and religion, marriage, vacations and travel, hopes and dreams, goals met, memorabilia, pets, friends, music and songs, favorite books or magazines, movies and TV shows, your political opinions, regrets, birth of grandchildren, health, and other memories or thoughts of this time.

Pages 12–13: later adulthood: Photos, retirement, life review, celebrations and major events, historical events, vacations and travel, hopes and goals, birth of grandchildren or great-grandchildren, hobbies and leisure activities, community or volunteer involvement, health, political viewpoints, church or religious activities, marriage, family reunions, memories of relatives, and any other comments you'd like to include.

Pages 14–15: pedigree and family group, with a pocket page for any important papers you'd like included.

Last page: from the heart explain what it was like to create this heritage album for yourself and your family. As the artist and creator of the scrapbook, you should sign and date this page. You might want to include an oral history on audio tape or videotape to companion the heritage album.

Our Family Legacy

A more comprehensive format than the "Our Family" outline. You can store originals in this type of heritage book, but remember that you need to be aware that disasters do happen. I advise you have top-quality preservation copies made of all legal documents and place the copy into your scrapbook.

Page 1: table of contents

Page 2: pedigree chart

Page 3: family tree (pedigree chart arranged as a family tree)

Page 4: family group 1

Pages 5–6: photos of each member of the family group (you may only need one page, but plan for two and adjust as you create the scrapbook)

Page 7: pocket page: Insert all important family documents for this family group

Page 8: memorabilia for this family group

Repeat pages 1–8 until all family groups are included.

Last page: from the heart, tell your all your family members what it was like to create this heritage album just for them. You might want to thank and acknowledge any relatives or friends who helped provide information, photos, or memorabilia. A dedication can be added on this page, and you'll want to sign and date the page, too. You might want to include an oral history on audio tape or videotape to accompany the heritage album.

This Is Your Life

This style of heritage book closely follows the same page outline as "My Life Story," but it is a heritage book created for an individual in your family or a close friend. The journaling can be done from your own viewpoint or by combining the voices from all family members. This is a wonderful gift to a family member who may be celebrating a life milestone such as marriage, a special birthday, retirement, anniversary, or birth of a child or grandchild. It is a caring and thoughtful way to let someone know how important he or she is to the family or your life.

This is a wonderful gift to a family member who may be celebrating a life milestone such as marriage, a special birthday, retirement, anniversary, or birth of a child or grandchild.

Page 1: photo of person you are honoring

Pages 2–3: pedigree of this person and pocket page with all family groups

Pages 4–5: photos of this person with other family members or friends, including all ages of this person's life

Pages 6–7: your favorite photos (or everyone helping's favorites) with journaling to say why you have such fond memories of the photo or event captured on film. If possible, have each comment handwritten by the person contributing the photo.

The remaining pages should follow the "My Life Story" outline, but you'll include the events from the honored person's life rather than your own.

Ending pages: leave several blank pages near the end of the heritage book. Allow family and friends to hand write personal notes or messages to the honored person. You can start a round-robin with blank pages (send the blank page with an archival pen to relative A and ask that relative A sent it to relative B), with a deadline to have the blank page returned to you. Also, if presenting this heritage scrapbook at a party or celebration, you can allow the attendees to sign the scrapbook, too. Just remember to bring along several pens with acid-free, archival ink.

Last page: create a "The Day You Were Born" or "The Meaning of Your Name" page, a time line of historical events that happened in this person's life, or a poem that reminds you of this person. From the heart, journal a few words about what it was like to create this heritage album just for him or her. Try to acknowledge anyone who helped you put together the scrapbook. Sign and date the page. You might want to include an oral history on audio- or videotape to go with the heritage album.

OTHER OPTIONS FOR FAMILY HERITAGE SCRAPBOOK THEMES

It is amazing how many ideas will come to you for your own family heritage scrapbook when you brainstorm with other enthusiasts and hobbyists. Surfing the Internet and interviewing family and friends will also inevitably lead to some ideas. The sky is truly the limit! In the following sections I have gathered some additional themes for your unique scrapbook.

The sky is truly the limit!

Kissing Cousins

Okay, you don't have to kiss every single one of your cousins, but I got your attention didn't I? Cousins can make any family tree fuller, with more family stories, memories, and photos to share. So why not dedicate a family heritage page to these wonderful people who make up our extended families? Family group records are key to this type of heritage scrapbook by giving the reader of the album a clear idea of how all the cousins are related. You'll find a great Relationship Chart about how cousins are related to each other in the back of the book.

Single Family Unit or Family Tree Branch

This scrapbook presents the history of a single family, with a pedigree chart, photos, memorabilia, and copies of any important documents. Another great idea is to focus on one branch of the family tree, such as your mother's or father's side of the family.

Ancestral Descendants

Select an ancestor, and go in reverse pedigree order. For example, instead of starting with yourself and tracking back to a relative who landed on the *Mayflower,* begin with that person and follow his or her family pedigree until you reach your grandparents. Or you can make the theme less encompassing by going from a great-grandpa to his children to his children's children.

Decade

Why not cover a decade within your family? This type of scrapbook works best with photographs and bits of memorabilia, rather than pedigree charts. For practical reasons, this decade scrapbook works best for decades within the twentieth and twenty-first centuries. You can cover your family during the Roaring Twenties, the Flower Power 1960s, or the new millennium.

A Moment in Time

Search and find birth or under-a-year-old baby photos and birth certificates for every member of your family. Or find photos and memorabilia for age 1 or maybe the terrible twos. Consider making a scrapbook depicting everyone in kindergarten or first grade, or everyone's high school graduation photo or wedding day, with copies of each couple's marriage certificate (state and church documents).

The Men or Women of the Family

Imagine the pictorial you could create with a focus on either the men or the women within your pedigree chart or family group, detailing as many generations as you like. This type of scrapbook really allows you to get personal with each member of the family. Include likes and dislikes, hobbies, careers, community work, volunteerism, histories of the day each was born, historical events within their lifetimes, fashion, hairstyles, friends, and anything that will bring each person off the page and into one's heart.

Family Treasure Chest

Every family, no matter how small, has family treasures, artifacts, or heirlooms. Somehow in the rush and hustle of everyday life these treasures can get misplaced and sadly even thrown out or given away, often making it impossible to track them down. This family heritage book can mean a great deal to future family generations by preserving such treasures.

Every family, no matter how small, has family treasures, artifacts, or heirlooms.

Start by using the Heirloom Log in the back of the book. Take photos of each piece, or ask the relative who has the item to send a photograph. Journal what each item means to the owner of it, describing, when possible, who made or bought the item and where and why the item came into the family.

Keep this family heritage scrapbook as up-to-date as possible, but take your time with this type of scrapbook. It may be that an item has been lost or given away but is still fondly remembered. Make copies of it to send to the head of each family unit or group.

ABCs of Family

ABCs are not just great for children but fun for adults, too, in this personalized album. You can use both photos and memorabilia to illustrate the alphabet in a way your family will cherish. The letter *A* may be illustrated with a photo of Aunt Annie or an anteater photo taken during a trip to the zoo you visited during a family vacation. Use a single letter per page or per two-page spread, or give each letter half of a scrapbook page. Embellish with great decorative papers and borders.

A FEW MORE DECISIONS TO MAKE

The style and feel of your family heritage scrapbook is important. You want consistency in your scrapbook, and that consistency will be created by your selected style. The scrapbook should flow smoothly from page to page from beginning to end. You'll need to consider and decide several factors that will lend to the overall style and appeal of your pages as a unit, as a story being told:

1. Have an opening or introduction followed by the body of the book and ending with a recognizable finish or conclusion. If you are going to use one of the model scrapbook outlines previously mentioned, these three essential parts of your heritage album are already included.

2. Select whether you want a very formal look or a less formal look to your scrapbook.

   ❦ Formal will include the use of ivory or cream background papers with black or gold matting, borders, any journaling, and photo corners.

   ❦ Semiformal can feature pastels of lavender, blue, green, pink, mauve or rose, or rich royal colors of garnet red, navy blue, and hunter green. You can also use delicate, elegant patterned papers.

❧ Least formal can entail any of the wide variety of plain or decorative archival papers available.

3. Consider color-coding your mats or inks, assigning a specific color to an individual or family group. You can also include double matting.

Example: Mom and Dad are green; children are blue. A photo of you or your sibling(s) would then first be matted with green, then blue (double-matted).

❧ Use one color for each generation to mat the photos. For the ones in your direct line, double-mat the photos using a coordinating print. That way the children's grandparents are in one color; parents, aunts, and uncles in another; and cousins in yet another color.

❧ Use one color for paternal lineage and another for maternal lineage.

❧ Another method of coding is to place a small acid-free sticker beside the photos. A small flower, for instance, may represent one family group, while a small ladybug represents another family group.

4. Simple or complex design? Most beginners should stick with simple layouts for each family heritage scrapbook page, with very special events or celebrations pages being more complex and elaborate in design and detailing. Your time and schedule are factors in this decision. Don't get overwhelmed by designing masterpieces for every single page of your scrapbook.

BASIC SCRAPBOOKING TECHNIQUES

Some techniques are universal to creating any type of scrapbook or memory album. The two most crucial are cropping and matting. Cropping is a technique that will help you make your photos less busy and bring into focus the face or moment you want represented on a page. Matting is a way to bring color or unity to the items you place on a page, including not just photographs but also documents, memorabilia, and journaling. Other techniques such as paper piecing, embossing, stenciling, or line work just make any family heritage scrapbook more interesting, fun, and exciting to read and enjoy. These additional techniques also allow you to express your creativity and add a touch of art to your scrapbook. Art and craft make up a large part of the leisure and recreation activities within families, which should be reflected within the scrapbook. And that's what you are doing. You are creating a small but very important masterpiece when you create a family heritage scrapbook.

You are creating a small but very important masterpiece when you create a family heritage scrapbook.

Cropping Photos

For most beginners, cropping a photo is the most difficult aspect of scrapbooking. The reason for this anxiety is not that cropping is difficult to do but rather more psychological. It can be a little nerve-racking to crop your first photo, which is why I highly recommend you practice your cropping skills on copies of original photos or duplicates of more current photos in your collection. Trust me, one of the most frightening things you may ever do is to take a utility knife and ruler to precious family photos.

Yet, the process of cropping itself is very simple. Your goal is to remove any unwanted background or unwanted blank space in a photo. The cropped photo will be more pleasing to the eye, and the focus will be on the person or people in the photo rather than a busy background. Other reasons to crop include these:

✿ To make a photo fit into a specific space size on a page

✿ To help emphasize part of a photo, such as a person's face

✿ To remove distracting elements from a photo

✿ To remove torn or ragged edges of a photo

✿ To remove white margins from a photo cut from a photo sheet.

✿ To create a special effect, such as mosaic, puzzle, or piecing

Cropping Techniques

As briefly discussed in chapter 7, there are several ways to crop a photo and several cropping tools to help make the job easier. The most basic cropping tool is a pair of scissors or craft utility knife and metal-edge ruler. When using scissors to crop, you lightly trace a pencil line onto the photo and cut away the unwanted areas of your photo. You use this same method with decorative scissors or plain shears. With the craft utility knife and ruler, you line the ruler up (edge to cut to the right of the ruler or reverse for left-handers) and use the knife to cut away the undesirable portions of the photo. Once you have cropped several photos with success, you'll relax with the technique and enjoy the results of cropping.

Using too many different overall shapes for cropping is distracting and will take attention away from the photos.

Many cropping templates are available, including templates for circular, oval, square, triangle, and heart-shaped crops. The templates are best served when cropping with regular or decorative scissors. You should stick to only one or two styles of cropping to keep continuity and flow within your heritage scrapbook. Using too many different overall shapes for cropping is distracting and will take attention away from the photos. Square/rectangular and oval are the most popular cropping shapes for family heritage albums.

You can also crop with the circular and oval cropping tools on the market. Your cropping tool should come with a see-through template that allows you to see exactly where the tool will crop. You place your photo under the template and decide on the size gauge you'll need to set on the cropping tool. Adjust the cropping tool to the measurement needed. You then place the photo on a self-healing cutting pad. Place the cropping tool over the photo, and turn the cutting blade slowly and with even pressure.

Again, I suggest that you always practice on photo duplicates. You can practice using your cropping tool on paper; just remember that a photograph is thicker than most papers, so cropping on paper is not the same feel as cropping a photo. For that reason, you will still need to practice using the cropping tool on duplicate photos before attempting to crop an original photograph.

Conventional wisdom says
never crop old or precious photographs.

To Crop or Not to Crop with Older Photographs

Conventional wisdom says never crop old or precious photographs. It's not smart to crop these photos because even the most experienced of croppers can make a mistake. And cropping is irreversible. However, if an old photograph has torn or ripped edges, you might want to trim the damage if it will not crop any people in the photo. I recommend that you consult with an expert in photograph restoration before you attempt to crop the photo and ask for advice. You can also have the photo copied by a printer or duplicated by a photo developer. Ask yourself how you will feel if you accidentally miscrop a photo. Your answer will guide you to how you will handle the situation.

You can get the same effect of cropping without cutting your photo by using the window mat explained in the next section under "Traditional Matting." You lay the window mat face-down and use photo corners to attach the photo to the mat. Next turn the mat over and use photo corners to mount the photo on the page.

Professional Photo Cropping

You have yet another option for cropping a photograph. By having your photo shop enlarge a photo, you may be able to crop the photo through this process. Take the time to explain exactly what in the photo you want highlighted or to be the focus of the photo. Through enlarging the photograph, the developer can adjust placement and remove the busy background or unwanted arm or shoulder that seems out of place, with the end result of a finished photograph that needs no mechanical cropping on your part.

Matting Photos

Matting your photographs can really bring them to life with a touch of color, especially black-and-white photographs. But photos are not the only items that can be matted in your family heritage scrapbook—you can also mat memorabilia. A word of caution, however: Understand that once a piece of memorabilia is matted, in most cases you will never see the back of the item again. Therefore, don't mat anything that has a front and back that you wish to keep available for reading. It is better to mount this type of item using photo corners or a pocket page.

When selecting the color palette of the mats, keep in mind your overall color theme for your scrapbook. Your color selection may vary greatly depending on whether your photo is black and white or a color print. Experiment by placing the black-and-white photo onto different colors of archival paper. Do certain colors accent and complement the black and white? Do some colors wash out or overwhelm the black and white? Run the same experiments with your color prints. This is also a time to call in a second or third opinion if you aren't confident in your color theory skills by asking some family members for their opinions.

When selecting the color palette of the mats, keep in mind your overall color theme for your scrapbook.

Matting Techniques

Most heritage scrapbooking experts suggest the following general matting and color tips are best when working with black-and-white photos. You might notice, as I did, that information from the experts is sometimes conflicting. You'll also notice that there are more don'ts than do's, but don't let that get you down! (Pun intended.) The don'ts are advised just to make sure you avoid making the most common beginner's mistakes. Consider each point a suggestion, not a rule.

- Choose two complementary colors and no more. One will be your background page, and the other will be your matting color. You can double- or triple-mat using the color combination.

- Ivory with gold accents gives an antique feel, while white with black or silver accents gives a clean, professional feel to pages.

- Mount/mat all photos on ivory paper.

- Do not mat old photos on heavy card stock or cardboard. This type of paper is too heavy for older photos.

- Paper should not overpower the photos, so avoid the shocking brights available.

- Do not cut or crop photos with decorative scissors. Only cut the paper mats.

🐝 Combine browns, tans, and rose archival papers for a muted look and feel.

🐝 Coordinate black, white, classic navy, and light blue archival papers for a masculine, strong look and feel.

🐝 When using the mount matting technique, the first mat should never be a decorative paper but rather a solid color.

🐝 A touch of color here and there is good, helping emphasize an extra special photo or piece of memorabilia.

🐝 Don't round corners or cut photos into shapes unless absolutely necessary. Keep photos in original shapes to maintain historical value, lend continuity, and give a classic look.

🐝 Since both adults and kids will pass this album around, you don't want it to seem intimidatingly formal.

Traditional Matting

Think of a traditional mat as a paper frame for your photos. This is most likely the type of matting you will use for some of your older photographs. Rather than cutting away unwanted or busy backgrounds, you place a traditional mat over the top of a photo and cover those undesirable areas while still being able to view the rest of the picture through the window of the mat.

You can buy traditional mats (sometimes categorized as die cuts in craft or scrapbooking stores), or you can make your own. The easiest way to make your own traditional mats is by using a circular or oval cropping tool. Using the cropping tool's see-through template, decide what size the window of the mat needs to be to properly show the photograph. Then use the cropping tool to cut that size window or opening. You can adjust the cropping tool to a bigger circle or oval to cut out the rest of the mat, or you can use scissors or a utility knife/ruler to cut a square or rectangular mat. See figure 8.5 for an example of traditional matting.

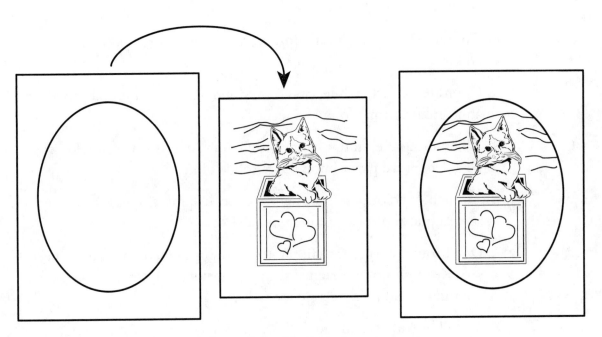

Figure 8.5. Traditional matting.

Mount Matting

Matting photographs with a mount mat is a simple way to add color to a scrapbook page. There are two schools of thought for the mount mat. The first is to cut a mat slightly larger than the photograph. The photograph can then be mounted on top of the matting paper using your favorite adhesive. The second is to mount your photo onto a much larger piece of paper and trim away the excess with scissors, a utility knife and metal ruler, or a personal trimmer. Either way, the result is a single mat.

To add more color and interest, you can double-mat by repeating the matting process with another piece of paper, in either contrasting or coordinating colors. The width of each mat's border is your judgment call. Experiment with several duplicate photos until you get a feel of the style you prefer and wish to use throughout your family heritage scrapbook. A triple mat can be very striking, too. You can use as many layers of matting as you like, but be aware that too many layers is distracting and adds bulk to the overall scrapbook.

ADDING THAT ARTISTIC TOUCH

By now you've learned the mechanical techniques in scrapbooking. It's time now to think about some creative touches to incorporate into your family heritage scrapbook. None of these techniques is difficult, but some do take more time than others. Just start out with simple attempts and build your skill and confidence. You can add one or all the following techniques to your scrapbook as long as you keep some consistency with the overall feel of your book. Pockets, flaps, pullouts, and even pop-ups actually help you add more information, including memorabilia and journaling, to a page. The other techniques described here are more decorative in nature.

Pockets

Creating a pocket on a scrapbook page is a great way to make a pretty, polished—and safe—home for documents or memorabilia (e.g., greeting cards, vacation brochures, location maps, playbills, airline tickets, etc.) in your family heritage album. The size of your pocket will depend on the size of your document or memorabilia. The entire page can be part of the pocket, or you may use several smaller pockets on a page. It is important to make the pockets sturdy to hold up to the removing of the contents many, many times over the years.

Flaps

Flaps are a great way to give you additional room on a page for journaling or a fun way to "hide" a photo until the reader of your scrapbook lifts the flap. They can be made from decorative papers or even pretty greeting cards. You simply adhere the back of the flap to the scrapbook page securely.

Sliders

Sliders are strips of paper that will slide out of a pocket. Like flaps, they can be used to create additional space for a body of journaling or to create captions for all photos on a page or two-page spread in one area. You may also wish to use sliders to mount copies of documents that are reduced in size so the documents can be incorporated into the page layout.

Pop-ups

Pop-ups are a way to have photographs "pop" out from the background paper or an open flap. You can create a single pop-up, or, by making an accordion fold, you can have many photos pop up. A single pop-up can be done using a blank greeting card, cardstock, or heavyweight paper. Figures 8.6 through 8.10 will guide you through the steps. This is a fun way to add dimension to a page layout.

Hand Lettering

Hand lettering is not writing, according to the experts of this technique. It is drawing. If you can understand the difference, you're two steps ahead of the game. It requires a very steady hand, a good eye, and nerves of steel, but some of us are not artists! This technique does take time and patience. However, you can create truly one-of-a-kind pages that may be the most personal and meaningful to your family.

Scrapbooking manuals and booklets, art books, and calligraphy books contain dozens of alphabets (letter styles), or you can use your own imagination thinking up a new one. Most hand lettering is done with a pen or marker. You can find markers with calligraphy tips in various sizes and shapes. Just make sure any ink is acid-free and of archival quality.

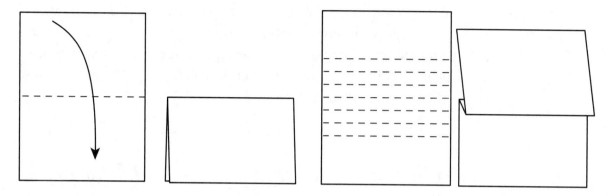

Figure 8.6.   Start with one piece of paper and fold in half.

Figure 8.7.   Fold again in ½- or ¼-inch widths.

Figure 8.8.   Side view after folding.

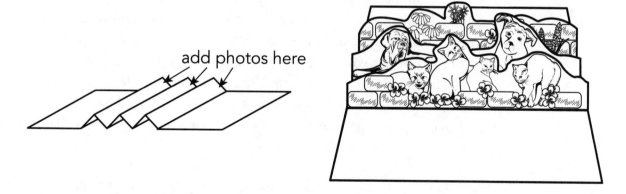

Figure 8.9.   Photo placement.

Figure 8.10.   Finished accordion.

You can opt to trace the letters onto your page and then draw over these lines with your pen or marker. Always be aware of spacing for it is key to straight and flowing hand lettering. As one expert explained, always plan ahead, use a spacing ruler if you need one, and measure twice, then put ink to paper.

You can create truly one-of-a-kind pages that may be the most personal and meaningful to your family.

Basics of Hand Lettering

1. Supplies needed: pen(s) or marker(s), pencil, ruler, alphabet guide (if you're not attempting a free-form style of your own), and paper or the page you wish to hand letter.

2. If you have never done any hand lettering before, please practice the following technique several times before you attempt it on your family heritage scrapbook page. You'll want to get a feel of spacing and drawing out a lettering space guide. And never create hand-lettering work on a page onto which you have already adhered any photos or paper memorabilia unless you are very artistic or have achieved a good skill level for hand lettering. Hand lettering should be done *before* you add photos, journaling, or memorabilia to a page. You can also hand letter on a piece of paper, trim, and then mat the hand lettering rather than create it directly on the page.

3. Carefully trace the letters onto the page, or lightly trace ruled lines with spacing on the page. Draw over the traced letters with your pen or marker, or fill in the letters on the spacing guide you lightly created

on the page. You may use an acid-free, archival paint marker, but read the labeling closely. Look for the label to mention specifically that the pen's ink or paint is *opaque*. Allow the page to dry several hours.

4. Erase any pencil lines that are showing and not covered over by ink or marker. Use only an artist's-quality eraser. Make sure the eraser is clean, by wiping it several times over a clean sheet of scrap or copier paper. Most markers are dye inks and will be transparent. As in many watercolor paintings, you may always see a certain amount of pencil lines.

 ## HANDS-ON WORK BEGINS!

Designing and making a family heritage scrapbook inspire so many ways to get creative. The techniques described and explained in this chapter are wonderful basics that should make your scrapbook interesting to read and view by all members of the family. Don't forget that if you feel less than confident about trying the methods in this chapter, you can always go to a local art, craft, rubberstamping, or scrapbooking store for help from these retailers. However, I want to give you the best all-around education in scrapbooking right here. Plenty of great examples of page layouts and applications of basic techniques have been presented to assist you, too.

The next chapter is brimming with many step-by-step instructions to create family tree, family pedigree, ancestor, descendent, grandparent, family, wedding, and other interesting pages for your own heritage album. I hope you have as much fun creating your own pages as I did in creating these examples for you.

9

Creating Your Heritage Scrapbook

Composing the Pages

lthough this book focuses on more than just creating your family heritage scrapbook, the scrapbook is the heart of the message. Gathering, sorting, and organizing your family photos and artifacts is a great way to reconnect, reminisce, and remind you of the importance of your family life. There is no better presentation of all this information and memorabilia than the completion of a family heritage scrapbook. This chapter will give you step-by-step instructions for creating a variety of heritage scrapbook pages, ranging from an individual's pedigree chart to surname distribution to the passions of each family member. Each of the projects in this chapter is featured in the color insert in the center of the book—refer to the insert for clarity when creating.

✿ A Note about the Instructions

A few key words within the page design instructions help simplify the steps. Refer back to this guide if you are unsure what a term or reference might mean within the instructions.

Paper: Always refers to archival, acid-free, lignin-free papers as described in this book.

Paper size: Will be 8½ by 11 inches unless I specifically recommend using 12 by 12 papers. However, any page design can be adapted to the other size.

Background paper: Indicated by {B}; the foundation of the page, the paper onto which the photos, journaling, or memorabilia is adhered.

Number of sheets of paper needed: The maximum number of sheets of paper needed for a page layout. Please understand that in many cases you can use scraps of papers rather than a whole sheet. Never throw out your scraps leftover after a page is designed. You can use these scraps to mat titles, captions, bodies of journaling, photos, and memorabilia.

Cutting tools: The cutting tools of your choice (see chapter 7) unless otherwise stated. I may recommend using a specific cropping tool for ease of design.

Adhesive: The adhesive of your choice unless otherwise stated (see chapter 7). There may be designs for which tape is better to use than liquid glue. However, all adhesive must be acid-free.

Drum Roll, Please: Opening Pages

Here is a variety of pages that displays many of the things you've learned throughout this book. Again, refer to the color insert for a photo of each one.

Welcome to Donegal

Materials

3 sheets of paper
    1 decorative: faux sponged ivy {B}
    2 coordinating solids
Cutting tools
Adhesive
Color-copied map
Journaling: caption

Instructions

1. Color copy and trim your map if necessary.

2. Double-mount mat the map with two solid colors of paper that coordinate with the background paper.

3. Adhere the map to top left of the background page.

4. Create a caption. This computer-generated caption journals the ancestor's immigration into the United States. The font used for the first few words of the caption is an older style to attract the eye. In the sample, the first few words are in all capital letters to catch the reader's eye.

SURNAME DISTRIBUTION

Materials

3 sheets of paper
   1 decorative: faux sponged ivy {B}
2 coordinating solids
Cutting tools
Adhesive
Color-copied map
Journaling: caption

Instructions

1. Color copy and trim your map(s) if necessary.

2. Single-mount mat the map.

3. Create a flap.

4. Adhere the matted map to the top of the flap.

5. Adhere a second map to the inside of the flap.

6. Adhere the flap to the top right of the background paper.

7. Create a caption. This computer-generated caption journals the ancestor's immigration to the United States. To attract the reader's eye, in this sample the font used for the first few words of the caption is an older style and in uppercase letters.

FAMILY COAT OF ARMS

Materials

8 sheets of paper
    1 decorative: light blue crystals (12 × 12) {B}
    1 decorative: violet crystals (12 × 12)
    5 coordinating: assorted with 1 cream and 1 silver vellum
    1 metallic: silver
Cutting tools
Adhesive
Journaling: title and three-generation family tree
Color-copied coat of arms

Instructions

1. Trim or crop the coat of arms.

2. Triple-mount mat the coat of arms. The fourth (front) "mat" is actually a flap.

3. Adhere the matted coat of arms to the center front of the flap. In this sample, an additional coordinating sheet of paper has been used inside the flap.

4. Create a family tree. This sample uses a three-generation chart.

5. Create a title and print it on cream paper; trim.

6. Single-mount the mat onto silver metallic paper.

7. Adhere the family tree and title onto the inside of the flap.

8. Adhere the flap to the center of the background paper.

THE MULLERS

Your opening family heritage page can be a photo of your oldest known ancestors, as shown in this sample. Three different styles were used to create this page so you could see how different papers can complement an older black-and-white photo. Here are three examples of color themes using the same photograph.

Classic Black-and-White
Materials

3 sheets of paper
    1 decorative: large rose print vellum {B}
    1 decorative: small rose print vellum
    1 coordinating: black
Cutting tools
Craft knife and metal-edged ruler
Pencil or disappearing ink pen
Adhesive
Journaling: title
Copy of black-and-white wedding photo

Instructions

1. Crop photo if needed.

2. Single-mount mat the photo on small rose print vellum and trim, leaving a half-inch border.

3. Place the matted photo onto the black paper, and trim to size. This black paper will help bring out the small roses in the vellum print.

4. Line up the matted photo onto the background paper, centered in the middle of the page.

5. Mark off where slots should be cut by making a very faint dot to the left and right of each corner.

6. Line the ruler up between the two dots and cut a slot.

7. Slip the photo into slots.

8. Create a title by computer or hand, and single-mount mat it to the center bottom of the page. Please note that there is no adhesive on the back of this matted title where it overlaps the photo's mat.

PEDIGREE OF JAMES THOMAS GIVEN

The pedigree chart is computer generated using Family Tree Maker software. The three-generation chart was printed on vellum paper and then trimmed.

Materials

3 sheets of paper
    1 decorative: scrolled brown/gold (12 × 12) {B}
    1 decorative: tan
    2 vellum: celebration and gold
Cutting tools
Corner slot paper punch
Adhesive
Pedigree chart
Journaling: title

Instructions

1. Punch four corner slots.

2. Slip the corners of the printed chart into the punched corner slots. (*Option:* Adhere the chart to corner slots with a small touch of glue adhesive.)

3. Adhere the pedigree chart to tan decorative paper and trim.

4. Adhere the matted pedigree chart to the center bottom of brown decorative paper.

5. Create a title.

6. Trim and then double-mount mat the title.

7. Adhere to the top center of the page.

THE GIVEN FAMILY TREE

Materials

2 sheets of paper
   1 decorative: family tree chart {B}
   1 coordinating: 12 × 12
Cutting tools
Adhesive
Archival black marker

Instructions

1. Fill out the chart with your family information.

2. Mount onto decorative 12 × 12 paper.

PAGES FEATURING FAMILY RELATIONSHIPS

Families are made up of so many different kinds of relationships: mothers and daughters, fathers and sons, brothers and sisters—and a few family friends thrown in! These pages can help the readers of your family heritage scrapbook have a better understanding of how family members are related and some insight into how your family feels about the family connections. Most likely this will be an area where older black-and-white photos are mixed with more recent color photographs. These pages are the perfect place to put some of your emotions into words for your family.

HELENE MULLER OBERMAYER

Pastel Treatment
Materials

> 4 sheets of paper
> 1 decorative: peach vellum {B}
>> 3 coordinating: navy, pink, and purple satins
> Cutting tools
> Colored chalks
> Adhesive
> Journaling: title
> Archival black marker, fine-tip pen
> Photo
> Copier or scanner with ink-jet printer

Instructions

1. Print a copy of the original photo on high-quality paper; trim.

2. Using pink coloring chalk and a small applicator sponge, apply chalk to the cheeks of the baby. Apply several light coats.

3. Spray the entire copy with several light coats of a clear Krylon sealer and allow to dry for twenty-four hours.

4. Triple-mount mat the copy; then adhere it to the center of the peach background paper.

5. Create a title on white paper; trim.

6. Adhere the title to the bottom center of the vellum background paper. In this sample, the year of the photo was hand printed in the lower-right corner of the second mat.

Fancy Corners
Materials

3 sheets of paper
    1 decorative: printed vellum {B}
    2 coordinating: mauve and beige
Cutting tools: paper edgers
Colored chalks
Adhesive
Journaling: title
Archival black marker, fine-tip pen
Photo
Copier or scanner with ink-jet printer

Instructions

1. Print a copy of the original photo on high-quality paper; trim.

2. Using pink coloring chalk and a small applicator sponge, apply chalk to the cheeks of the baby. Apply several light coats.

3. Spray the entire copy with several light coats of a clear Krylon sealer, and allow to dry for twenty-four hours.

4. Double-mount mat the copy, with the light color as the first mat and the dark color as the second mat.

5. Create four mauve and four beige corners; trim the mauve corners with decorative scissors.

6. Adhere the mauve corners over beige corners.

7. Adhere the corners to the matted copy, then adhere this to the top center of the vellum background paper. You can adhere the corners to the matted copy because it is a paper copy, not a photograph of the original, copied onto paper.

8. Create a title on beige paper and trim.

9. Adhere the title to the strip of beige paper. The year of the photo in this sample was hand printed on white paper, trimmed, and matted with a scrap of black paper and adhered to the bottom center of the title.

SILHOUETTE BABY BLUE AND PINK

Kenny, 1958
Materials

5 sheets of paper
   1 decorative: plaid {B}
   2 decorative: dots and border (for pocket)
   2 coordinating: cream and blue
Cutting tool: oval cropper
Adhesive
Christy's Crafts Silhouettes
Journaling: title and size-reduced birth certificate
Photos

Instructions

1. Using the oval cropper, crop photos and use to create two medium (slightly larger than the photo) and one large mats (slightly larger than medium mats).

2. Single-mat one photo, and double-mat the remaining photo.

3. Trim the dotted decorative sheet of paper slightly smaller than the size of the background paper.

4. Adhere this dotted paper to the center of the background paper.

5. Cut a strip of cream paper to create a side border for the page.

6. Adhere silhouettes of boys to this strip. (Please note that true silhouettes are black rather than other colors.)

7. Adhere the silhouette border to the left side of the page. If creating the two-page spread, you will use a girl silhouette in the top right corner of the dotted paper. If creating just the boy page, use a boy silhouette.

8. Create a pocket for the double-matted photo.

9. Adhere the double-matted photo onto the pocket.

10. Create a sliding strip for the pocket.

11. At the top of the sliding strip (front), journal the child's name and year of birth.

12. Adhere a reduced copy of the birth and/or baptism certificate to the front of the strip.

13. Slide the strip into the pocket.

14. Adhere the remaining oval matted photo to the top center of the page.

Maria, 1959
Materials

5 sheets of paper
  1 decorative: plaid {B}
  2 decorative: dots and border (for pocket)
  2 coordinating: cream and yellow
Cutting tool: oval cropper
Adhesive
Journaling: title and size-reduced baptism certificate
Photos

Instructions

1. Using the oval cropper, crop the photos and create two medium (slightly larger than the photo) and one large mats (slightly larger than medium mats).

2. Single-mount mat one photo, and double-mount mat the remaining photo.

3. Trim the dotted decorative sheet of paper slightly smaller than the size of the background paper.

4. Adhere this dotted paper to the center of the background paper.

5. Cut a strip of cream paper to create a side border for the page.

6. Adhere silhouettes of girls to this strip. (Please note that true silhouettes are black rather than other colors.)

7. Adhere the silhouette border to the left side of the page. If creating the two-page spread, use a boy silhouette in the top left corner of the dotted paper. If creating just the girl page, use a girl silhouette.

8. Create a pocket for the double-matted photo.

9. Adhere the double-matted photo onto the pocket.

10. Create a sliding strip for the pocket.

11. At the top of the sliding strip (front), journal the child's name and year of birth.

12. Adhere a reduced copy of the birth and/or baptism certificate to the front of the strip.

13. Slide the strip into the pocket.

14. Adhere the remaining oval matted photo to the top center of the page.

STEPHANIE JO GIVEN FRIDAY

Materials

4 sheets of paper
    1 decorative: fern {B}
    3 coordinating: beige, solid green, ivy
Cutting tools
Adhesive
SpotPen black and white hand-coloring markers
Journaling: title
Photos

Instructions

1. Crop the photo.

2. Following the manufacturer's instructions, hand-color the black-and-white photo.

3. Create four photo corners from ivy paper.

4. Single-mount mat the photo with corners onto beige paper.

5. Create a title; trim and adhere it to the bottom center of the background page.

FATHERS AND SONS; BROTHERS AND FRIENDS

This page took some planning. You will have to play around with photos and determine whether any photos should be cropped. Do not place and adhere any corners until you have firmly decided where photos will be placed on the pages and double-checked that all the photos will fit.

Materials

4 sheets of paper
  2 decorative: faux marble sponged (12 × 12) {B}
  2 coordinating: gold dots and cloud
Cutting tools
Five different-colored plastic corners (clear, gold, silver, white, and black)
Journaling: title and body
Photos

Instructions

1. Create the journaling. This sample has a title with a body mounted onto a flap, plus there is journaling inside the flap that explains who is in all the photos and their family relationships. Also included inside the flap is the color-coding used with the corners: each color represents a different branch of the family tree.

2. Once you have created your journaling and flap, adhere it to the top left of the first page of the two-page spread.

3. Using the colored corners, adhere all photos to the pages.

MOTHERS AND DAUGHTERS⋆

Materials

4 sheets of paper
    1 decorative: small floral print {B}
    1 decorative: pink satin
    2 coordinating: solids
Cutting tools
Adhesive
Journaling: title and body
Photos

Instructions

1. Crop and single-mount mat the photos.

2. Create a title and body of journaling. Note in this sample that the title and body of journaling are one.

3. Print this journaling onto decorative pink satin paper.

4. Trim and triple-mount mat this journaling with a darker color, a lighter color, and again the darker color.

5. Adhere the photos and journaling to page. Note that there is no adhesive on the back of the smaller photo that overlaps the larger photo. The corner will be loose but protected when the inserted into a page protector. Even though these photos are copies and not originals, it is better not to allow any adhesive to come into direct contact with a photo front.

⋆ Reprinted with permission of *Snapshot Memories* magazine, Primedia Publications.

IMRO REUNION 2000

Please note that the photo on the top page has been enlarged to a 5 × 7 and then cropped. It is double-mount matted with coordinating pressed flower papers.

Materials

6 sheets of paper
   2 decorative: pressed flowers {B}
   3–4 coordinating: pressed flowers with a solid
Cutting tools
Adhesive
Journaling: title and caption
Photos

Instructions

1. Crop the photos. In this sample, the bottom-page photo is first mounted onto a flap and then mount-matted onto another coordinating pressed flower paper. Inside this flap is a third smaller photo plus the photo captions.

2. Create a title; single-mount mat it onto a solid color.

3. Adhere to the bottom center of the page.

GRANDMOTHER'S GIFT BY THE SEA

Materials

4 sheets of paper
   1 decorative: seashell print {B}
   3 coordinating: solids
Cutting tools
Adhesive
3L Memorabilia Pocket
Journaling: title and body
Photos
Memorabilia: seashell

Instructions

1. Crop and double-mount mat the photos.

2. Create a body of journaling and double-mount it. In this sample, the first mat is trimmed away on the left side. The second mat is wider, yet just a touch shorter in vertical length of the lighter coordinating paper.

3. Create a mat for the memorabilia pocket. Notice in this sample, the seashell is white and would be lost on the page without this darker matting behind it.

4. Adhere photos and journaling to the page.

 ## OTHER ASPECTS OF FAMILY

So many pieces go into being a part of a family. And as much as things can change over time, some things never really do, such as family bonds and love. These pages were designed to celebrate some of the everyday joys of family and home.

A CLAN OF IRISH FOLK SMILE

Materials

3 sheets of paper
   1 decorative: faux sponge rust {B}
   3 coordinating: faux blue and green speckled with solid gray
Cutting tools
Adhesive
Journaling: body
Photos

Instructions

1. Crop the photos.

2. Single-mount mat the photos with blue paper.

3. Create a pocket with green paper.

4. Adhere the pocket to the bottom center of the background paper.

5. Adhere the largest photo to the top of the pocket.

6. Adhere the remaining photos to the top of the background paper. (Note on this sample there is a gap between the top of the pocket and the bottom of the top photos.)

7. Create a title.

8. Double-mount mat the title and adhere it at the center of the background paper.

9. Create a slider. (Note in this sample "A Clan of Irish Folk Smile" may look like part of the title but is really the top of the slider! When the slider is removed, the photo captions can be read.)

A PLACE CALLED HOME

Materials

5 sheets of paper
    2 decorative: blueprint and brick {B}
    3 coordinating: navy, medium blue, and red marble
Cutting tools
Adhesive
Journaling: title and captioning
Photos

Instructions

1. Crop the photos.

2. Double-mount mat left-page photos with a mixture of coordinating papers.

3. Double-mount mat right-page photos with a mixture of coordinating papers, with top right and bottom right photos mounted on flaps.

4. Create small page titles and adhere to the pages.

5. Create captions for the inside of flaps explaining the different homes on the pages.

ALWAYS IN MY HEART

Materials

5 sheets of paper
    1 decorative: burgundy tapestry {B}
    1–3 coordinating: solids of cream, vellum, and burgundy
Cutting tools
Adhesive
Gold corners
Journaling: body
Photos
Memorabilia: funeral card

Instructions

1. Crop the photos.

2. Double-mat the main photo (of the person being remembered) with cream and a scrap of vellum. Note that gold corners are placed onto the photo before mount matting is done.

3. Attach the funeral card, with a gold corner, to a burgundy flap. The card can be removed to read it and then placed back into the corners at any time. Inside the flap are the photo captions.

4. Adhere the remaining photos to the background paper with gold corners.

5. Create and adhere a title of the person with years of birth and death.

CLAUDE BYRUM GIVEN
BLACK AND WHITE

Materials

5 sheets of paper
    1 decorative: black and white embossed roses {B}
    4 coordinating: black, white, gray, and white satin
Cutting tools
Corner paper punch
Adhesive
Journaling: title and body
Photo

Instructions

1. Crop the photo and quadruple-mat with gray as first mat, then alternate with black.

2. Create four black photo corners. Using scraps of gray, punch corner designs and trim to a triangle that fits over the top of each black corner. Adhere a decorative gray corner punch to the top of each black corner. Adhere the corners to the matted photo.

3. Add a fifth, final mat using white satin. Adhere the photo to the bottom center of the background paper.

4. Create a title and body of journaling on white paper. Trim and adhere to the top center of the background page.

IN MEMORIAM

Materials

6 sheets of paper
    2 decorative: painted vellum butterfly and iris {B}
    2 decorative: faux sponged green
    2 coordinating: black and mint sponged
Cutting tools
Adhesive
Journaling: body
Photos

Instructions

1. Crop and single-mat photos with black or mint.

2. Mount the bottom left photo onto a flap.

3. The body of journaling placed inside of the flap is a map to get to the cemetery and how to find relatives' headstones.

❧ JUST THE BEGINNING . . .

These pages are just a few examples of all the possibilities you have when you put your family research and photographs into your family heritage scrapbook. Hopefully, your creative appetite has been whetted and you'll have your own variations of these examples to create.

However, a family heritage scrapbook is not the only way to celebrate and present your family history. Chapter 10 will discuss some of the most popular memory crafts, especially quilting, including tips from two of the foremost experts in the field. You'll learn how to make photo transfers of your family photographs so that they can be used for a memory quilt, pillows, or T-shirts. Chapter 10 will also touch on Christmas ornaments, family frames, or a unique cover for family reunion videotapes or a family history CD slide show.

10

Memory Quilts and Memory Crafts

What do quilts have to do with creating a family heritage scrapbook? It was through their quilts that women of the family often communicated their thoughts and recorded their memories. Quilts are often made for special occasions, and, as with any handmade gift, they are treasured forever and have certain memories associated with them—the occasion, the quilt maker, and the relationship between maker and recipient.

The James Collection is an assortment of quilts housed at the University of Nebraska. Among the collection is a signature quilt that is a perfect example of how quilts are indeed a form of scrapbooking. This particular quilt, dated 1916, is from an unknown maker in Pennsylvania and features a portrait of the church along with the pastor's and parishioners' names embroidered in red. Such quilts were often used to raise funds when people paid to have their names embroidered on the quilt. It was then raffled or given to the pastor. Such quilts serve as valuable sources for local and church history.

> *Quilts are often made for special occasions, and, as with any handmade gift, they are treasured forever and have certain memories associated with them— the occasion, the quilt maker, and the relationship between maker and recipient.*

Other quilts have been made to show family trees; some are made to remind someone of home or of years of service to an organization. Whatever the occasion, quilting has always been an outlet for recording history.

To truly give you the lowdown on memory quilts, I went straight to the experts. Ami Simms is one of the most authoritative sources on the subject. She's owner of Mallery Press and is the author of seven quilting books, including *Fun Photo-Quilts & Crafts* and *Creating Scrapbook Quilts*. She's been quilting since 1975, when she learned the craft from an Amish woman. She's made nearly a hundred quilts and her work has been featured in several magazines and other publications. She's also a quilting teacher and lecturer and has appeared on national television. In addition, she created the WORST Quilt in the World Contest.

SITES TO VISIT

Learn more about memory quilts and photo transfers on these sites:

www.MalleryPress.com
This is Ami Simms's Web site where you can purchase her books, Photos-To-Fabric transfer paper, Springmaid's Southern Belle fabric, and other photo transfer products. Ami also has a newsletter. To subscribe, contact her via e-mail at amisimms@aol.com, or sign up on her Web site.

www.memoryquilts.com and **www.pictureplayquilts.com**
This Web site shows sample quilts and offers products for sale. The company also has a photo transfer service.

www.kayewood.com
This site is from another well-known quilting expert, Kaye Wood. Here you'll find a variety of products, including many of Ami Simms's books, as well as others.

Here's what she had to say:

Q: *How was quilting used in the early days as a way to create memories?*

A: Any project that takes as long to make as a quilt is bound to capture the memories of the maker. To paraphrase from a book I no longer can remember the title of, we sew parts of ourselves into our quilts. The quilt embodies the life of the maker; what she was thinking about; the events that occurred during the time she planned and made the quilt; indeed, what happened afterward as the quilt was used. Quilts are chockfull of memories.

Often you'll find quilts made to commemorate a person or event. When these events are political, we regain the intent of the maker because we recognize a historical event. Unfortunately, when these events are of a more personal nature, we don't "see" it in the quilt because we don't share the quilter's personal history. The clues are subtle, maybe influencing a patch here or a fabric there. They are not any less meaningful for the quilter but harder for outsiders to figure out.

❀ PHOTO TRANSFER QUILTS

Those quilts that are easily recognizable as a "memory" quilt are often made in a pictorial style. That is, appliquéd images tell the story. With the advent of modern photo transfer techniques, memory quilts have become immensely popular. First, you don't have to know how to draw; second, you don't even need to know how to appliqué. Everybody has snapshots, and if they don't, they can go out and make them! I love to watch people's faces when they see their first photo quilt. You can almost SEE the gears turning. They see the possibilities, realize they can probably do it, and feel tremendously empowered.

Most first-time photo quilters explain that they are making a quilt for someone's fiftieth wedding anniversary. That's probably the most popular theme. After that come graduations, weddings, other milestone events, mourning quilts, and finally travel quilts.

Q: *When did you begin photo quilting?*

A: I made my first memory quilt in 1990 when I had the opportunity to teach quilting in Australia. For me it was the trip of a lifetime, so far from home, to such an exotic place. I was so honored to be invited and I wanted to remember everything. When I was a college student on foreign study in Italy I kept travel journals illustrated with postcards, pictures, brochures, and postage stamps. After all that work, I hardly looked at them. Later in life, I gave up the writing and just stuck to pictures. We have a lot of photo albums. Don't look at those much either. In trying to capture every memory of my adventure Down Under, I knew I wouldn't have time to write, and a photo album was nice, but I wanted something more. I remembered seeing a show-and-tell where Roberta Horton shared a "memory" quilt she had made of a trip to Japan. I guess she really planted the seed.

When I arrived in Australia my friend and fellow "tutor" Marsha McCloskey and I decided to make memory quilts. It was a tremendous departure for me, not just in theme, but in technique. At that time I was one of those anal quilters (people who know me well say I still am!) who plans everything out ahead of time. If my fabric was talking to me, I wasn't listening. I told it where to sit and that was that! I didn't have a design wall. I worked with pencil and paper and plugged in the colors like a paint by number. I had just finished my St. Basil's Cathedral quilt this way the previous year (take a look at www.mallerypress.com /Artists/AmiSimms/StBasils.html to see what I mean).

So I made my memory quilt totally on the run. No plan. No fabric or supplies either. It was one of the most difficult quilts I've ever done because it felt so awkward. Still it was one of the most satisfying to make (especially when it was all done), and it opened my mind to more exploration.

The next breakthrough for me came from a teaching trip to New Zealand where I met a woman who was transferring black and white photocopies of photographs to fabric using turpentine and a wooden spoon. She then embellished the transferred photos with embroidery and textile paint.

Yet another teaching trip took me to the next step. In Banff, Alberta, Canada I met Anita Sperber, who had a business transferring photographs to fabric. Then everything came together, and I began making photo quilts. People who saw the quilts in progress went bananas, so after the first three or four I decided to write a book. *Creating Scrapbook Quilts* provided quilters with twelve examples and a recipe for puzzling together photo transfers no matter what their size or their shape. Simple sashing strips and the seemingly unplanned appearance to the quilts make them very alluring, especially for beginners. The fact that the quilt is done when you run out of pictures was also appealing.

The major drawbacks to making photo quilts at that time (1993), however, were the methods available. Choices were limited to the liquid transfer media, which was messy, time-consuming, difficult to get good results, and didn't stand up to laundering very well; the transfer services were expensive and required you to send your valuable photographs "out" to be transferred; and Marjorie Croner's method uses mending tape as a printing plate to transfer photocopies to fabric. (See her book *Fabric Photos* from Interweave Press.)

In 1996 transfer paper started getting popular. Feed the stuff through a color copy machine, and you could photo-transfer anything that could be photocopied. It was a tremendous breakthrough.

In 1999 I wrote *Fun Photo-Quilts & Crafts* for a more structured approach for beginners who were hesitant to tackle a quilt with a lot of photos in it, or who might want to explore other ways of capturing photo memories. It has over 25 projects including wall quilts, pillows, coasters, mouse pads, garments, and Christmas ornaments—all with photo transfers.

In fact, I'm still not free from the pull of photo transfers in my quilts. My book *Picture Play Quilts* is about quilts for kids. Each of the quilts in the book is made with conversational fabrics. To spice those up I suggest using photo transfers of the child who is to receive the quilt—siblings, parents, grandparents, pets—anything that would make the quilt special.

Q: *Why do you enjoy making memory quilts?*

A: The idea of making a scrapbook quilt satisfied all my needs. I could put photographs together in a visual display that pleased me and thus remember an event or pay tribute to a person, or make a statement. The cost was no longer prohibitive, the process easy. Photo transfers made with the transfer paper in the color copy machines were permanent and washable. Best of all, I didn't have to take a book off the shelf to look at it. With my photo quilts hanging on the wall, I looked at them all the time. Not only that, but the original photographs weren't harmed at all in the process. In a sense I was even preserving them, although in another media. I was making "copies" on cloth.

> *"The idea of making a scrapbook quilt satisfied all my needs. I could put photographs together in a visual display that pleased me and thus remember an event or pay tribute to a person, or make a statement."*

Snapshots aren't the only things that can be transferred to fabric. Any flat image is fair game and even some that aren't. What does that mean? Any paper I collect on a trip (trash that other people throw away, like ticket stubs, paper napkins with logos, business cards, drinking straw wrappers, paper chopstick holders, fortune cookie fortunes, restaurant receipts, candy wrappers, bus tickets)—all that becomes "memorabilia" worth saving. And, I get to make the scrapbook or photo album, too!

Q: *What particular photo transfer methods do you recommend?*

A: There are several options on the market now: transfer papers made for color copy machines, transfer papers made for color computer printers, and solutions for pretreating fabric for "direct" printing with computer printers. I still like the transfer paper made to be used in a color copy machine. I'm confident that the computer printer methods will improve, but until they do, I think most people will get the best results from a $30,000 machine they bring their transfer paper to, rather than their home computer setup. The technology is more sophisticated. The clarity is superb; enlarging and reducing images is easy; the completed transfers from Photos-To-Fabric transfer paper are completely permanent and washable. You can even stitch through them and iron over them when you build your quilt. Large office supply stores like Office-Max, Staples, Office Depot, and Mailboxes Etc. have state-of-the-art color copy machines with prices per copy usually ranging from $.89 to $1.20 per copy.

For whatever method you prefer, use the smoothest cotton to transfer onto. Don't prewash it; use it right off the bolt. Springmaid Southern Belle 200 thread count is the best I've seen to date. (It is also marketed as Memory Cloth.) It's readily available and makes a terrific photo transfer.

Sandy Bonsib is another expert on memory quilting. She's a quilt maker, teacher, and author of *Scrapbook Quilts/Quilting Your Memories* and *Quilting Your Memories: Inspirations for Designing with Image Transfers*, both published by That Patchwork Place. In an interview with *Craftrends*, a trade magazine for the scrapbooking, craft, and quilting industries, Sandy offered her insights on memory quilting. She says there are three ways to transfer photos to fabric:

1. Using transfer paper with a laser color copier

2. Using photo transfer paper with an ink-jet printer

3. Transferring directly to fabric

She says transferring photos to fabric often results in the photo losing clarity. With ink-jet paper at home, she says the transfer tends to be thicker on fabric because of the extra coating needed to make ink-jet inks, which are water-soluble.

Like Ami Simms, Sandy Bonsib would much rather make a trip to a copy shop and use photo transfer paper on a laser color copier. She claims this method gives the best color.

Simms believes that transfers made using fabrics mounted on "carriers" that help feed fabric through a printer often don't offer satisfactory color reproduction. Plus, they may not stand up to repeated laundering.

Remember, not everyone has the same opinion. If you choose to experiment with photo transferring, test the methods available to you and use the one with which you're most comfortable and that provides you with the best results.

 ## Creating Memories Face-to-Face

One way to get everyone involved is to plan a family reunion. The final chapter of this book will focus on this great way to gather more family history and reconnect with family members. You'll learn about how to get organized and send out a friendly invitation to gather family and friends to a reunion that will be fun and exciting. Whether you have six or sixty relatives, a family reunion is a wonderful family event.

One way to get everyone involved is to plan a family reunion.

 ## Other Types of Memory Crafts

For centuries families have been making memory crafts that are appreciated by generations to follow. Memory quilts are a fine example of this type of craft, but you can use numerous other ways to express family heritage through art and craft—ways that work hand in hand with the creation of a family heritage scrapbook.

Photographs tend to be a part of a memory craft, but this is not an absolute rule. You can create a family heirloom by stitching the family tree on a cross-stitch or needlepoint sampler. This sampler can be

(continues on page 272)

N INTERNATIONAL MEMORY QUILT

Perhaps the largest "scrapbook" in the world is the NAMES Project AIDS Memorial Quilt. It's constructed of approximately forty-three thousand three- by six-foot panels that would measure 48.82 miles if laid end to end. (That's greater than the distance between Providence, Rhode Island, and Boston, Massachusetts.) Panels are made by family members, friends, spouses, significant others, coworkers, and others to commemorate a person who has died of AIDS. They work in groups or individually, and they come from diverse backgrounds. As people gather together to make panels for the AIDS Memorial Quilt, this tradition gives comfort in a time of grief.

The quilt was conceived in 1985 by Cleve Jones, an activist who organized annual candlelight marches honoring assassinated San Francisco Supervisor Harvey Milk and Mayor George Moscone. In planning the 1985 march, Jones learned that more than a thousand San Franciscans had been lost to AIDS, so he asked fellow marchers to write on placards the names of friends and loved ones who had died of AIDS. At the end of the march, Jones and others stood on ladders taping the placards to the walls of the San Francisco Federal Building. Jones thought the wall of names looked like a patchwork quilt. That's what inspired him to plan a larger memorial, and a little over a year later, he created the first panel for the NAMES Project AIDS Memorial Quilt in memory of his friend Marvin Feldman. In June 1987, Jones teamed up with several others to formally organize the NAMES Project Foundation.

Today more than 83,000 names are on the quilt, representing 20 percent of all U.S. AIDS deaths. It weighs more than 50 tons and measures 773,280 square feet, the equivalent of 25 football fields. More than thirteen million people have visited the quilt as it's toured the country, and its displays have raised nearly $3 million for direct services for people with AIDS.

The quilt is the largest example of a community art project in the world and has redefined the art of quilt making in response to contemporary circumstances. It was nominated for a Nobel Peace Prize in 1989, and that year, *Common Threads: Stories from the Quilt* won an Academy Award as the best feature-length documentary film of 1989.

According to the NAMES Project, some of the memorabilia used in the quilt include a hundred-year-old quilt, afghans, Barbie dolls, buttons, car keys, champagne glasses, cowboy boots, cremation ashes, credit cards, first-place ribbons, flags, fur, hats, human hair, love letters, leather, jewelry, jeans, Mardi Gras masks, merit badges, needlepoint, paintings, pearls, racing silks, records, silk flowers, shirts, stuffed animals, tennis shoes, wedding rings, and much more.

Though the quilt panels are a permanent part of the AIDS Memorial Quilt, all panels have been photographed and archived on the NAME Project's Web site at www.aidsquilt.org. The viewers can search for the panel by the person's name to view it. The quilt is also carefully and meticulously mapped out, so when it's on display someone can easily find a specific panel.

As you create your family heritage scrapbook, think about quilting in all its forms and how it illustrates a unique form of scrapbooking, and consider what a powerful memorial the AIDS Memorial Quilt is. It stresses the importance of remembering our loved ones in a wonderfully creative way. And that's exactly what you want to do with your scrapbook.

(continued from page 269)

framed or made into a pillow. The woodburner can create a family tree onto a wood plaque or get very creative and even burn the images of a family coat of arms or crest onto the wood. A decorative painter or artist might paint a family tree. The options really have no limits. Families keep such heirlooms for generations. Each new home enjoys the wonder of an ancestor's talent.

The options really have no limits. Families keep such heirlooms for generations. Each new home enjoys the wonder of an ancestor's talent.

If you feel you lack skill or artistic talent, don't get discouraged from being creative, however. Today, thanks to technology, photographs can be transferred to multiple mediums from fabric to wood. In most cases, with the help of a computer and printer, you can include family photos when making book inscriptions, stationery, refrigerator magnets, widow decals, and so much more. Some pieces will be the family masterpiece, and some creations will be enjoyed in the moment of a family gathering or reunion. It's a shame to use our precious photos only in scrapbooks that are viewed then placed back onto the bookshelf or living room coffee table—not when we have so many great ways to showcase the photos.

Consider faux finishing or découpaging a picture frame for a photo of an ancestor. Think about photo transferring the last group shot of your family's reunion onto a T-shirt given to this year's gathering. Explore how to create a family slide show that can be burned onto a CD and then use your imagination to create the CD's label and case. Add some color to a family newsletter by using a photo transfer on the cover of a pocket folder that will hold the volumes and keep the newsletters organized. Make family memories and heritage a part of your home's décor!

Maria and I want to encourage you to keep being creative with family memories after you've completed your family heritage scrapbook. Get the whole family involved with creative ways to show off family photos, history, memorabilia, and stories. Try making your own journal or diary with some basic bookbinding. Have a family recipe weekend, and use family recipes to create every meal. Make your own family trivia game by placing family questions onto index cards; the first person to answer twelve questions correctly wins. Whatever creative memory craft you choose, continue to share the pleasure of family beyond your scrapbook pages.

11

Family Reunions

Staying Connected All Year Long

Many people shudder at the very mention of family reunions. They have visions of strange distant relatives who they never knew and whom they would prefer to keep at an arm's length—if not even further removed. Many families have their skeletons they would prefer to lock up, but, as the television character Julia Sugarbaker of *Designing Women* once said (and I paraphrase), "Some families keep their crazy relatives locked up. In the South, we put them on the front porch!" Most likely, though, the so-called "skeletons" are far outnumbered by interesting, charming, and truly wonderful human beings.

My mother's family, the Trummels, began holding family reunions sometime back in the 1940s, and I don't think they've missed a year since. In the beginning it was held twice a year, once during the Christmas holiday and once in June. The reunion began as a Father's Day celebration in honor of my great-grandfather, and was held on Father's Day weekend for many years. As the younger generations grew older and started their own families, the reunion moved to another weekend, but stayed in June. As I mentioned in the Preface, the reunion is currently held once each year in June and hosting is rotated among family members.

I remember my mom's aunts and uncles pulling up in their mobile homes and parking in my grandparents' front yard a few days before the actual reunion. Family members came at different times over the weekend depending on where they were coming from—some had to drive several hours while others lived closer. One thing I found peculiar, though, was that the host was expected to feed all of their guests for however long they stayed! For the reunion day, family members each brought something to contribute, but for the other days, the host was prepared with a refrigerator and freezer full of food. These days some hosts elect to have the affair catered.

There's a family "business" meeting each year. Sometime during the afternoon, the surviving siblings of my late grandfather and the offspring of the deceased gather to discuss next year's reunion—where and when it will be—and to share news about their respective families: graduations, births, job accomplishments, weddings, and other important events. Anyone who didn't attend would get caught up on family news in the family's Round Robin newsletter.

❧ PLANNING AND ORGANIZING

Everyone has their own idea on how to do things, but there's nothing like learning from other people's successes and failures. Here are some guidelines to planning a reunion based on my own experience.

Everyone has their own idea on how to do things, but there's nothing like learning from other people's successes and failures.

Tip 1: Decide Who to Invite

Make out your guest list before deciding on a date so that you can learn whether the date will be suitable for the majority of people, especially those who will need to travel a good distance or have other personal circumstances to consider.

Tip 2: Pick a Date

Consider whom you're planning to invite. More than likely children will be involved, so their school calendar must be considered. Keep in mind what family members do for a living. Is that a convenient time for them to get off work? You can't accommodate everyone's schedule, so you have to do your best to determine what works best for the majority.

Tip 3: Reserve Space and the Date

If you plan to rent a hall or have the reunion at a resort or any place other than your home, be sure the space is available the day(s) you want it. You may have to be flexible by a week or two; just be sure it's still convenient for the majority. Then let everyone know when you're planning the reunion so they can reserve the date. You don't have to have specific plans, but you need to let them know the date well in advance. When I was planning my reunion, I first mentioned my plans in October for a reunion the following July. By the time I sent out Christmas cards, the date was picked and I could mention it in the card so people could begin planning vacation time or saving money for the trip.

Tip 4: Arrange Accommodations

Chances are you can't accommodate everyone at your residence. If you're holding the event in a hotel, resort, or other place with sleeping rooms, be sure to reserve a block of rooms. You'll probably have to make a wild guess as to how many rooms, but they can always be canceled.

Call the hotel's sales office and ask whether they give group discounts. Even with a small group, sometimes you can receive a price break on five rooms; I obtained $20 savings per night per room for my reunion guests. The hotel will ask you to sign a contract specifying a cancellation policy that allows you to cancel extra rooms without penalty. Usually the hotel will automatically cancel the rooms at a certain date without penalty. However, any rooms reserved and then canceled after that date will be charged a cancellation fee.

Guests should be instructed to make their own reservations. That reminder can be done in the invitation (see tip 7).

Tip 5: Plan the Menu

The timing for this part of the reunion planning process will depend on whether you plan to use a caterer and how busy that caterer may be. Decide who you want and work within their parameters. Of course, if you're preparing the food yourself and/or having others bring a dish to pass, that makes things easier. However, if others bring a dish, you don't want duplicates, so be specific when telling them what to bring. Don't just say vegetable or salad. What if three people all brought baked beans and three all brought cole slaw?

This is also where you need to remember who your guests are. Do any have special meal requirements? Are there vegetarians in the group? I needed a heart-healthy menu, so I specified that with the caterer, who was more than accommodating. Also consider the type of cuisine. Most of my family grew up in Illinois and love their meat and potatoes! Since the caterer also grew up there, she knew exactly what I meant and made sure she didn't prepare anything too unusual. Most people are willing to try something out of the ordinary, but many prefer to stick to the tried-and-true.

Tip 6: Plan Activities

What will people do all day? Will some be making a weekend out of it or perhaps staying even longer? Include a list of local points of interest with your invitation: historical sites, nearby state or national parks, museums and art galleries, botanical gardens, the zoo, shopping centers, and so forth. If people are in town for two, three, or more days, you don't need to entertain them every minute, but give them suggestions. If they're like my family, they'll toss those suggestions around, try to come up with a consensus, and everyone does the same thing. Or maybe spending each day together is a bit much for some people and they'd prefer to do something on their own for an afternoon. Just be sure they know what there is to do.

As for the reunion itself, make sure there's something for everyone. A swimming pool, cards, board games, and a few rented movies for different age groups are all great ideas for reunion activities.

Tip 7: Set a Time and Send Invitations

Once you have the place figured out, determine a time of day for the event and send the invitations. I sent mine four months in advance, then followed up with a "what-to-bring" letter about six weeks before the reunion. Sending invitations can be a daunting task depending on

Who's in the Kitchen with Grandma? Creating a Family Cookbook

Maria's mother-in-law, Elizabeth, still grumbles that no one has the recipe to Grandma Nerius's famous chocolate cake. "In those days a family recipe was heavily guarded," she explained. "You didn't share your best recipe with anyone because we always tried to outdo each other at family gatherings. But we had all hoped that Grandma Nerius had at least written the recipe down somewhere. Sadly, she never did. She kept promising, but I guess she never got around to it. That was the best chocolate cake any of us had ever tasted. And try as we might, we just can't duplicate it."

Does your family have famous and favorite dishes or desserts? Why not start a family cookbook at your next family reunion? Don't let treasured recipes disappear, leaving future generations with only memories to digest. You have a few options to get organized:

❈ Send out a recipe card sheet (a card that includes the recipe name and who it is for, the ingredients and directions, where the original recipe came from, and the history of the recipe) with each reunion invitation. Ask each family member to fill out the sheet (one recipe written four times) with a favorite recipe. This recipe card sheet should be returned to you immediately, and then make enough copies of this recipe for each family attending the reunion. Making four copies at once will save time and money. Simply cut and trim the recipe cards from the sheet. You can print on card stock from your home printer or use a local print shop.

❈ Ask family members to send to you their top three family recipes. Enter these recipes into a computer database or software designed for recipes, and print out a complete set for each family attending the reunion. Or type up the recipes and get copies for the family members at a print shop.

❈ Post the family recipes on your family's homepage or Web site. If your family has an Internet mail list with a file area, you can upload the recipes to this site for all family members to download at their convenience.

the number of people you're inviting. If you don't have addresses for all your cousins, for example, send invitations only to the oldest generation and ask them to please inform their offspring.

Our invitation was very simple, created on the computer with the basic fonts available. It's best to create your own so you're sure to include everything necessary. Preprinted invitations are often small and don't leave enough room for the details you need for an event like this. Besides, by doing them on the computer, you only have to "write" it once and print as many copies as you need or photocopy it. You could also take your invitation to a quick printing place depending on the number of copies you need made.

Remember when you're preparing the invitation that others have no idea what you're planning, so be as detailed as possible. Be sure to include these points:

❀ The occasion (such as "D. E. Trummel Family Reunion")

❀ When

❀ Where

❀ What to bring

❀ RSVP (your phone number, address, date to respond, and number of people)

❀ Accommodation information (include phone numbers and information about any special arrangements that may have been made)

❀ List of local attractions

❀ A map

Tip 8: Gather Memories

What would a family reunion be without fond memories? And because this book is all about recording your family heritage, reunions provide the perfect opportunity to gather information. Ask each family member to write one hundred to three hundred words—about a page—recounting fond memories of a relative and to bring it to the reunion. Then gather around and read them aloud, no doubt inspiring everyone to chirp in with their own version of the story!

What would a family reunion be without fond memories? And because this book is all about recording your family heritage, reunions provide the perfect opportunity to gather information.

Another terrific way to gather family history—and have a lot of fun at the same time—is to pass around trivia questions (see the sidebar on page 284). Some of the questions can go back several generations, but they don't have to. Compiling your own list of questions and distributing it at your reunion is a great way to get family members talking about old times and generations past. It's also a good way to teach younger generations about family history.

Tip 9: Tend to Details on the Day of the Event

Make sure the caterer arrives in plenty of time to get things ready before the guests arrive. If you're preparing the food yourself, be sure to allow time to have everything ready so you're not rushed at the last minutes. It's important to *relax!* You want everyone else to have fun, but you should, too! Don't worry if everything isn't perfect. Tell everyone what's available on the entertainment front, and let them decide for themselves what they want to do. Engage people in conversation and get them talking about themselves and their families. This will help you tremendously in planning your heritage scrapbook. You will compile pages and pages of history and stories to plug in with the photos and mementos.

Take lots of photos! Be sure to take a couple of group shots. With groups too large for one group photo, consider grouping people by generation—for instance, Mom with her siblings in one photo and grouped with their spouses in another. Immediate families can be grouped as well. If it's a really large group, consider hiring a photographer. That way you won't have to worry about forgetting to take photos. It's up to you. As with most aspects of collecting and preserving family history, there are no set rules. Do what you think is best based on what you need for your heritage scrapbook.

Next Generation, New Traditions

In the year 2000, I started a new family reunion tradition: I invited my parents and my mom's siblings and their offspring for our own "immediate family" reunion. It's really the same concept as the larger Trummel clan, but this one was for my grandfather's offspring.

It could have been a tremendous undertaking had I let it get that way, but I didn't. Since I live in Denver and have two cousins who live in nearby Boulder, it seemed that Colorado was a logical central location for our family who is spread over three other states: Illinois, California, and Wyoming.

I have twelve cousins on my mom's side of the family—ten who are married and eight who have children. With all of those cousins, two aunts and their spouses, an uncle and his spouse, my parents, and my own brother and sister-in-law and their three kids, I knew I could possibly end up with a crowd big enough to field three or four football teams! And living in a high-rise condominium building involved some strategic planning (there was no front yard for mobile home parking).

Fortunately, many of my family members are much like me and don't rely on planning every single detail. Those that do just had to put up with my way of doing things—heck, I was the host!

(continues on page 286)

$\mathscr{F}$AMILY HISTORY TRIVIA QUIZ

A great activity for reunions is a family history trivia quiz. Offered here are some general questions that can fit into the life and lifestyles of most families; think up additional ones that may be more applicable to your own family. Mix and combine questions with older and younger generations' time lines to keep everyone interested.

❋ What are the name(s) of the first generation of family member(s) who immigrated to the United States?

❋ What country did they immigrate from?

❋ Name two relatives who were not born in a hospital.

❋ Name the first relative born in a hospital.

❋ Which family member's home had the first indoor bathroom?

❋ What was the occupation of Grandpa (Family Surname)?

❋ What was Grandma (Family Surname's) maiden name?

❋ What was Great-grandmother (Family Surname's) hobby?

❋ What was the family's first new car?

❋ Who was the first sibling to leave home?

❋ Who was the first family member to graduate from high school? college?

❋ What is your favorite family childhood memory?

- What were the names of the family pets?

- Who is the official "saint" of the family?

- Who was the first grandchild to have children?

- Grandpa listens to classical jazz, while his grandson listens to _____?

- Great-grandpa walked how many miles to school in the snow each winter?

- How many states do the [Family Surname] live in today?

- Who has the most coveted family recipe?

- Who should organize the next family reunion?

- What was [Relative] on his or her first Halloween?

- Who is the youngest cousin, and who is the oldest cousin?

(continued from page 283)

Living in a high rise actually made planning easier. I reserved one of the building's party rooms that had a full kitchen and a big-screen television and opened onto the swimming pool area. There are also grills right outside the door for cooking. Since people were driving or flying great distances, I arranged for a caterer and asked others to bring only food and drink that would travel easily, or to keep in mind something they could easily pick up at the local grocery store once they arrived in town.

I had a good idea when I started out that many of my cousins probably wouldn't make it since most of them are in Illinois and Indiana with young children. I ended up with 18 people, including myself. All of my aunts and uncles came, as did my parents and my brother and two of his kids. (My sister-in-law stayed home with my older nephew, the high-school baseball star who was playing in a summer league and being recruited for college.)

One lesson I learned and will share with you is that it's important to remember what age groups will be represented at your reunion. My mother and her siblings and their spouses range from ages 47 to 73, the first cousins ranged in age from 13 to 47, and the third generation ranged from 20 months to 20 years. Not having children, I planned for the adults and figured the parents would worry about the kids. I knew the pool would be attractive to the teenagers and the 12-year-old, and I was right. The pool was attractive to young and old alike, and the parents of the toddler took care of him, but I found that conversation isn't enough amongst adults 35 to 73! Fortunately my cousins immediately recognized my shortcomings and headed for the nearest store to buy some board games. I'd forgotten how much this family enjoys games! Somehow that gene skipped me and it didn't occur to me to have such entertainment on hand.

✻ CREATING A FAMILY WEB SITE

You'll find as you search the Internet that many of the sites offer help for building a family Web site. This can be done a couple of ways. If there's a techie in the family, he or she can build the site. It really isn't that complicated for someone who knows something about computers. The other option is to research all the options you find as you're surfing the Web and determining which suits you best.

By developing your family's own Web site, you can post a notice about upcoming reunions and special occasions. You can also post photos and create an online scrapbook. By recording your family's heritage online, you have the opportunity to share with family members almost instantaneously your creative endeavor. Not everyone is always able to attend family reunions to see the scrapbooks in person. Putting them online lets them share in the moment, too.

By developing your family's own Web site, you can post a notice about upcoming reunions and special occasions. You can also post photos and create an online scrapbook.

Take your time determining what works best for you. And remember, there isn't necessarily a right or wrong way. What's important is what works best for you. To help you determine what might work for your family, here are some sites to check out:

www.dcn.davis.ca.us/~vctinney/reunions.htm
> This site offers links to a number of other sites, some of which are also listed here. It presents samples of online reunion announcements and provides links to family Web sites.

www.reunionsmag.com
> This is the site for the quarterly print magazine called *Reunions,* a magazine "dedicated to the joy of family, class, and military reunions.

Content focuses on helping organizers be well-educated, wise reunion consumers." The Web site includes articles from the magazine that provide invaluable information for anyone planning a reunion.

www.mindspring.net/community/featurepgs/familyplan/
Here you'll find *Using the Internet to Plan a Family Reunion*. It includes a tool for searching for long-lost relatives, as well as a checklist and planning suggestions. There are links to a main event planner, reunion planner, reunion services, and others, plus sites suggesting activities. It even provides links for information on preserving the reunion memories with a Web photo album.

www.familyreunion.com.
You can use this site to post announcements about your reunion, and the site provides a resource guide that allows you to search for ideas, tips, products, services, and more. Plus, you can share your reunion story, reunion-planning idea, and other reunion-related information. There's also a chat room and a travel center that provides low-cost travel services.

One very useful tool that ties into this book very well is Genealogy Central, which allows you to research your lineage, reconstruct your family tree, and find long-lost relatives. You can also purchase books on the site—books on reunions and genealogy and a list of new or out-of-print books, magazines, calendars, software, CDs, and gifts.

www.homestead.com
This site offers a family newsletter service and will set up your family news Web site for an initial setup and monthly fee.

www.family-reunion.com
This site offers a Family Reunion Resource Guide, listing accommodations and travel suggestions, correspondence samples (including software for invitations), decorations, a guide to researching family history, food, gifts and awards, entertainment ideas, location information, photography tips, publications, rentals, software, and special considerations.

FAMILY NEWSLETTERS

Don't let any insecurities you might harbor about writing scare you away from creating a family newsletter. Family newsletters aren't intended to be entered in any literary competitions. The important thing is to share family news. Here are four ideas for creating newsletters:

1. Perhaps the simplest way to do a family newsletter is to use a round-robin approach. It starts with one member of the family (usually the oldest) who simply writes a letter telling about what's happening in his or her family. That's sent to the second oldest, who adds his or her own family update and sends it on to the next person. It continues that way until it gets back to the originator, who removes his or her original letter and writes a new update. It usually takes several months for the round-robin to make its rounds so there's always something new to add.

2. You could also do an electronic round-robin, by writing an e-mail and sending it on to the next person, who adds information and forwards it on. Remember, though, that doing it this way won't take much time, and by the time it gets back to the originator, that person may not have much to add.

3. You could do an actual four-page newsletter and lay it out with headlines just like a newspaper, but then someone would have to take responsibility for gathering information, designing the newsletter, and mailing it. I don't recommend this format.

4. If your family is technologically savvy, you might try an online newsletter. Create a family Web site and have family members post their information there. Remember, though, that unless you create some protection, these Web sites are open to the public. Anyone could wind up reading your family's private news.

www.minutiaesoftware.com/reunion.htm

This reunion planner will cost you $59.95, but it calls itself the "ultimate tool for planning and coordinating your family, college, high school, company, or military reunion." It's a pretty sophisticated software that includes a budget planner, the capability of printing photo name badges, the ability to send e-mail, and more.

 A FINAL TIP

Planning a family reunion doesn't have to be difficult. It can be time-consuming and perhaps a bit stressful, but there's nothing wrong with asking your relatives to help, especially if other family members live in the same city or town. One can be in charge of accommodations, one in charge of securing a location, and one in charge of invitations.

If you're tackling it alone and need some help, check out the Internet. When searching online for reunions, you will no doubt find lots of helpful sites if you're planning a class reunion, but most of those sites will also offer help with family reunions. In fact, most of them will provide links to even other sites that offer yet more help. A list of reunion Web sites can be found in the sidebar on pages 287–288 and in Appendix A.

PIECES OF TIME SHARED: A FAMILY REMEMBERS

Here are some of the wonderful memories we shared at the 2000 Trummel family reunion.

John Trummel, uncle, August 2000

My wife says my family is boring. And she is probably right. I come from good solid German-English Midwestern farm stock. My father was one of eight kids raised during the Depression on a farm in mid-state Illinois. By the standards of those days, the kids were very successful, and I'm sure they exceeded all of their own expectations. Six of the eight graduated from the University of Illinois, and the other two took to the land and became farmers. The eight siblings settled in Illinois, Indiana, and Wisconsin, all within a few hours of one another.

"As a kid I remember going to family reunions."

As a kid I remember going to family reunions. They were held twice a year—in June and again in December. In the summer, the reunions were often in a city or county park, but in the winter they were always at someone's house. The host duties were passed in sequence from one sibling to the next. Everyone would arrive midmorning and begin preparing lunch, which, of course, was potluck. It generally consisted of a meat dish, scalloped potatoes, vegetable casserole, rolls, and Jell-O. Dessert was ice cream and pie. Lemonade and iced tea were the strongest drinks on the table.

The cousins and I played after lunch. I lived in town, and my favorite reunions were those held in the summer at one of the farms. We would run all day through the fields and go down to the creek or up into the hayloft to play.

For the adults, the reunions were a time to catch up. After lunch they would sit and talk quietly about what they were doing, and often laugh over old stories. There was no swearing, and the TV was never on in the background. During the afternoon there was a business meeting of sorts where each family member reported in on family news—births, deaths, graduations, and other milestones in life.

On the surface, my father's family didn't appear to be very close. They were reserved, and I never remember them hugging. That wasn't

Who's Got Mail?
Tips for Starting a Family Mail List Online

One of the best ways to keep in touch with relatives is starting a family mail list. Dozens of Web sites offer this free service. You'll have to put up with some discrete advertising, but the mail list can be invaluable to staying connected with various family groups. Granted, not every family member will have access to the Internet, but in most cases at least one member of the family branch does have access and will pass on family news to the rest of his or her family.

A mail list can be set up as a monthly newsletter or as a very active mail center with daily posts from any member of the list. If you are familiar with electronic bulletin boards or Internet newsgroups, a mail list is similar in most respects except that all posts will be delivered directly to your e-mail address. Many sites also allow for a file area where text or graphics can be stored on the site for downloading, ability to create polls (which is great when planning family reunions), and the ability to create databases of family recipes or mailing addresses.

A mail list can be private so that only people you approve can access the list's information. Or the mail list can be public, meaning that anyone can access the information. You might consider starting one of each: one is private and for members to share personal information such as home phone numbers; the second is open to the public and placed in the site's general directory. The reason for this second mail list is so that anyone with an interest in your family surname can get basic information to help him or her figure out whether he or she might be part of your extended family.

Check out these sites for more information on creating a family mail list:

www.egroups.com

http://eleccomm.ieee.org

http://internetemaillist.com

www.hotbot.com

www.free-market.net

their way. But beneath that, they were family. That was it: They were family. They respected each other. They didn't gossip about family. They didn't brag about kids, or vacations, or what they were doing, and they never borrowed money from family. If someone needed help you would offer, but you didn't push and didn't pry. These people made their best effort to live a decent life and tried to instill those values in their children. Overall, they may be a pretty boring bunch, but they're not a bad foundation on which to build your life.

John Trummel on Keeping a Journal

When my daughter was 5 and my son less than 1 year old, I read an article about an 87-year-old Kansas farmer who had kept a journal for 50 years. It wasn't a diary. It was a journal of his life and, in the context of what we see as history, nothing out of the ordinary. In the journal he would record day-to-day events and note things like the price of wheat, what it took to plant a crop, and the things that were going on around him.

I thought about this for some time, and then I began to write my own journal. My daughter is now 18, my son is 13, and I've been making entries in my journal for 13 years. I don't write often, once every month or so, usually when I'm on a business trip and I have time in the airport or on the plane or in the motel at night.

I write about my family and what they are doing. I wrote about my daughter's first-place finish in the kindergarten science fair, and about coaching soccer with my son. I've recorded my wife's activities, too—getting her teaching certificate and starting her first teaching job. I write about my reaction to things I've observed and people I've talked to in airports. And I also write about events of the day. I was watching the news in a motel room in North Dakota one night in 1987 when the stock market dropped 500 points, and commentators were comparing it to the 1929 crash. I wondered how significant an event this would be over time. I wrote about the fall of the Berlin Wall and the change of presidents. I wrote about a hitchhiker I gave a ride to one time along a stretch of interstate highway in Wyoming.

I write this journal because I want there to be some connection between generations. I think all kids have trouble understanding their parents because they judge things in the context of their own life experience, just as we as parents judge the actions of our own kids. I want my kids to have some view, however limited, of the world as I've seen it.

"I want my kids to have some view, however limited, of the world as I've seen it."

It is important to me that I try to make this connection between generations. I hope these things I've written mean something to my kids. Will they care? Who knows. The wonderful and frustrating thing about parenting is that the product of a job well done is an individual with his or her own sense of values. I can tell my kids that it is important for them to read this. And they may find that to be true, or they may just have a few laughs and throw the whole thing away. In either case, there is a connection.

Sharon Harker, aunt, July 2000

The way I remember seems to be in generalities rather than a specific story. I remember my grandparents milking cows in the old barn, the smell of the hay and the warm milk mixed with the smell of the cattle; their dog Reggie; the garden and fruit trees; climbing roses on the fence; Grandpa in his rocking chair, smoking a cigar; Grandma in the kitchen making homemade noodles; my sister Mary Jo falling off her bike in loose gravel and scraping her knee.

Growing up, I remember going to a one-room school (I learned phonics there) for a year; Dad going to the University of Illinois to get his teaching degree; Dad's laugh—he loved a good story; Mom making us clean house on Saturday (we would listen to *Grand Central Station* on the radio, and Mom had to get after us for stopping our work to listen); the vacations at the lake; Mom helping me match stripes on a dress with a gored skirt (it had to be perfect); Christmas in Oreana, Illinois, when an orange was a luxury; the year the house in the country near Sheldon burned; Mom and Dad playing Bridge with friends; building the house in Yorkville, Illinois; moving—Danville to Decatur to Oreana to Scotland (Illinois) to Sheldon to Yorkville; our dog Gypsy; crossing the Fox River every school day; ice skating on the Fox.

Judith Svoboda, aunt, July 2000

I remember going to my grandparents' farm when I was a kid. My grandparents were opposites in many respects. Grandma was petite and English. Grandpa was tall and German. According to my father, Grandpa was *very* German—stubborn, demanding, and stern. This side of his character was not observed by his grandchild. I recall him sitting in a large oak chair, smoking a cigar. To this day I recall that image whenever I smell cigar smoke. This was also a man who would crack black walnuts by the quart and give them to his grandchildren. My grandparents did not have an easy life. Compounding the hardships of the farmers' Depression in the 1920s was the fire that destroyed their home. In spite of these setbacks, my grandparents raised eight successful children, managing on the most meager of funds. Six graduated from the University of Illinois.

Judith Svoboda on Christmas

Warm and fuzzy family memories: What better qualifies than memories of Christmas? First are all the Christmas pageants presented to the church congregation. One year the Yorkville Methodist Church played host to Knights of the Round Table as they came, swords clanging, to welcome the Christ Child to the world. Over the years, that Child was also greeted with the voices of Pa Trummel and Elsa Marshall as they sang so beautifully out of tune. Neither ever got one tone right.

There are also the most beautiful of snowy nights when my parents and I walked to the services—no vehicles could get through—pulling my younger brother on a sled. Norman Rockwell couldn't have done it better.

Then there was Christmas morning—very *early* Christmas morning— when I caught my aunt shaking my girls to wake them up so the gift opening could begin. Caught in the act, she turned so as not to meet my eye, but I could see the most sheepish of looks on her face.

And there was my mother's last Christmas, when her daughter and her family presented her with a quilt made so lovingly by each family member.

Perhaps the saddest and most memorable Christmas was 1944, my parents' 13th wedding anniversary, the day their home burned to the ground. We lost almost all of our possessions, including a beloved dog. But I remember most the little details, such as being asked by a bank clerk if the clothes I wore were the only ones I had, and being asked if I wanted a poached egg and not knowing what that was.

I remember the cowgirl outfit my mother made. It was spared because it was hidden in the shed. Mostly I remember the Anderson family, who took us in and provided a Christmas Eve for us. They gave me a doll that I kept into adulthood, discarding it only when it literally disintegrated. I still have the doll clothes my mother made for it the following Christmas.

Judith Svoboda on Family Get-Togethers

I am blessed with amazing siblings. In spite of age differences (17 years between youngest and oldest), different career choices, and geographic distances, we have remained close. The love and respect we have for one another is due in large part to the example set by our parents and grandparents.

Family functions have always been a large part of our social life. Annual family reunions have been regularly scheduled for at least half a century. The family still enjoys a round-robin letter, with cousins filling the void left by deceased parents.

My grandmother's diary, written in the 1940s, makes constant references to family get-togethers. She speaks of family celebrations and simple Sunday afternoon visits as she discusses egg prices and canning projects.

I personally remember regular visits to grandparents' to celebrate holidays and weddings. And, amazingly, these visits were pleasant! Everyone seemed to enjoy the others' company. And they laughed and shared memories, often about themselves.

This is the tradition we came from and one we are carrying on—laughter. We have a repertoire of family stories that have been told and retold—common experiences that make up our family lore. Families are connected because of a common ancestry, but the glue that holds a family together is the fact that its members share so many common experiences. There is a tradition, a collection of stories, that each member can connect to.

Deborah Svoboda, cousin, July 2000

Ahh, the Trummels. My miscellaneous childhood remembrances of Grandma and Grandpa's house. As a suburban forest dweller, I found the sites in Yorkville very unusual. I can remember being very surprised that there were no sidewalks in front of Grandma and Grandpa's house. Didn't *every* house get built with one in front? What an unusual place, I thought. And where were the fences? Did their backyard not end?

And what? Walk to Jo and Bum's house? Sure, through the backyard, I was told. Where was I? This was not California, the place of my birth and upbringing. Yes, Virginia, this was not Santa Clara.

I can remember the smell of the cornfields on the way into town. That hot grass smell and the miles and miles of corn. As we approached Yorkville, I tried to see the path that my mom had taken to school. It had to be uphill both ways and able to receive six feet of snow. I never could figure out where that path was. There's Fast Eddie's! And there on the right was Grandma and Grandpa's place—a white cottage, basically, but the coolest house I had ever seen. As you walked in, there was the living room to the left and the dining room just ahead. Tucked in the corner to the left was the kitchen.

Where's the liquid silver? It's in the kitchen drawer, as usual. Continue through the kitchen and go into the garage. I don't remember the car, but I do remember the enormous freezer. What do you put in there? It must be for lots of ice cream. What else would you need that much space for?

Back into the kitchen, where I remember finding a bottle of dandelion wine with Gramps. He said Uncle John had made it when he was in college. It must have been a fine wine by then, because college was a long time ago, right? Wait, dandelions? He made wine out of dandelions? What was he thinking? I was very young, but I knew that dandelions were only weeds to blow the little fluffy parachutes off of.

Now into the dining room, where many a game of Hearts was played; graze the living room; go left and toward the bedrooms. Grandma and Grandpa's room was on the left; John's old room was just beyond that. He had that cool bookcase with the glass doors that opened down. He also had interesting things to look at—lots of rocks and baseball cards. A very boy's room, I used to think.

Across from his room was the guest room. I had the bed that seemed to be 10 feet off the ground. Boy, was that ever cool! Back down the hall, was there another room? Well, there was the bathroom across from Gram and Gramp's room, and voilà, back to the front door.

I always tried to envision Jo dating an older man; Sharon studying to be a nurse; and Mom running around being the youngest, coming home and admitting to stealing fruit from the neighbor's tree. Then there was the surprise visit from the stork, the ever-so-hip Uncle John. This may not have been Santa Clara, but it was a very homey place indeed.

Over the years at family gatherings, my brother and I have had the opportunity to hear many of the same stories over and over. Each time we hear them, we laugh until we cry. Sometimes a little extra embellishment is added, but usually it's the same old story. Somehow, though, hearing about how Mary Jo and her "four fat friends" broke Judy's new sled still causes us all to double over in laughter.

I often wonder if my niece and nephews have heard some of those stories. I wonder if they know their grandfather was driving a gasoline truck that got hit by a train the day after Christmas. (Thankfully, he wasn't injured.) I wonder if they have heard about the time, when their grandparents were dating, that their grandmother ordered fried chicken but he ordered just coffee. That's all he could afford.

I wonder if they know that their grandfather worked in a factory while attending college after he was married, and that he didn't receive his bachelor's degree until their father was in high school.

Now that you've heard about my reunion experience and have a list of resources to help you plan yours, do it! It's well worth the effort. Just remember to take plenty of photos and add them to your family heritage scrapbook. Including photos of more than one generation will help link future generations to their past.

Family reunions are such a valuable source of family history, and recording that history in a heritage scrapbook creates a valuable keepsake that will last for generations and that will keep memories alive forever. Don't let the good times, or even the difficult times, fade from memory. Create your own family heritage scrapbook, and may your family live eternally.

Appendix A

Online Information

GENEALOGY ORGANIZATIONS

Active family history societies and other organizations can provide you with tools, aids, and information to make your genealogical pursuit easier.

GENEALOGY LINK PAGES

These sites have thousands of links to genealogy information you might need.

Ancestry.com
    www.ancestry.com/

Ellis Island Foundation
    www.ellisisland.org/history.html

Family Search Internet Genealogy Service
    www.familysearch.org

Federation of Genealogical Societies
    www.fgs.org/~fgs/

Finding Your Family Stories
    www.wizard.net/~loiselle/geneol.html

The Genealogy Home Page
    www.genhomepage.com/

Genealogy Online
www.genealogy.org

Helm's Genealogy Tool Box
www.genealogytoolbox.com/

Library of Congress
lcweb.loc.gov/homepage/lchp.html

Links from Cyndi
www.CyndisList.com

National Archives
www.nara.gov/

National Genealogical Society
www.ngsgenealogy.org/

Roots-L Home Page
www.rootsweb.com/roots-l/

Take Me Home, USA
www.takemehomeusa.com

❀ TIME LINES

If you put "time line" and "history" into your favorite Internet search engine, you will see there are several time lines on the Web relating to various areas and subjects.

Age Gauge
web.superb.net/boy/age1.html

Chinese History
www-chaos.umd.edu/history/time_line.html

Christy's Garden of History
(mainly European)
www.smokylake.com/Christy/History.htm

History of Ideas
www.rahul.net/renoir/timeline/

The History Place
historyplace.com/index.html

Irish Timelines
wwwvms.utexas.edu/~jdana/history/timelines.html

sunsite.unc.edu/gaelic/Eire/7.8.2.html

Jewish History
www.nmajh.org/timeline/index.htm

Maryland African American History:
library.advanced.org/10854/time.html

Medieval History (includes family trees):
www.btinternet.com/~timeref/

Russian History
ourworld.compuserve.com/homepages/DouglasHartman/
chronology.htm

JOURNALING INFORMATION

This is an assortment of sites that include tips and articles on journaling for scrapbooks and other memory crafts.

207.158.243.119/html/journals___diaries.html

www.campsark.com/index.html

www.deardiary.net/

www.geocities.com/SoHo/9993/

www.journalkeepers.com/

www.poewar.com/

songfile.snap.com/

www.tapestryintime.com/

www.triggers.com

www.turningmemories.com/

www.turningmemories.com/clinic.htm

www.writingthejourney.com/about/sitemap.htm

❦ GRAPHICS, CLIP ART, AND FONTS

Most of these sites contain free downloadable or printable graphics, clip art, or fonts. Many also have dozens of links to more sites.

www.3dcafe.com/

www.abstractfonts.com/

www.arttoday.com/

www.countryclipart.com/

desktoppublishing.com/fonts-free.html

www.fontaddict.com/

fonts.tom7.com/

fonts.tedesign.net/

www.thefreesite.com/

www.freeyellow.com/members2/sascha/software.html

www.geocities.com/Heartland/Hills/6631/mhgmain.html

www.geocities.com/Heartland/Meadows/7597/cgindex.html

www.geocities.com/Heartland/Plains/4539/graphics.htm

www.graphicgarden.nu/

www.larabiefonts.com/

magnagraphics.com/fonts

members.tripod.com/~jane2bob/

PRESERVING KEEPSAKES

Preserving anything from movie tickets to old home movies to the family slides can be found on the sites listed here. Most sites will include links additional preservation sites.

lcweb.loc.gov/preserv/aware.html

lcweb.loc.gov/preserv/presfaq.html

www.lib.az.us/archives/preserve.htm

palimpsest.stanford.edu/aic/disaster/tentip.html

www.pro.gov.uk/preservation/default.htm

www.seedsofknowledge.com/photos.html

www.unesco.org/webworld/mdm/administ/en/guide/guidetoc.htm

Appendix B

Glossaries

 GENERAL FAMILY HERITAGE SCRAPBOOKING

Words found in this glossary cover the basics of scrapbooking, photography, papers, and tools. You'll need to have a good understanding of these words throughout your family heritage adventures!

Acetate: Acidic plastic that causes photographs and documents to deteriorate and fade.

Acid: Substance that produces hydrogen ions when dissolved in water. Acids have a pH of less than 7.0. Acid is produced in paper when the paper and paper-making chemicals in the paper deteriorate or when acid is absorbed from its environment. Over time, acid breaks the paper fibers down, causing the paper to deteriorate and become brown and brittle.

Acidic: Item contains acid or has a pH level lower than 7.0.

Acid-free: Term describing materials with a pH value of 7.0 or higher. Materials with a pH level of 7.0 are neutral, and those with a pH level greater than 7.0 are alkaline.

Acid migration: Transfer of acid from one acidic material to another less acidic material, either by direct contact or by absorption of acidic gases from the surrounding atmosphere.

Adhesive: Any substance that allows two or more surfaces to adhere to one another.

Alkaline: A term used when something contains alkali or has a pH level of more than 7.0. It is the opposite of *acidic*. In paper products, an alkaline substance is added to the pulp during the manufacturing process, which gives permanence and durability.

Alkaline chemical: Also referred to as *alkali*. Substance that reacts with acid. Alkaline is added to paper pulp at a level sufficient enough to neutralize acids. All buffered paper also has a reserve of alkaline that can react with acids absorbed from the atmosphere or produced by the future degradation of the paper. This makes the paper alkaline (or acid free) and will reduce future deterioration of the paper.

American National Standards Institute, Inc. (ANSI): An organization that publishes industry standards that relate to the quality of goods manufactured in the United States.

Archival: Originally this term meant that a material or product is permanent, durable, or chemically stable and that it can therefore be used safely for preservation purposes. No standards exist that describe how long an "archival" product will last.

Back-printing: Information printed on the back of a picture by the photofinisher that may include negative number, date, or other information.

Buffer: Alkaline substance (usually calcium carbonate) added to the paper to make it acid-free.

Buffered: Term used in the paper industry designating that an alkaline filler has been added during the paper-making process, which makes the paper acid-free. It also increases the smoothness of the paper surface, improves brightness and opacity, and helps prevent ink from feathering.

Calcium carbonate: Primary filler added in the paper-making process that makes paper acid-free.

Card stock: General term for heavier papers commonly used for the covers of catalogs and brochures, and frequently used in scrapbooking. The correct term for heavier-weight paper is *cover stock*.

Chlorophenal red: Chemical that indicates whether the paper is acid-free.

Coated paper: Paper with a finishing layer on one or both sides of the core sheet.

Colorfast: Pigment or dye that is resistant to environmental exposure, such as light, acid, heat, and other atmospheric conditions.

Condensation: Humidity that is trapped and forms a vapor, causing mold, water stains, and deterioration of stored valuables.

Conservation: Care and treatment that attempts to stabilize items such as paper documents, photographs, textiles, or memorabilia through chemical means or by strengthening items physically, which results in sustaining the items' survival for as long as possible in their original form.

Copy negative: A negative made by reproducing a photograph or reproducing artwork.

Cropping: Altering the boundaries of a finished photograph by trimming or masking the photograph. This can also be done using the negative and requesting that only a portion of the scene in the negative be used.

Deacidification: Alkaline-salt process that raises the pH level in paper. It impregnates the paper with a high-alkaline reserve and neutralizes existing acids while preventing the development of future acids.

Die cut: A shape or letter cut from paper with a special die-cutting machine. Accu-Cut and Ellison are best known for their die-cutting machines.

Digital: Process that uses numerical digits to create a uniform picture on a computer.

Digital camera: Camera that creates a photograph in digital form.

Dye: Colored substance (soluble) that is added to ink, paper, and textiles. Generally, dye colors are not permanent enough to be used for fine-art applications where long-term lightfastness is required.

Emulsion: Silver-gelatin image layer of the processed film.

Encapsulation: A safe process for protecting valuable newspaper articles and other paper documents.

Fiber-based paper: Photographic paper used to develop black-and-white photographs. Because of the way it is made, fiber-based paper can have a life expectancy of two hundred years (if taken care of and processed correctly). Formerly, it was the standard type of photographic paper, but today, fiber-based paper is mainly used for fine-art black-and-white prints and is available upon request.

Film: A photographic emulsion coated on a flexible, transparent base that records images or scenes.

Foreground: The area between the camera and the principal subject.

Frame: One individual picture on a roll of film. Also, a tree branch, arch, or other object that frames a subject.

Fugitive dye: A dye that is not permanent. It will fade when exposed to light, run when water is applied, and transfer color to other items.

Hand tinting: Also referred to as *hand coloring*. A process of applying colors with oils or dyes to the surface of a black-and-white photograph, giving it the appearance of a colored photograph.

Interleaving: An acid-free sheet that is placed between pages in a scrapbook when no sheet protector is used. The sheet prevents photos from touching another one, which could result in scratching and damage to the emulsion.

Lamination: Permanent bonding of two layers of plastic film to one or two sides of a flat item. This process is done by applying high heat and pressure (which makes it irreversible) and is not recommended for valuable items.

Lightfast: Material not affected or faded by sunlight, fluorescent tubes, and light bulbs.

Lignin: Substance that gives plants and trees their strength and rigidity and also binds wood fibers together. When wood is broken down to make paper, the lignin becomes unstable. Paper that contains large amounts of lignin, such as newsprint, is very acidic and will turn yellow when exposed to light and humidity.

Lignin-free: To be considered lignin-free, paper can contain a maximum of 1 percent lignin.

Migration: Transfer of chemicals to neighboring materials.

Mylar D: Uncoated, clear, polyester plastic made by Dupont. It is chemically stable and does not release harmful gases. Mylar D is used in sheet protectors and photograph sleeves and is safe for encapsulation.

Negative: The developed film that contains a reversed tone image of the original scene.

Neutral pH: The center reading of 7.0 on the pH scale of 0 to 14. It is neither acidic nor alkaline. For manufacturers, the acceptable pH neutral range is from 6.5 to 7.5.

Nonbleeding: Ink, dye, or paint that does not spread from the original mark on the paper's surface. Nonbleeding depends on both the degree of sizing in the paper and the use of solvents (other than water) in ink.

Nonmigrating: Material and its properties will not transfer or spread to a neighboring item.

pH: Measurement of the degree of acidity and alkalinity. On a scale ranging from 0 to 14, pH 7.0 is neutral, above 7.0 is alkaline (or acid-free), and below 7.0 is acidic.

Permanence: A material's ability to maintain its strength and color over an extended period of time (in some cases, several hundred years) without significant deterioration under normal use and storage conditions.

Permanent: Describes materials that are chemically stable (i.e., not prone to deterioration under normal use and proper storage conditions).

Photo-safe: Any material that is chemically stable.

Plasticizer: Unsafe softening agent added in the manufacturing of plastics to make them flexible.

Polyester: Clear, uncoated, strong plastic used in preservation procedures. Polyester is used in making folders, book jackets, and sheet protectors and used for encapsulation.

Polyethylene: Chemically stable, but naturally slippery plastic with little tendency to cling. It is normally manufactured without antiblock and antislip agents. Polyethylene is used primarily in the manufacturing of photographic sleeves and poly bags.

Polypropylene: Clear and pliable, a stable plastic used in the manufacturing of photographic sleeves.

Polyvinyl acetate (PVA): Plastic with properties that cause photographs and documents to deteriorate and fade.

Polyvinyl chloride (PVC): Unstable plastic, generally called *vinyl* or *Naugahyde,* that may exude oily plasticizers or emit corrosive and acidic hydrogen-chloride gas. It is easily identified by its strong plastic odor. Avoid all sheet protectors, binders, photo enclosures, corners, or any other product made from vinyl with your photographs, negatives, and memorabilia.

Preservation: The act of stabilizing an item from deterioration by using the correct methods.

Retouching: Altering a print or negative after development by use of dyes or pencils to alter tones of highlights, shadows, and other details or to remove blemishes.

Reversible: Preservation process or treatment that can be undone without changing the object to return it to its original state.

Safety film: Film introduced in the 1950s that replaced the volatile cellulose-nitrate film. Called *safety film* because it is made from an acetate base that is not flammable so it will melt but not burn.

Sepia: Brownish color produced on photographs in the photographic process.

Sizing: Coating applied to a surface that increases water resistance, and eliminates abrasiveness and fuzz while improving bonding strength.

Slipcase: Open-ended box that holds a binder. It serves to put your album or photos in dark storage protecting the contents from dust and light.

Solvent: Any substance that dissolves another substance to form or create a solution.

Spotting: Retouching a processed print with a pencil or brush (with watercolors or dyes) to eliminate spots left by dust or scratches on the negative.

Substrate: Surface or medium on which inks may be applied such as paper, canvas, or plastic.

Unbuffered: During the paper-making process, the buffering step is eliminated. If a buffer or alkaline compound is added during the paper-making process, the paper is acid free. When interleaving photographic materials, an unbuffered paper works better. An unbuffered sheet is vulnerable to migrating, and atmospheric acids, and pollutants.

Water-soluble: Substance that dissolves in water.

BASIC GENEALOGY GLOSSARY

These are specific terms used by both professionals and enthusiasts of genealogy. Order and consistency in terms are necessary since genealogy is a global interest. At times it might seem like this is a foreign language, but you'll catch on quickly.

Abstract: A written summary of the main points in a document.

Administrator: The court-appointed person who handles the business of a deceased person's estate or the affairs of an incompetent person (female: *administratrix*).

Agricultural schedule: A separate part of the federal census, listing the farmers, with statistical information about their farms and crops; 1850–1880.

Archives: A repository containing primarily the retired official records of public or private agencies.

Bible records: Vital records written in the family record pages of a Bible.

Burned county: A common term for a courthouse whose records have been lost or destroyed through fire, flood, vermin, or neglect.

Census: The counting or listing of inhabitants of a certain region; done by a *census enumerator* commonly on a federal or state basis.

Church of Jesus Christ of Latter-Day Saints: Commonly known as Mormons; interested in family history because of their religious beliefs.

Collateral relatives: People who share an ancestor but do not descend from one another.

Compiled service record: Military records that have been abstracted from various original documents, into one record, and filed alphabetically by the soldier's name.

Compiled source: Information abstracted from various original documents into one record; secondary source.

Conflicting information: Data that come from different sources but do not agree; must be evaluated.

Emigration: The act of moving from one country to another.

Enumeration order: The sequence in which census entries were recorded; house to house.

Estate: The property held by a person at the time of his or her death.

Evidence: Facts that indicate whether something is true; proof.

Executor: The person who is named in a will to handle the affairs of an estate after the death of the deviser (female: *executrix*).

Extract: To copy a record, or portions of a record, verbatim from a body of records.

Family group record: page (often a preprinted form) listing a family unit: father, mother and children of that union, with the dates and places of birth, death, and burial given for each individual, in addition to other information and source documentation.

Family history: The study of the genealogy of one's family with emphasis on accumulating information on the events and circumstances of their lives, rather than mere dates, places, and lineage.

Family History Center: A genealogy library operated by the LDS Church (Mormons), where any visitor can access the extensive records amassed by the LDS Family History Library in Salt Lake City, Utah.

Family History Library: The repository of the largest collection of genealogical materials in the world; operated by the LDS Church, located in Salt Lake City, Utah. Open to the public, it distributes copies of microfilmed records to Family History Centers.

Family Tree Maker: A widely used genealogy computer program from Broderbund.

Genealogical society: An organization of people associated because of their common interest in the genealogy of the families in an area (county, state, country) or an ethnic or a family group.

Head of household: The term used for the person whose name appears first in the census enumeration of a family or group of people living together; before 1850, the only peoples' names who appear in the census enumeration.

Heirloom: An object passed down, generally within the family, from generation to generation, often of worth only due to sentimental value.

Heir: A person designated by a will or by the court to receive the property of the deceased.

Historical society: An organization of people associated because of their common interest in the history of an area (county, state, country).

Immigration: The act of moving into one country from another.

Industry schedule: The additional part of the federal census detailing the business activities of those enumerated within each county; also called *Products of Industry*.

Interlibrary loan: One library borrowing, for a patron's use, books from another library system. Genealogical books are often not available through interlibrary loan.

Intestate: Without a will or a person who dies without a will.

Inventory: A list of the property held by a person at the time of his death; usually compiled by several court-appointed people, who submit the list to the court for approval.

In-law: Person related by marriage or by another legal tie.

LDS: Church of Jesus Christ of Latter-Day Saints; Mormon.

Legal notice: An advertisement in a newspaper fulfilling the requirements of the law for notification of other interested parties or the public.

Library of Congress: A repository located in Washington, D.C., originally created to serve the needs of Congress, now open to the public.

Local history: The events of the past that impact a certain area; often includes family histories.

Loose papers: The original legal documents (decrees, inventories, depositions, receipts, claims, petitions, etc.) usually gathered into packets as they relate to one person or action and filed at a courthouse.

Maiden name: The surname a woman is given at birth.

Manuscript collection: An assortment of unpublished related papers, letters, or documents held by a library or archives and usually unindexed.

Microfiche: Cards made of photographic material containing reduced images of printed material; used with a special reader that illuminates and enlarges the images.

Microfilm: Rolls of photographic material containing reduced images of printed material; used with a special microfilm reader that illuminates and enlarges the images and allows the spool of microfilm to be rolled forward and rewound onto the spool.

Militia: Organized armed forces of an area subject to a call to arms in an emergency.

Mortality Schedule: An additional part of the federal census detailing the deaths in each family within the preceding twelve-month period.

NATF–80 Form: A form used when submitting a request for military, military pension, or bounty land records from the National Archives.

National Archives: The repository for documents relating to the history and people of the United States.

Negative research: A search of a source that yields no information yet reveals information of a sort by the very fact that nothing was found. It gains importance from the knowledge that the source will not have to be searched again for the same reason.

Obituary: An announcement of a person's death, giving details that may include information about the deceased's origins, biographical data, survivors, religion, and burial information; usually both a primary and secondary source.

Pension: A stipend provided to an elderly or disabled military veteran or to his/her widow or children, upon proof of military service.

Periodical: A publication produced at regular intervals, such as quarterly or monthly.

Personal Ancestral File (PAF): A widely used genealogy computer program; available from the LDS Church.

Personal property: Possessions held by a person, which may include livestock, gold watches, carriages, and slaves; as opposed to *real property,* which refers to land.

Plantation account: Records kept pertaining to the business activities of a plantation, either narrative or tabular; often included vital statistics of slaves.

Population Schedule: The main part of the federal census, listing the inhabitants (the free inhabitants, before 1870) of an area, with varying degrees of other personal data.

Primary source: A record containing information recorded at or about the time of the event, as opposed to compiled or secondary information. Primary sources are generally more reliable than secondary sources.

Query: An advertisement of sorts, requesting an exchange of data with readers who are interested in the history of the same family.

Research calendar: A list of sources searched showing surnames sought and results.

Reunion: An organized gathering of people descended from a common ancestor, bearing the same surname or bound together by some common tie.

SASE: Self-addressed stamped envelope; an envelope provided to another person or correspondent by a researcher, already addressed back to that researcher and stamped with first-class postage, for the convenience of the correspondent.

Secondary source: A record containing information compiled long after the events discussed; generally not as reliable as a *primary source*.

Slave: Usually a black, mulatto, or mixed-race person, bought and sold as property, kept in servitude with no individual rights.

Slave Schedule: An additional part of the federal census (1850 and 1860), listing the slave owner's name, with a tally, by age, sex, and color, of the slaves owned by that person; no names of slaves are given.

Source citation: A note, footnote or endnote stating where the information given was derived.

Surname: Last name; usually the same as the surname of the father.

Tax record: A list of people liable to pay taxes in a given area, with a list of their property, real and/or personal; usually compiled annually on a county level.

Topographic map: A map showing the physical contours of a region of land; landmarks, churches, schools, roads, and cemeteries are sometimes shown.

Widow's pension: The monthly or annual stipend received by a woman due to her husband's qualifying service or employment; often refers to a military pension.

Will: A legal instrument directing the disposition of a person's estate, the handling of a person's affairs, and the appointment of an executor for the estate and/or a guardian for dependents after a person's death.

Witness: A person who signs his or her name to (or makes his or her mark on) a document, attesting to the correctness of the statements or information in the document or that the principal's signature is genuine.

Appendix C

Organizations and Societies

 ### THE NATIONAL ARCHIVES

The National Archives includes information and data on Freedman's Savings and Trust Company, African American genealogical research, immigration records, naturalization records, passport applications, post office records, and Social Security records. The Web site also includes helpful general genealogical information, including the regional centers.

National Archives and Records Administration
Seventh and Pennsylvania Avenues, NW
Washington, D.C. 20408
Telephone: (301) 713-6800
www.nara.gov/genealogy/

 ### LDS FAMILY HISTORY LIBRARY

The Family History Library was founded by the Genealogical Society of Utah in 1894, and it now houses the largest collection of genealogical material in the world. The society is dedicated to acquiring and preserving copies of the records of mankind. The Church of Jesus Christ of Latter-Day Saints (LDS) has financed the society's methodical work.

Salt Lake City Family History Library
35 N.W. Temple, SLC, UT 84103
Information phone number: (801) 240-2331
Hours: Mon. 7:30–6 P.M., Tues.–Sat. 7:30–10 P.M.; closed Sun.
Web site: www.lds.org

SPECIALTY ORGANIZATIONS

The following organizations focus on a particular aspect of genealogy or preservation.

Association for Gravestone Studies
278 Main Street, Suite 207
Greenfield, MA 01301
Phone: (413) 772-0836

Association of Moving Image Archivists
c/o National Center for Film and Video Preservation
PO Box 27999
2021 N. Western Avenue
Los Angeles, CA 90027

FAIC Conservation Services Referral System
1717 K Street NW, Suite 301
Washington, D.C. 20006
Phone: (202) 452-9545
Fax: (202) 452-9328

Library of Congress
Motion Picture Broadcasting and Recorded Sound Division
Washington, D.C. 20540-4500
National Archives and Records Administration

Motion Picture Sound and Video Branch
8601 Adelphi Road
College Park, MD 20740-6001

National Media Lab
PO Box 33015
St. Paul, MN 55133-3015

Oral History Association
Dickinson College
P.O. Box 1773
Carlisle, PA 17013
Phone: (717) 245-1036
Fax: (717) 245-1046

Scrapbooking for Parents of Special Needs Children
Linda Magnuson, Publisher
304 S. Lake Land Drive
League City, TX 77573

 # CULTURAL AND ETHNIC ORGANIZATIONS

The following groups are broken into cultural and ethnical backgrounds.

African

African-American Genealogy Group
PO Box 1798
Philadelphia, PA 19105-1798

African-American Family History Association
PO Box 115268
Atlanta, GA 30310
Phone: (404) 344-7405
Publication: *AAFHA Newsletter*

Afro-American Historical and Genealogical Society
PO Box 73086
Washington, D.C. 20056

Schomburg Center for Research in Black Culture
515 Malcolm X Blvd.
New York, NY 10037-1801

Australian

Australian National University Historical Society
PO Box 112
Canberra, 2600

Federation of Australian Historical Societies
PO Box 40
Civic Square, Canberra, 2608

Library of Australian History
PO Box 795
North Sydney, 2059

Royal Australian Historical Society
133 Macquarie Street
Sydney, 2000

British

Genealogical Institute
PO Box 22045
Salt Lake City, UT 84122

International Society for British Genealogy and Family History
PO Box 3115
Salt Lake City, UT 84110–3115

Canadian

Alberta Genealogical Society
10440 100 8th Avenue, Room 116
Edmonton, Alberta T5H 3Z9

National Archives of Canada
395 Wellington Street
Ottawa, Ontario K1A 0N3
General information: (613) 995-5138

Ontario Genealogical Society
40 Orchard View Boulevard, Suite 102
Toronto, Ontario M4R 1B9

Chinese

China Institute in America
125 E. 65th Street
New York, NY 10021

Chinese Culture Foundation of San Francisco
750 Kearny Street, Third Floor
San Francisco, CA 94108

Chinese Historical and Cultural Project
PO Box 70746
Sunnyvale, CA 94086-0746

Chinese Historical Society of America (CHSS)
650 Commercial Street
San Francisco, CA 94111

Cuban

Cuban Genealogical Society
PO Box 2650
Salt Lake City, UT 82110-2650

Dutch

Dutch Family Heritage Society
2463 Ledgewood Drive
West Jordan, UT 84084

Holland Society of New York
122 E. 58th Street
New York, NY 10022

Joint Archives of Holland
Hope College Campus
Holland, MI 49423

French

American-French Genealogical Society
78 Earle Street
Woonsocket, RI 02895

American-French Genealogical Society
PO Box 2113
Pawtucket, RI 02861-0113

French-Canadian Heritage Society, Detroit Chapter
1056 Balfour Road
Grosse Point, MI 48230

La Société de Cajuns
108 E. 155th Street
Galliano, LA 70354

German

German-American Family Society
3871 Ranfield Road
Brimfield, OH 44240

German Genealogical Digest
PO Box 700
Pleasant Grove, UT 84062

German Genealogical Society of America
2125 Wright Avenue, Suite C9
Laverne, CA 91750

German Research Association
PO Box 711600
San Diego, CA 92171-1600

Mid-Atlantic Germanic Society
PO Box 2642
Kensington, MD 20891-2642

Hungarian

American Hungarian Library and Historical Society
215 E. 82nd Street
New York, NY 10028

Irish

American Irish Historical Society Library
991 Fifth Avenue and 80th Street
New York, NY 10028

Irish Ancestral Research Association
PO Box 619
Sudbury, MA 01776

Irish Families
PO Box 7575
Kansas City, MO 64116

Italian

Italian Genealogical Group
7 Grayon Drive
Dix Hills, New York 11746

POINT—Pursuing Our Italian Names Together
PO Box 2977
Palos Verdes, CA 90374

Italian Genealogical Society of America, Inc.
PO Box 8571
Cranston, RI 02920-8571

National Italian American Foundation
666 11th Street, NW, Suite 800
Washington, D.C. 20077-0380

Japanese

Japanese American Resource Center and Museum
535 N. Fifth Street
San Jose, CA 95112

Latin Countries

Institute of Genealogy and History for Latin America
316 W. 500 N.
St. George, UT 84770

Native American

Am-Toola Publications
East 4516 Sixth Avenue
Spokane, WA 99212

Histree
PO Box 5982
Yuma, AZ 85366-5982

American Indian Culture Research Center
PO Box 98
Marvin, SD 57251-0098
Phone: (605) 398-9200
Fax: (605) 398-9201

Norwegian

Norwegian-American Historical Association
Saint Olaf College
Rolvaag Memorial Library
1510 Saint Olaf Avenue
Northfield, MN 55057-1097

Norwegian Genealogical Group
1046 19th Avenue, SE
Minneapolis, MN 55414

Vesterheim Genealogical Center and Naeseth Library
415 W. Main Street
Madison, WI 53703-3116

Mexican

Chicano Research Collection
Department of Archives and Manuscripts
Hayden Library, Arizona State University
Box 871006
Tempe, AZ 85287-1006

Hispanic History and Ancestry Research
9511 Rockpoint Drive
Huntington Beach, CA 92646

Los Fundadores and Friends of Santa Clara County, California
1509 Warburton Avenue
Santa Clara, CA 95050

Polish

Polish Genealogical Society
984 Milwaukee Avenue
Chicago, IL 60622

Polish Historical Society
4291 Stanton Avenue
Pittsburgh, PA 15201

Russian

American Russian History Society
1272 47th Avenue
San Francisco, CA 94107

Russian Historical and Genealogical Society
971 First Avenue
New York, NY 10022

Spanish

Saint Augustine Historical Society
271 Charlotte Street
St. Augustine, FL 32084

Spanish American Genealogical Association
PO Box 5407
Corpus Christi, TX 78405

Swedish

American Swedish Institute
2600 Park Avenue
Minneapolis, MN 55407

Scandinavian-American Genealogical Society
PO Box 16069
1650 Carroll Avenue
Saint Paul, MN 55116-0069.

Swedish American Genealogist
PO Box 2186
Winter Park, FL 32790

Royal Swedish Embassy
Watergate 600
600 New Hampshire Avenue NW
Washington, D.C. 20037

 # RELIGIONS AND CHURCHES

So much of our family history may be documented through the family religion or faith. Many churches keep very good records of members. The following list is of the main branch or headquarters of specific religions. This is only a sampling of what is available. You may need to research your family's specific branch of a church for more help.

Anglican Church of Canada
General Synod Archives
600 Jarvis Street
Toronto, Ontario M4Y 2J6
Canada

Church of England Historical Society
G.PO Box 2902
Sydney, New South Wales 2001
Australia

Orthodox Church in America
6850 N. Hempstead
Syosset, NY 11791

Altoona Johnston Diocese
126 Logan Boulevard
Hollidaysburg, PA 16648

American Jewish Archives
3101 Clifton Avenue
Cincinnati, OH 45220

American Jewish Historical Society
2 Thornton Road
Waltham, MA 02154

Association of Jewish Genealogical Societies
PO Box 50245
Palo Alto, CA 94303

Central Archives for the History of the Jewish People
Sprinzak Bldg., Hebrew University
PO Box 1149
91010 Jerusalem
Israel

American Lutheran Church Archives
333 Wartburg Place
Dubuque, IA 52003

Evangelical Lutheran Church in America
8765 W. Higgins Road (mailing address)
Chicago, IL 60631-4198

Archives and History Center of the United Methodist Church
Methodist Historical Society
36 Madison Avenue
Drew University
PO Box 127
Madison, NJ 07940

United Methodist Historical Center
c/o Saint George Church
235 N. 4th Street
Philadelphia, PA 19106

Family History Library
Church of Jesus Christ of Latter-Day Saints
35 N.W. Temple Street
Salt Lake City, UT 84150

Mormon Historical Association
PO Box 7010
323 KMB
Brigham Young University
Provo, UT 84602-4446

Presbyterian Historical Society
425 Lombard Street
Philadelphia, PA 19147-1516

American Catholic Historical Society
PO Box 84
Philadelphia, PA 19106

Appendix D

Supplies and Resources

 ## RECOMMENDED SUPPLIERS

Bill and I combined have worked more than thirty years in the craft and creative industries. We take very seriously the word *recommended*. This listing is not complete by a long shot! There are hundreds and hundreds of suppliers of just about every material and tool imaginable to the family heritage scrapbooker. We did our best to give a broad spectrum of suppliers and regret having to leave even one great company out of this listing. You should be able to find additional supplies online, through magazine advertisements and articles, and on the Thomas Register available at most public library reference desks or at www.thomasregister.com/.

Suppliers for a variety of materials and tools used in heritage scrapbooking can be found in this listing. An asterisk (★) has been placed by companies that have supplied products for this book. Some of the companies listed may refer you to a local dealer in your area for the actual purchase of a supply. Most companies do have Web sites and great customer relations departments for answering specific product questions. In some cases a supplier may have more than one product line; this list will include a [bracketed] listing if this is the case.

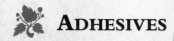 ## ADHESIVES

3L Corp.★ [page protectors, memorabilia pockets, photo corners]
685 Chaddick Drive
Wheeling, IL 60090-0247

Beacon Adhesives/Signature Crafts
125 MacQuesten Pkwy S.
Mount Vernon, NJ 10550

Delta Technical Coatings
2550 Pellissier Place
Whittier, CA 90601

Pres-On Merchandising Corp
1020 S. Westgate Drive
Addison, IL 60101

Sailor Corporation of America
121 Bethea Road, Suite 307
Fayetteville, GA 30214

Therm O Web
770 Glenn Avenue
Wheeling, IL 60090

❈ ALBUMS AND PAGE PROTECTORS

Archival Products
PO Box 1413
Des Moines, IA 50305-1413

Avery Dennison★
50 Pointe Drive
Brea, CA 92821

Century Plastics
PO Box 2393
Brea, CA 92822-2393

Conservation Materials, Ltd.
240 Freeport Blvd.
Sparks, NV 89432

Conservation Resources International, Inc.
8000-H Forbes Place
Springfield, VA 22151

DMD Industries, Inc.★ [albums, journals, diaries, cards, bookmarks,
    die-cuts, and papers]
1205 ESI Drive
Springdale, AR 72764

Get Smart Products
PO Box 522
Manhasset, NY 11030

Pioneer Photo Albums, Inc.★
PO Box 2497
Chatsworth, CA 91313-2497

Webway Photograph Albums
c/o Antioch Publishing
PO Box 28
888 Dayton Street
Yellow Springs, OH 45387

The Preservation Emporium
2707 N. Stemmons Freeway
Dallas, TX 75207

❧ TOOLS

Accent Design
3690 W. 1st Avenue
Eugene, OR 97402

Archival Products
2134 E. Grand
PO Box 14
Des Moines, IA 50305

Crafty Cutter
179 Niblick Road, Suite 334
Paso Robles, CA 93446

Cut It Out
4543 Orange Grove Avenue
Sacramento, CA 95841

Dover Publications
31 E. 2nd Street
Mineola, NY 11501

Family Treasures
24922 Anza Drive
Valencia, CA 91355

Fiskars Inc.★ [adhesives, stamps, decorative-edge scissors, corner and
    paper punches, and markers]
7811 W Stewart Avenue
Wausau, WI 54401

Grafix
19499 Miles Road
Cleveland, OH 44128

Janlynn Corp.
34 Front Street
Indian Orchard, MA 01151-5848

Jason Imprinting Systems
108 Friendship Road
Clanton, AL 35045

Lasting Impressions for Paper Inc.★ [brass templates]
585 W. 2600 S., Suite A
Bountiful, UT 84010

Lighthouse Memories★
PO Box 187
Bloomington, CA 92316

🌿 PAPER

Carriage House Paper
79 Guernsey Street
Brooklyn, NY 11222

Colorbok Paper Products
2716 Baker Road
Dexter, MI 48130

COSCA Studio and Paper Mill
Route 4 Box 279
Ellensburg, WA 98926

Daniel Smith, Inc.
4150 First Avenue South
PO Box 84268
Seattle, WA 98124-5568

Dieu Donne Pepermill, Inc.
433 Broome Street
New York, NY 10012

Hot off the Press★ (All papers used in the heritage page designs were
    from Hot off the Press unless otherwise stated.)
1250 NW Third, Dept. B
Canby, OR 97013

The Japanese Paper Place
887 Queen Street West
Toronto, Ontario
Canada M6J 1G5

Oblation Earthworks
6503 SW Luana Beach Drive
Vashon Island, WA 98070

Paper Adventures★ (sparkle papers)
PO Box 04393
Milwaukee, WI 53204

Paper Journey
450 Raritan Center Parkway
Edison, NJ 08837
Phone: (800) 827-2737

Paper Peddlers
P.O. Box 57697
Jacksonville, FL 32241-7697

PaperDirect, Inc.
205 Chubb Avenue
Lyndhurst, NJ 07071

800 A PAPERS
PaperSource, Ltd.
1506 W 12th Street
Los Angeles, CA 90015
(213) 387-5820

Patersen-Arne★ (colored vellums)
3690 W. First Avenue
Eugene, OR 97402
Phone: (541) 485-1406

The Paper Source
232 W. Chicago Avenue
Chicago, IL 60610

Pinestreet Papery
42 1/2 Caledonia Street
Sausalito, CA 94965

Pixie Press★
2950 E Flamingo, Suite K
Las Vegas, NV 89121

Planet Paper
716 Thornwood Drive
Odenton, MD 21113-1565

Royal Stationery
2080 Lookout Drive; PO Box 8240
North Mankato, MN 56003

Strathmore Paper
39 S. Broad Street
Westfield, MA 01085

Twinrocker Handmade Paper
PO Box 413
Brookstone, IN 47923

❧ PENS, MARKERS, STAMPING, INKS, AND JOURNALING MATERIALS

Chatterbox Inc.
252 Main Street
Star, ID 83669

Clearsnap★
PO Box 98
Anacortes, WA 98221
www.clearsnap.com

EK Success★
PO Box 1141
Clifton, NJ 07014

Embossing Arts Co.
PO Box 439
Tangent, OR 97389

Hampton Art Stamps
19 Industrial Blvd.
Medford, NY 11763

Hero Arts Rubber Stamps Inc.
1343 Powell Street
Emeryville, CA 94608

The Pencil Grip
PO Box 67096
Los Angeles, CA 90067

Personal Stamp Exchange
360 Sutton Place
Santa Rosa, CA 95407

Ranger Ink★
15 Park Road
Tinton Falls, NJ 07724

Rembrandt: Ultra Pro
6049 Slauson Avenue
Los Angeles, CA 90040

Rubber Stampede
967 Stanford Avenue
Oakland, CA 94608

Sakura of America
30780 San Clemente Street
Hayward, CA 94544

Sheaffer Pen
1506 Providence Highway, Suite 29
Norwood, MA 02062

Speedball Art Products Co.
PO Box 5157
Statesville, NC 28687

Staedtler, Inc.★
21900 Plummer Street
Chatsworth, CA 91311

Stampendous, Inc.
1240 N. Red Gum
Anaheim, CA 92806

Stewart Superior Corp.
2050 Farallon Drive
San Leandro, CA 94577

Tsukineko Inc.
15411 NE 95th Street
Redmond, WA 98052

Uchida of America Corp.
3535 Del Amo Blvd.
Torrance, CA 90503

Yasutomo
490 Eccles Avenue
So. San Francisco, CA 94080

Zebra Pen Corp.★
105 Northfield Avenue
Edison, NJ 08837

Paper Punches, Stickers, and Die Cuts

Accu/Cut Systems
1035 E. Dodge Street
Fremont, NE 68025

Christy's Crafts★
PO Box 492
Hinsdale, IL 60521
Phone: (630) 323-6505

Design Originals
225 Cullen Street
Fort Worth, TX 76107

Ellison Craft & Design
25862 Commercentre Drive
Lake Forest, CA 92630
Phone: (800) 253-2238

McGill Punches★ (All paper punches used in heritage page designs were
    from McGill, including slotted corner punches.)
131 E. Prairie Street
Marengo, IL 60151
Phone: (800) 922-9884

Mrs. Grossman's
3810 Cypress Drive
Petaluma, CA 94954

Provo Craft★
285 E. 900 South
Provo, UT 84601

Sanford
2711 Washington Blvd.
Bellwood, IL 60104

Seitec: Cache Junction★
1717 S. 450 W.
Logan, UT 84321

Stickopotamus, Inc.
PO Box 86
Carlstadt, NJ 07072-0086

✿ PHOTOGRAPHY AND COLORING BLACK-AND-WHITE PHOTO TOOLS

Craf-T Products★
PO Box 83
Fairmont, MN 56031
Phone: (507) 235-3996
www.craf-tproducts.com

Christmas Ornaments and Snow Globes
Kelly's Crafts
4350 Wade Mill Road
Fairfield, OH 45014
Phone: (513) 738-5364, ext. 207

Kodak
4 Concourse Parkway, #300
Atlanta, GA 30328

Marshall Photo Coloring Division of Brandess
701 Corporate Woods Parkway
Vernon Hills, IL 60061

SpotPen, Inc.★ (acid-free chalks for coloring)
140 E. Madrid, Suite A
Las Cruces, NM 88004
Phone: (505) 523-8822

GENEALOGY, VIRTUAL SCRAPBOOKING, AND OTHER COMPUTER SOFTWARE

Claudia's Clip Art
435 S. 300 E.
Salt Lake City, UT 84111

Dogbyte Development★
66 W. 88th Street, #3E,
New York, NY 10024

Family Tree Maker★
PO Box 7865
Fremont, CA 94537
Phone: (800) 223-6985

L N S Software Solutions LLC
25825 104th Ave. SE, PMB 321
Kent, WA 98031

 ## SPECIALTY SUPPLIERS

Color Wheels

The Color Wheel Company★
521 N. 19th Street, Unit B
Philomath, OR 97370
Phone: (541) 929-7526

Templates and Rulers

C-Thru Ruler Co.
6 Britton Drive
Bloomfield, CT 06002

Environmental Lighting Concepts★ (full-spectrum lighting)
3923 Coconut Palm Drive
Tampa, FL 33619

Unique Writing Tool
Nu Century★
955 Foothill Drive
Providence, UT 84332

Archival Mist (removes acid from paper)

Preservation Technologies★
111 Thomson Park Drive
Cranberry Township, PA 16066

un-du (removes photos in old magnetic albums)

Un-du/Doumar Products Inc.★
12784 Perimeter Drive, Suite B-100
Dallas, TX 75228

Adding Human Voice to Any Heritage Project

Voice Express★
42 Oak Avenue
Tuckahoe, NY 10707

STORAGE AND ORGANIZATIONAL TOOLS

Crop-In-Style/Platte Productions★
9660 Cozycroft Avenue
Chatsworth, CA 91311
Fort Atkinson, WI 53538

Hopper Cropper★
Leeco Industries Inc.
8855 Cypress Woods Drive
Olive Branch, MS 38654

Preserve, Inc.
PO Box 28, Old Chelsea Station
New York, NY 10011-0028

Appendix E

Helpful Documents and Forms

 ## LETTER TO REQUEST INFORMATION FOR PEDIGREE CHART

Include the Pedigree Chart (next page) with the following cover letter:

[Date]

[Your name]
[Your street address]
[Your city, state, and zip code]

[Name of contact]
[Street address of contact]
[City, state, and zip code of contact]

Dear _____:

I am gathering information and need your help to create a family heritage scrapbook. I've enclosed a "family tree" chart filled in with information I already know about our family. Please take a look at it and fill in any information you might now about names, dates, or places. I'd love to hear any family stories or traditions you might be able to share so I can include the information in the scrapbook.

I've enclosed a self-addressed, stamped envelope to make responding easier. Please take your time and return this at your convenience—I can't wait to hear from you. I will be happy to share any of the information I've gathered with you.

I appreciate your time and help.

Sincerely,
[Your name]

❋ PEDIGREE CHART

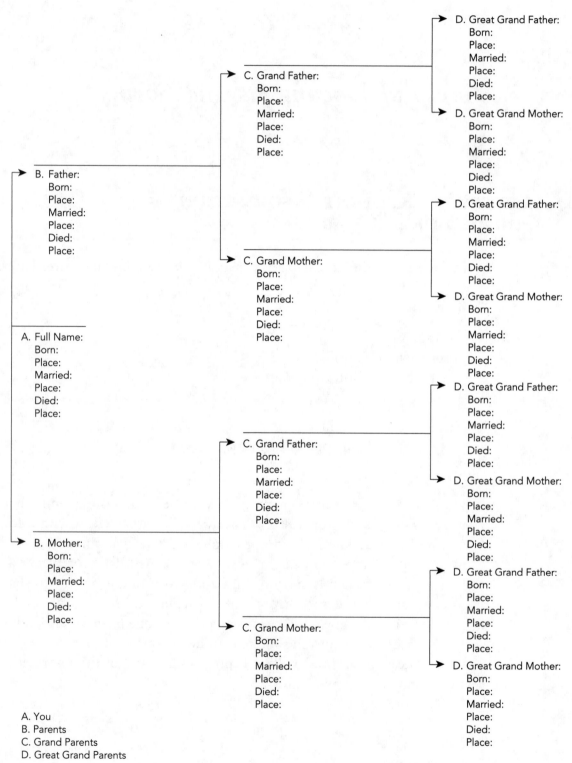

A. You
B. Parents
C. Grand Parents
D. Great Grand Parents

FAMILY GROUP RECORD

FAMILY GROUP RECORD OF _____

HUSBAND'S NAME

Born (date):   Place:

Married (date):   Place:

Died (date):   Place:

Father's name: Mother's name:

WIFE'S NAME:

Born (date):   Place:

Married (date):   Place:

Died (date):   Place:

Father's name: Mother's name:

CHILDREN (in order of birth):

❶ Name: Sex: Spouse:

Born (date):   Place:

Married (date):   Place:

Died (date):   Place:

❷ Name: Sex: Spouse:

Born (date):   Place:

Married (date):   Place:

Died (date):   Place:

❸ Name: Sex: Spouse:

Born (date):   Place:

Married (date):   Place:

Died (date):   Place:

❹ Name: Sex: Spouse:

Born (date):   Place:

Married (date):   Place:

Died (date):   Place:

❺ Name: Sex: Spouse:

Born (date):   Place:

Married (date):   Place:

Died (date):   Place:

Other marriages of husband or wife:

Children:

Documentation:

RECORD OF DOCUMENTS

Family Member: _____

Family Group: _____

Resources Checklist

VITAL RECORDS

Birth: _____

Marriage: _____

Death: _____

CENSUS RECORDS (COPIES)

1790 _____

1800 _____

1810 _____

1820 _____

1830 _____

1840 _____

1850 _____

1860 _____

1870 _____

1880 _____

1880 (soundex) _____

1890 _____

1900 _____

1900 (soundex) _____

1910 _____

1920 _____

1930 _____

GOVERNMENT RECORDS

_____

_____

_____

_____

_____

CHURCH RECORDS

_____

_____

_____

_____

_____

CORRESPONDENCE RECORDS

_____

_____

_____

_____

BOOKS OR OTHER PRINT SOURCES

_____

_____

_____

_____

_____

Husband's name: _____

Wife's maiden name: _____

Other Documentation

Bible _____

Passenger lists _____

Immigration _____

Naturalization _____

School _____

Orphanage _____

Voting records _____

Tax lists _____

Court records _____

Military records _____

Pension records _____

Land records _____

Deeds & abstracts _____

Divorce _____

Newspaper clippings _____

Mortuary _____

Cemetery _____

Gravestones _____

Obituary _____

County histories _____

Occupational _____

Societies _____

Job awards _____

Associations _____

Drivers license _____

Wills _____

Guardianships _____

Written Interviews

_____

_____

_____

_____

_____

Oral Interviews

_____

_____

_____

_____

Family Comments or Traditions

_____

_____

_____

_____

_____

_____

_____

_____

_____

_____

_____

_____

_____

_____

_____

_____

_____

_____

_____

RESEARCH LOG

Family Member Researched:

Query/questions to answer:

Date of search	Contact/ source	Description of source (author, title, year, pages)	Results/ comments	Document number/code

❧ CORRESPONDENCE LOG

Family group or surname: _____

Date	Contact	Query	Reply date	Results

HEIRLOOMS LOG

Heirloom: *Original owner:*   *Current owner:*   *Will be given to:*

🍂 MAIDEN NAMES LOG

County: _____ State: _____ Date Search: _____

Surname	Maiden Name	Given Name	Family Group

GENEALOGICAL RESEARCH LIBRARY

The chart below shows relationships formed from common ancestors. Box 1 (on the horizontal scale and the vertical scale) is the Common Ancestor box. To find relationships to common ancestors, use the chart. For example, if you want to find the relationship between a son and a great grandson of that common ancestor, you go to box 2 on the horizontal scale (son) and find the meeting point of box 4 on the vertical scale (great grandson). The relationship of the great grandson to the son would be grand nephew.

	1	2	3	4	5	6	7	8	9	10
1	Common Ancestor	Son or Daughter	Grandson or Daughter	Great Grandson or Daughter	2nd Great Grandson or Daughter	3rd Great Grandson or Daughter	4th Great Grandson or Daughter	5th Great Grandson or Daughter	6th Great Grandson or Daughter	7th Great Grandson or Daughter
2	Son or Daughter	**Siblings (Brother or Sister)**	Nephew or Niece	Grand Nephew or Niece	Great Grand Nephew or Niece	2nd Great Grand Nephew or Niece	3rd Great Grand Nephew or Niece	4th Great Grand Nephew or Niece	5th Great Grand Nephew or Niece	6th Great Grand Nephew or Niece
3	Grandson or Daughter	Nephew or Niece	**First Cousin**	First Cousin Once Removed	First Cousin Twice Removed	First Cousin Three Times Removed	First Cousin Four Times Removed	First Cousin Five Times Removed	First Cousin Six Times Removed	First Cousin Seven Times Removed
4	Great Grandson or Daughter	Grand Nephew or Neice	First Cousin Once Removed	**Second Cousin**	Second Cousin Once Removed	Second Cousin Twice Removed	Second Cousin Three Times Removed	Second Cousin Four Times Removed	Second Cousin Five Times Removed	Second Cousin Six Times Removed
5	2nd Great Grandson or Daughter	Great Grand Nephew or Neice	First Cousin Twice Removed	Second Cousin Once Removed	**Third Cousin**	Third Cousin Once Removed	Third Cousin Twice Removed	Third Cousin Three Times Removed	Third Cousin Four Times Removed	Third Cousin Five Times Removed
6	3rd Great Grandson or Daughter	2nd Great Grand Nephew or Neice	First Cousin Three Times Removed	Second Cousin Twice Removed	Third Cousin Once Removed	**Fourth Cousin**	Fourth Cousin Once Removed	Fourth Cousin Twice Removed	Fourth Cousin Three Times Removed	Fourth Cousin Four Times Removed
7	4th Great Grandson or Daughter	3rd Great Grand Nephew or Neice	First Cousin Four Times Removed	Second Cousin Three Times Removed	Third Cousin Twice Removed	Fourth Cousin Once Removed	**Fifth Cousin**	Fifth Cousin Once Removed	Fifth Cousin Twice Removed	Fifth Cousin Three Times Removed
8	5th Great Grandson or Daughter	4th Great Grand Nephew or Neice	First Cousin Five Times Removed	Second Cousin Four Times Removed	Third Cousin Three Times Removed	Fourth Cousin Twice Removed	Fifth Cousin Once Removed	**Sixth Cousin**	Sixth Cousin Once Removed	Sixth Cousin Twice Removed
9	6th Great Grandson or Daughter	5th Great Grand Nephew or Neice	First Cousin Six Times Removed	Second Cousin Five Times Removed	Third Cousin Four Times Removed	Fourth Cousin Three Times Removed	Fifth Cousin Twice Removed	Sixth Cousin Once Removed	**Seventh Cousin**	Seventh Cousin Once Removed
10	7th Great Grandson or Daughter	6th Great Grand Nephew or Neice	First Cousin Seven Times Removed	Second Cousin Six Times Removed	Third Cousin Five Times Removed	Fourth Cousin Four Times Removed	Fifth Cousin Three Times Removed	Sixth Cousin Twice Removed	Seventh Cousin Once Removed	**Eighth Cousin**

SAMPLE LETTER REQUESTING DOCUMENTATION

[Date]

[Your name]
[Your street address]
[Your city, state, and zip code]

[Name of institution]
[Street address of institution]
[City, state, and zip code of institution]

Dear Sir or Madam:

I am currently researching my family history and would like to request copies of [document you're requesting]. If you aren't the correct contact, please direct me to the appropriate person.

I have enclosed a self-addressed, stamped envelope for your use, and will reimburse you for any research or copy expenses.

I appreciate your help.

Sincerely,
[Your name]

Index

A

Acid-free paper, 10, 176
Acts of nature, 98
Adhesives
    choosing, 238
    damage, 185–187
    types, 129
AIC. *See* American Institute for
    Conservation of Historic
    and Artistic Works
Albums. *See also* Scrapbooks
    flex hinge, 181–182
    page protectors, 185
    pages, 179
    post style, 182–183
    selecting, 177
    sizes, 177–178
    spirals, 180–181
    three-ring, 178–179
Ambrotype, 130
American Institute for Conserva-
    tion of Historic and Artistic
    Works, 98
Ancestral file, 89–90
Archer, Frederick Scott, 130
Archival, definition, 10
Archival mists, 100
Archives, 10
Artifact tracker, 24

B

Bigamy, 42
Binders. *See* Albums
Bonsib, Sandy, 268–269
Books
    clip art, 198–199
    lettering, 198
    preservation, 111–112

C

Cabinet cards, 131
Calendars, 24, 168
Cameras
    film speed, 145–146
    loading, 145–146
    types, 145, 150
Carte de Visite, 130–131
Cemeteries
    gravestone rubbings, 68–69
    New England, 72
    records, 34
    statuary, 64
    visiting, 64–66
Census records, 34, 82–84
Children, journaling by, 169
Christ, Jesus, 64
Church of Jesus Christ and Latter
    Day Saints, 88–89
Church records, 35
City histories, 35
Clip-art books, 198–199
Coding systems, basic, 14–15
*Common Threads: Stories from the
    Quilt,* 271
Compact discs, 272
Computers, 163
Conservation, 10
Conservators, 97
Cookbooks, family, 280
Correspondence
    function, 173
    preserving, 108–109, 171
    records, 24
    research via, 66–67
County histories, 35
Creating Scrapbook Quilts, 265
Croner, Marjorie, 266
Croppers, 195–196

D

Daguerreotype, 130
Dates, listing, 15
*Dictionary of American Family
    Names,* 77
Die cuts, 203, 205
Digitizing, 103
Directories, telephone, 35
Disasters, man-made, 98
Disderi, photographer, 131
Disowned family members, 42
Ditties, 170
Documentation, 62–63
Documents. *See* Records
Doty, Edward Jr., 37
Double-stick tape, 186

E

Essays, personal, 170
Everton Publisher's list, 76

F

Fabrics, 118
Families
    group records, 22–23
    group sheets, 10
    history
        definition, 10
        for reunions, 281–282
        shared memories
            Deborah Svoboda,
                297–299
            John Trummel, 290–291
            Judith Svoboda, 295–297
            Sharon Harker, 294–295
        trivia quiz, 284–285
Family History Center, 10
Family History Library, 10, 88–89
Flaps, 231

Flowers, symbolism of, 64
Furniture, 114–115

G

Gender errors, 43
Geographical Names Information
    System, 87–88
Gloves, white, 96
Glue sticks, 187
GNIS. *See* Geographical Names
    Information System
Gravestone rubbings, 68–69

H

Hand lettering, 232, 234
Harker, Sharon, 294–295
Heirlooms, 24, 114–115
Horton, Roberta, 265
Humidity, 106, 129

I

Indexes
    census, 82–84
    soundex, 84–86
    SSDI, 34, 86–87
Inks
    colors, 189
    on photos, 132
    types, 187
Internet. *See also* Web sites
    clip art, 202
    research
        bulletin boards, 81
        mail lists, 77–79
        newsgroups, 83
        online services, 81–82
        public record access, 28
        surnames, 76
        tips, 71

J

The James Collection, 262
Jones, Cleve, 270
Journaling
    accuracy, 162
    beyond, 174
    children's words, 169
    components, 161–162, 164–166
    definition, 155

key elements, 160–161
observation, 156–157
oral, 173–174
in scrapbooks, 157, 160
subjects, 172
tips, 158–159
tools, 163
types, 166–168

L

Legal documents, 107–108
Lettering, hand, 232, 234
Lettering books, 198
Letters. *See* Correspondence
Light
    boxes, 163, 200–201
    effects on
        paintings, 121
        paper, 56
        photo taking, 147–148
Lignin-free paper, 10, 176
Lions, symbolism of, 64
Liquid paper glues, 187
Logs, 24

M

Maiden names, 60–61
Mail lists, 77–79, 292
Maps, 35
Markers, 187, 189
Matting, 227–231
Mayflower, 37
McCloskey, Marsha, 265
Memorabilia
    minimizing, 211
    paper, 100
    preserving, 132
    printed, 109, 111–112
Memorial rubbings, 68–69
Meyerink, Kory, 62
Mildew, 95–96
Military records, 10, 35
Milk, Harvey, 270
Moisture, 129
Mold, 95–96
Mormons. *See* Church of Jesus
    Christ of Latter Day
    Saints
Moscone, George, 270

N

Names. *See also* Surnames
    changing, 42–43
    duplicate, 43
    geographical (*See* Geographical
        Names Information System)
    life of, tracing, 12–13
    maiden, 60–61
Names Project, 270–271
Nash, Dr. Rick R., 76
National archives, 10
Neutral pH, 10
New England Cemeteries, 72
Newsletters, 289
Newspapers, 34

O

Oral journaling, 173–174

P

PAF. *See* Personal Ancestral File
Paintings, 120–123
Paper
    acid-free, 176
    background, 238
    cutter, 194–195
    displaying, 107
    lignin-free, 176
    memorabilia, 100
    page protectors, 185
    preserving
        clippings, 109, 111–112
        correspondence, 108–109
        legal, 107–108
        risks, 105–106
        storing, 106–107
    punches, 198
    PVC-free, 176
    restoration, 110
    selection, 183–185
    sheets needed, 238
    size, 238
Pedigree chart, 22
Penmanship, 163
Pens
    colors, 189
    specialty, 201, 203
    uses, 187
Personal Ancestral File, 10

Personal essays, 170
Personal trimmer, 194–195
Pests, 94–95
pH, 10
Photographs
    cleaning, 128
    coloring, 136
    common problems, 134–135
    corners, 192–193
    cropping, 224–227
    découpaging, 272
    documenting, 137–138
    faux finishing, 272
    finding, 126–128
    handling, 128–129
    image transfers, 264–269
    matting, 227–231
    organizing, 138–139
    red eye remover, 201
    squares, 186
    storage, alternative, 144
    taking
        composition, 148–151
        cropping while, 149
        equipment, 145–146
        focusing, 146–147
        hierarchy of attention, 151
        importance, 243
        lighting, 147–148
        people shots, 152–153
        timing, 151–152
    tape, 186
    types, 130–131
    words with, 153
    writing on, 140
Photo-safe, 14
Pockets, 231
Poems, 170
Polaroid, 150
Police, 35
Pollution, 94–95
Pop-ups, 232
Preservation
    challenges
        acts of nature, 98
        disasters, man-made, 98
        environmental, 105–106
        mildew, 95–96
        molds, 95–96

pests, 94–95
        pollution, 94–95
    copying, 113–114
    definition, 14
    fabrics, 115–116
    furniture, 114–115
    memorabilia, 132
    organization, 93
    papers
        clippings, 109, 111–112
        correspondence, 108–109
        displaying, 107
        legal, 107–108
        risks, 105–106
        storing, 106–107
    photographs, 128–129
    professionals, hiring, 97
    simplicity, 93–94
    slides, 99–100
    tips
        paper, 112
        records/documents, 108, 109
        videotapes, 104–105
    videocassettes, 100–105
Przecha, Donna, 42
Public records. See Records
PVC-free paper, 176

Quilts
    AIDS, 270–271
    care, 118
    photo transfer, 264–269

Race errors, 43
Records
    access, Internet, 28
    cemetery, 34
    correspondence, 24
    criminal, 35
    family group, 22–23
    military, 35
    preserving, 107–108
    religious, 35
    school, 34
    selecting, 27
Red eye remover, 201
Reflections instruments, 201

Research
    beginners tips, 26
    checklist, 16–20
    coding systems, 14–15
    crediting sources, 63
    duplication, avoiding, 63
    emotional aspects, 2–3
    evaluating, 28–29
    file, creating, 14
    free help, 29
    Internet
        bulletin boards, 81
        indexes, 82
        mail lists, 77–79
        newsgroups, 83
        online services, 81–82
        surnames, 76–77
        tips, 71
        web genealogies, 80
    interview questions
        ambitions, 48–49
        artifacts, 59
        background, 45–46
        careers, 48–49
        childhood, 46–47
        education, 51–52
        entertainment, 50–51
        friends, 50–51
        grandparent specific,
            58–59
        life experiences, 56–57
        life's lessons, 47–48
        marriages, 55–56
        philosophy, 57–58
        records, 59
        special occasions, 49–50
        traditions, 54
        transportation, 53–54
        warm-up, 41, 44–45
    interviews
        follow-up, 61–62
        guidelines, 33, 39
        self, 36
        setting up, 40–41
    narrowing, 25–28
    purpose, 4–8
    skeletons, 42–43
    sorting out, 6
    source list, 34–36

Research *(continued)*
   tools, 24
   via correspondence, 66–67
Resource checklists, 24
Restoration, 110
Reunions
   accommodations, 278–279
   activities, planning, 279
   date selection, 277
   details, last minute, 282–283
   family histories, 281–282
   invitations, 277, 279, 281
   new traditions, 283, 286
   reservations, 277–278
Roosters, symbolism of, 64
Rubberstamps, 204
Rubbings, 68–69
Rulers
   choosing, 189–190
   decorative, 201
   for line making, 163

Scales, symbolism of, 64
School records, 34
Scissors, 189–190
Scrapbooks. *See also* Albums
   creative touches, 231–234
   family pages, examples
      always in my heart, 256–257
      a clan of Irish folk smile,
         254–255
      Claude Byrum Given,
         257–258
      fancy corners, 246–247
      fathers and sons/brothers
         and friends, 251
      grandmother's gift by the
         sea, 253
      Helene Muller Obermayer,
         130–135
      Imro reunion 2000,
         252–253
      Maria, 1959, 249–250
      in memoriam, 158
      mothers and daughters, 252

a place called home,
    256–257
silhouette baby blue and
    pink, 247–248
Stephanie Jo Given Friday,
    250–251
journaling in, 157, 160
key ingredients, 15
layout, 208–212
memorabilia in, 188
opening pages, examples
   family coat of arms, 241
   the Mullers, 242–243
   pedigree of James Thomas,
     243–244
   surname distribution, 140
   welcome to Donegal, 239
penmanship, 163
styles, 222–223
techniques
   photos
      cropping, 224–227
      matting, 227–231
themes, examples
   ABC's of Family, 222
   ancestral descendants, 220
   decade, 220
   family treasure chest, 221
   family tree branch, 219
   kissing cousins, 219
   the men/women of the
     family, 220–221
   a moment in time, 220
   my life story, 213–216
   our family, 213
   our family legacy, 216–217
   single family unit, 219
   this is your life, 217–218
   virtual, 215
Simms, Ami, 262–264, 268
Sliders, 232
Slides, 99–100
Smith, Elsdon C., 77
Social Security Death Index, 34,
   86–87
Software, 200
Soundex, 84–86

Sperber, Anita, 265
SSDI. *See* Social Security Death
   Index
Stickers, 203, 205
The Story of Our Names, 77
Surnames
   definition, 14
   importance, 15
   searches, 76–77
   soundex formula, 84–86
Svoboda, Deborah, 297–299
Svoboda, Judith, 295–297

Telephone directories, 35
Templates, 163, 196
Textiles. *See* Fabrics
Tintype, 130
Tools
   adhesives, 186–187
   cutting, 189–186, 238
   journaling, 163
   top, 194
Trummel, John, 290–294
T-shirts, 272
*200 Years of Census Taking: Popula-
   tion and Housing Questions,*
   82

United States Census Indexes,
   82–84
Utility knives, 189–190

Veterans. *See* Military
Videocassettes, 100–105
Virtual, 215

Web sites. *See also* Internet
   creating, 286–288, 290
   family, 286–288, 290
   genealogies, 80
   memory quilts, 263
White gloves, 96